Baptism, Peace and the State in the Reformed and Mennonite Traditions

Edited by

Ross T. Bender and Alan P. F. Sell

What are the most significant points at issue between the Reformed and Mennonite communions? Baptism, peace and church-state relations. Is there a way forward? In the hope that there may be, the contributors to this book attempt to clear the way to closer relations between Reformed and Mennonites by careful scholarly discussion of the traditionally disputed questions.

The papers gathered here were presented at the second phase of the international dialogue between the World Alliance of Reformed Churches (Presbyterian and Congregational) and the Mennonite World Conference. There are Reformed and Mennonite studies of the three topics, together with the responses of a philosopher of religion, a sociologist, a systematic theologian and a church historian. In the Introduction the dialogue is set in its historical and contemporary ecumenical context, and the Conclusion, drafted by the dialogue participants, has been forwarded to the two world bodies for their consideration and action. This important work will be relevant to all future scholarly research into the growing debate between Reformed and Mennonite communions.

Ross T. Bender is Professor of Christian Education at the Associated Mennonite Biblical Seminaries, Elkhart, Indiana, and a former President of the Mennonite World Conference.

Alan P. F. Sell is the incumbent of the Chair of Christian Thought in the University of Calgary, Canada, and a former Theological Secretary of the World Alliance of Reformed Churches (Presbyterian and Congregational).

Baptism, Peace and the State in the Reformed and Mennonite Traditions

Baptism, Peace and the State in the Reformed and Mennonite Traditions

Edited by

Ross T. Bender and Alan P. F. Sell

Essays by

Alan P. F. Sell
Charles C. West
Marlin E. Miller
Max L. Stackhouse
Howard John Loewen
Iain G. Nicol

Harry Loewen
Hugo Meynell
Harry H. Hiller
Andrew D. MacRae
Tom Sinclair-Faulkner

Published by
Wilfrid Laurier University Press
for
The Calgary Institute for the Humanities

Canadian Cataloguing in Publication Data

Main entry under title:
Baptism, peace and the state in the Reformed and
   Mennonite traditions

BX
9419.5
.M46
B37
1991

Papers presented at a consultation held at the
University of Calgary, Oct. 11-14, 1989.
Co-published by Calgary Institute for the Humanities.
Includes bibliographical references and index.
ISBN 0-88920-204-4

1. Baptism — Reformed Church — Congresses.
2. Baptism — Mennonites — Congresses. 3. Peace —
Reformed Church — Congresses. 4. Peace — Religious
aspects — Mennonites — Congresses. 5. Church and
state — Reformed Church — Congresses. 6. Church and
state — Mennonites — Congresses. 7. Reformed Church —
Doctrines — Congresses. 8. Mennonites — Doctrines —
Congresses. 9. Reformed Church — Relations —
Mennonites — Congresses. 10. Mennonites — Relations —
Reformed Church — Congresses. I. Bender, Ross T.
(Ross Thomas), 1929- . II. Sell, Alan P. F.
III. Calgary Institute for the Humanities.

BX8123.4.A3B36 1991   280′.042   C91-093477-1

Copyright © 1991
Wilfrid Laurier University Press
Waterloo, Ontario, Canada
N2L 3C5

Cover design by Leslie Macredie

Printed in Canada

Baptism, Peace and the State in the Reformed and Mennonite Traditions has been produced from a manuscript supplied in camera-ready form by The Calgary Institute for the Humanities.

TABLE OF CONTENTS

PREFACE

Since an account of the historical background, nature, and purpose of the international consultation on "Baptism, Peace, and the State in the Reformed and Mennonite Traditions" is given in the Introduction which follows, this prefatory note may be devoted to cordial expressions of gratitude.

The Director of the University of Calgary Institute for the Humanities, Dr. Harold Coward, and his Board are to be thanked for their enthusiastic adoption of this project; for their recognition of its scholarly and international significance; and for their encouragement and assistance at all stages of the venture. The Administrator of the Institute, Mrs. Gerry Dyer, could not have been more helpful during the eighteen months of planning, during the consultation itself, and during the period of the preparation of this volume. She deserves high praise for her care and promptness in preparing this manuscript. Mrs. Cindy Atkinson, the Institute's Secretary, also contributed to the success of this project in numerous ways, and this is gratefully acknowledged.

The Reverend Paul N. Kraybill, Executive Secretary of the Mennonite World Conference, the Reverend Dr. Edmond Perret, former General Secretary of the World Alliance of Reformed Churches, and the Reverend Dr. Lukas Vischer, former Moderator of the Department of Theology of the World Alliance of Reformed Churches, are warmly thanked for the moral and financial support of their organizations. Additional funding was granted by the Social Sciences and Humanities Research Council of Canada, University of Calgary Conference Grant, and the Department of Religious Studies, University of Calgary, and thanks are expressed to these bodies.

The interest of the Department of Religious Studies of the University of Calgary was valued, and especial thanks are due to its Head, Dr. Ronald W. Neufeldt, who participated in the consultation sessions and chaired some of them.

The consultation participants were grateful for the hospitality arranged by the Institute for the Humanities, and for the official yet warm welcome they received on behalf of the University President, Professor Murray Fraser, and in his own name from Dr. Peter Krueger, the then University Vice-President (Academic), and from Dr. A. Brannigan, representing the Executive Council of the Calgary Institute for the Humanities.

The welcome presence at the sessions of a number of local ministers and laypeople was a constant reminder, if any were needed, that it ill behoves those who engage in dialogue at the international level to forget the grass roots.

Above all, thanks are due to the distinguished contributors of initial papers and responses, both for the calibre of their work and for their promptness in meeting deadlines. Finally, Dr. Ross T. Bender, the co-secretary of the consultation, is enthusiastically to be thanked for his support throughout, and for his editorial work. Not the least important aspect of the latter was his quest of consistent North American spelling — a minefield which this Englishman was far too timid to enter.

Alan P. F. Sell
The University of Calgary

FROM THE DIRECTOR

Established in 1976, the Calgary Institute for the Humanities has as its aim the fostering of advanced study and research in all areas of the humanities. Apart from supporting work in the traditional "arts" disciplines such as philosophy, history, ancient and modern languages and literatures, it also promotes research into the philosophical and historical aspects of the sciences, social sciences, fine arts, and the various "professional" disciplines.

The Institute's programs in support of advanced study attempt to provide scholars with time to carry out their work. In addition, the Institute sponsors formal and informal gatherings among people who share common interests, in order to promote intellectual dialogue and discussion. Recently, the Institute has moved to foster the application of humanistic knowledge to contemporary social problems.

The seminar *Baptism, Peace, and the State in Reformed and Mennonite Traditions*, October 12-14, 1989, brought together scholars of History, Religious Studies and Theology from the United States and Canada. This study has practical significance for the Mennonite and Reformed Churches as well as theoretical importance for the understanding of baptism, peace and the state within Christianity.

We wish to record our thanks to the Social Sciences and Humanities Research Council of Canada, The University of Calgary Conference Grant, the Religious Studies Department of the University of Calgary, the World Alliance of Reformed Churches and the Mennonite World Conference for their financial support. Without the careful attention to detail of Gerry Dyer, the Institute Administrator, and Cindy Atkinson, Institute Secretary, the Conference would not have been the success that it was.

H. G. Coward
Director
The Calgary Institute
for the Humanities

Chapter I

INTRODUCTION

Alan P. F. Sell

During the past thirty years a considerable number of bilateral and multilateral dialogues have taken place between the major Christian world communions. These dialogues are a product of, and a contribution towards, those improving inter-Church relations which are a prominent feature of this century's Christian history.

This volume marks a stage in the scholarly debate between the Reformed and Mennonite communions upon the theological and other issues which have traditionally divided them. The papers here gathered were presented and discussed at an international consultation on "Baptism, Peace, and the State in the Reformed and Mennonite Traditions," which was held at the University of Calgary, 11-14 October 1989. The pre-history of this consultation, and the way in which it was organized, are more than ordinarily interesting.

I.

Although both the Reformed and the Mennonites claim as their own the pre-Reformation Christian heritage, they emerged as distinct communions during the turbulent sixteenth century. The Mennonites, named after one of their Dutch leaders, Menno Simons (1496-1561), are heirs of the Anabaptists of Reformation times. The Reformed, who number Zwingli (1484-1531) and Calvin (1509-1564) among their forebears, are now represented around the world by the Reformed, Presbyterian and Congregational traditions. During the present century the Reformed tradition has passed into some sixteen United churches, including the United Churches of Canada (1925) and Zambia (1965), and the Uniting Church in Australia (1977). It must also be said that some in other communions, notably the Anglican and the Baptist, follow Reformed theology closely—in some cases more closely than do some of the Reformed.[1]

The Mennonites have been persecuted on a number of occasions in the course of their history. Some had no option but to migrate from their Swiss and Dutch strongholds. They settled in various parts of

Europe, and first reached America in the 1660s. In the 1870s some 18000 Mennonites came from the Ukraine to Canada and the American Midwest; and in the 1920s a further 23000 left the same region, bound in most cases for Canada. During the past century Mennonite missionary activity has resulted in the formation of new communities in many parts of the world. In Zaire, for example, there are some 100000 Mennonites. The Mennonite World Conference (1925) represents nearly one million Mennonites in about sixty nations.[2]

The Reformed family, comprising some seventy million members, is spread widely around the world. The bulk of the membership is in Africa and Asia, where missions from Switzerland, Holland, Britain, North America, and elsewhere became active from the late eighteenth century onwards. The World Alliance of Reformed Churches[3] results from the union in 1970 of the World Presbyterian Alliance (1875) with the International Congregational Council (1891).

To say that Reformed-Anabaptist relations were sometimes strained is to put it very mildly indeed. As Dr. Nicol points out at the beginning of his paper in this volume, Calvin indulged in "consistently negative polemic against the Anabaptists." Nor was this polemic simply the solo performance of an idiosyncratic theologian. On the contrary, in some of their most formal statements — their confessions of faith — Reformed groups condemned the Anabaptists. Thus, for example, in the Scots Confession (1560), "we damne the error of the *Anabaptists*, who denies baptisme to apperteine to Children, before that they have faith and understanding [Colossians 2: 11, 12; Romans 4: 11; Genesis 17: 10; Matthew 28: 19]."[4] In the Belgic Confession (1561), following a dispute between Micronius and Menno Simons over the person and work of Christ, the Reformed confessed "(in opposition to the heresy of the Anabaptists, who deny that Christ assumed human flesh of his mother) that Christ became a partaker of the flesh and blood of the children [Hebrews 2: 14]."[5] Concerning baptism they declare that "we detest the error of the Anabaptists, who are not content with the one only baptism they have once received, and moreover condemn the baptism of the infants of believers, who, we believe, ought to be baptized and sealed with the sign of the covenant [Matt. 19: 14; I Cor. 7: 14]."[6] Where subjection to the magistrate is concerned, "we detest the error of the Anabaptists and other seditious people, and in general all those who reject the higher powers and magistrates, and would subvert justice [2 Peter 2: 10], introduce a community of goods, and confound that decency and good order which God hath established among men [Jude, 8, 10]."[7]

Finally, in the Second Helvetic Confession (1566): "We condemn the Anabaptists, who deny that newborn infants of the faithful are to be baptized"[8]; "We condemn the Anabaptists who, in denying that a Christian may hold the office of magistrate, also deny that a man may justly be put to death by the magistrate, or that the magistrate may wage war, or that oaths are to be taken before a magistrate, and so on."[9]

In the present more charitable climate of current ecumenism, and even after allowing for the vastly different socio-religious attitudes of earlier times, such affirmations are nothing but an embarrassment to the heirs of those who drafted them, and an obstacle in the path of fruitful dialogue with the heirs of those formerly condemned. It was therefore an historic moment when, on 5 March 1983, a united service was held in Zurich Cathedral, at which representatives of the World Alliance of Reformed Churches, the Baptist World Alliance, and the Mennonite World Conference were present. There in Zurich, the scene of so much Reformed-Anabaptist animosity in the sixteenth century, the place where Felix Mantz was drowned for his Anabaptist views, the President of the Reformed Church of Zurich offered a prayer which included these words:

> Today we confess before You and our Mennonite and Baptist sisters and brothers how often we as Reformed Christians have failed to understand the message You desire to be mediated to Your Church by the testimony and work of our fellow Christians in the Free Church tradition. We bring before you all the injustice done to them in our country through the ages: persecution, oppression, execution and banishment. Lord our God, show your grace and mercy upon us. Forgive and help us today to begin anew in fellowship with one another through the power of reconciliation and love.[10]

This repudiation by the Reformed of the classical anti-Anabaptist anathemas paved the way for Reformed-Mennonite dialogue at the international level. The first joint consultation was held at Strasbourg, 17-18 July 1984. Sponsored by the World Alliance of Reformed Churches and the Mennonite World Conference, its findings were published under the title *Mennonites and Reformed in Dialogue* (Geneva: WARC 1986). A large part of the purpose of this meeting was to introduce either side to the other. Since the Reformed family is seventy times larger than the Mennonite, there are many parts of the world where the communions have no personal contact, and where their mutual stories are scarcely known. Again, the two communions are internally diverse, and this variety requires to be understood if intelligent dialogue is to be possible. The strands within the Reformed family (Reformed, Presbyterian, Congregational, United) have already been mentioned; but the Mennonites, too, were diverse from the beginning, and have experienced change in the course of their history. Their family includes those who are as visually distinct as the Amish, and others who, to the outward eye, could be mistaken for members of any mainline denomination.

A second objective of the first consultation was to view the now-repudiated condemnations in their historical context (in which connection the Mennonite Heinold Fast was gracious enough to say that "the Anabaptists...were not far behind the Reformed in damning their opponents")[11]; and to stimulate dialogue between the communions.

The improved ecumenical climate, the repudiation of the historic anathemas by the Reformed, and the fact that on both sides the theological and ethical lines are not quite so sharply drawn as once they were are omens favourable to future good relations. In 1986 the present writer, then serving as Theological Secretary of the World Alliance of Reformed Churches, visited Mennonite leaders and scholars in the United States with a view to ascertaining what further steps might be taken in Reformed-Mennonite dialogue. It quickly became clear that there was a pressing need for detailed scholarly analysis of the three traditionally "neuralgic" points at issue between the two communions: baptism, peace, and Church-state relations. Since the first consultation had taken place on European soil, it seemed entirely appropriate that the next phase of dialogue should be held in North America, where both Reformed and Mennonites are present in some numbers and where both display considerable internal diversity. Within weeks of assuming his present position at the University of Calgary, and with the blessing of the two world bodies, the writer approached the Board of the University's Institute for the Humanities to see whether it would be possible for the Institute to convene an international scholarly consultation in co-operation with the World Alliance of Reformed Churches and the Mennonite World Conference. The favourable response of the Director of the Institute, Dr. Harold Coward, and his colleagues, was greatly appreciated by all concerned. Thus the consultation was held, and in this volume are its papers and findings.

Without wishing to claim too much, it may truly be said that this consultation marked the first occasion on which Reformed and Mennonite scholars, representing their international families, engaged in detailed scholarly discussion of the theological and ethical points at issue between the two traditions; and, so far as is known, it was the first time that an institute in a secular university had joined in fostering scholarly work between two Christian world communions.

At the consultation pairs of papers were presented on baptism, peace, and the state by highly regarded scholars who represented their world bodies, and who were drawn from different branches of their respective families. Thus, Charles West and Iain Nicol belong to the Presbyterian branch of the Reformed tradition, the former in the United States, the latter in Canada, while Max Stackhouse is a member of the United Church of Christ in the USA. The United Church of Christ results from the union in 1957 of the Congregational Christian Churches, whose heritage stretched back to the Puritans, with the Evangelical and Reformed Church, the roots of which were in Germany. On the Mennonite side, Marlin Miller has standing within both the General Conference Mennonite Church and the Mennonite Church, while Ross Bender is a member of the latter; and Harry Loewen, Howard Loewen, and Ronald Neufeldt belong to the Mennonite Brethren Church. Of these churches, the Mennonite Church has Swiss-South German origins and embraces Mennonite and Amish traditions; the General Conference Church, constituted by evangelical progressives on 28 May 1860, encompasses a wider diversity of ethnic backgrounds than any other Mennonite conference; and the Mennonite Brethren Church results from revival movements and a heightened concern for godliness and evangelism among Mennonites who were living in Southern Russia in the 1860s.

The respondents were selected for their scholarly expertise and for their ability to bring insights from their subject areas to bear upon the initial papers. It was a welcome bonus that Hugo Meynell, the philosopher, is a Roman Catholic; that Harry Hiller, the sociologist, and Andrew MacRae, the systematic theologian, are Baptists; and that Tom Sinclair-Faulkner is a member of the United Church of Canada, which resulted from the union, in 1925, of Presbyterians, Congregationalists, and Methodists, and which holds membership in both the World Alliance of Reformed Churches and the World Methodist Council. That the roots of Iain Nicol and Andrew MacRae are in Scotland, where the former was ordained in the Church of Scotland, and the latter formerly served as Secretary of the Baptist Union — a numerical minority *vis à vis* establishment Presbyterianism, brought an added dimension to the discussion of Church and state. The extensive international experience of the two co-secretaries, and the English Dissenting heritage of one of them further widened the scope of the discussion.

Following the presentation and discussion of the papers and responses, a synthesis of the points made was drafted, and this appears as the Conclusion to this volume. In addition, the Reformed and Mennonite participants devised a set of nine resolutions designed to promote further joint activity between their communions at all levels. These were sent to the Executive Committees of the two world bodies, and are reproduced herein.

Having set the consultation in its historical context, and having indicated its nature and purpose, we may now briefly turn to the papers themselves.

II.

Those who engage in transconfessional dialogue frequently find that whereas they had thought that the focus would be almost entirely upon doctrinal and other issues which *divide* the communions in question, the spotlight is also relentlessly turned upon ambiguities and even discords *within* each participating tradition. The papers presented at this consultation admirably illustrate this point.

Thus, while all might reasonably have expected that between Reformed and Mennonites the discussion of baptism would focus upon paedobaptism *vis à vis* believers' baptism (and it did), it also becomes clear from Dr. West's paper that there are varied views of baptism *within* the Reformed family. Similarly, Dr. Miller affirms that "There have been and continue to be *several* Mennonite traditions with regard to baptism." Both West and Miller locate baptism (however construed) within an ecclesiology according to which the Church is conceived as a missionary body. The question as to how this mission is to be prosecuted in a pluralist world remains open and urgent. The common emphasis upon the ethical implications of baptism is a further noteworthy feature of the first pair of papers, as is Miller's emphasis upon the importance of church discipline. Despite its traditional prominence in their confessions and practice, this latter topic evokes a thunderous silence in many Reformed circles today (cf. Miller's note 38). Can this betoken a capitulation to the standards of "the world"? Or amnesia, or discomfort in respect of a classical doctrinal emphasis of much Reformed theology, namely, that there is a distinction of eternal significance between those who are "in Christ" and those who are not? However this may be, the matter is of sufficient importance to warrant close examination—as Dr. Sinclair-Faulkner's response makes plain. Put otherwise the question is, "What are the ecclesiological implications of Dr. Stackhouse's strong affirmation that 'There is no such thing as a born and bred Christian. Getting born is not religiously distinctive and no one is saved by being born, or born into a Christian family' "?

The pair of papers on peace likewise reveal differences of emphasis within as well as between the Reformed and Mennonite communions. If Stackhouse recalls the historic Reformed-Mennonite discrepancies on this issue, he also notes the spread of pacifist convictions in Reformed circles, and the military involvement of some Mennonites. Dr. Howard Loewen attends to those socio-political changes of recent decades which have both challenged Mennonites as to their peace practice and led to some ambivalent responses. It is noteworthy, as Dr. Sinclair-Faulkner points out, that Stackhouse finds it impossible to treat peace without reference to baptism and the family on the one hand and the state on the other. Equally significant is Howard Loewen's exposition of the biblical basis of a Mennonite peace theology which can be transformationist rather than separatist. As the consultation Conclusion makes plain, an abiding question is, "What actions, if any, ought a transformationist peace theology to prompt when those who espouse it are confronted by wicked powers?" Stackhouse's paper raises the issue; and in his contribution, Dr. Harry Loewen reminds us of the strand of Anabaptist thought represented by Hübmaier, which "does not say — as Calvin does — how a wicked government is to be replaced."

Yet again, where the state is concerned the inter-confessional edges are blurred. In the course of his exposition of Calvin's view of Church-state relations, Dr. Nicol alludes to the diversity within the present-day Reformed family on this matter, and he is right to do so. For there are Reformed national churches (of various kinds) in Scotland and in some of the Swiss cantons; there is the Congregational witness which, at this point, is closer to that of the heirs of the Anabaptists;[12] and in a few places in the world Presbyterians and Congregationalists, though not established churches, are nevertheless the folk-church of the region. From the Mennonite side Harry Loewen traces the development of *two* traditions among the Mennonites: that of involvement, and that of non-involvement in the political arena. This very diversity, he argues, facilitates rather than hinders Reformed-Mennonite dialogue.

III.

The issues between and within the Reformed and Mennonite communions were grist to the mill of the respondents. They, as requested, commented upon all or some of the themes as they saw fit. They left the authors of the initial papers in no doubt as to how they had been heard. Many incisive points clamour for further attention. In relation to the political order, how can churches achieve "that nice combination of detachment and commitment" which Dr. Meynell recommends? How may Christian communions best reckon with those socio-political factors to which Dr. Hiller points, which influence their doctrinal formulations and help to explain some of their internal diversity? Dr. MacRae presses the question, "Who constitute the Church?" Is Calvin's "both-and" ecclesiology, so clearly expounded by Dr. Nicol, preferable to the "either-or" ecclesiology of the Anabaptists (and classical Congregationalists—yet another blurred edge)? It would seem that in the absence of a clear answer we shall not know what the entity is which is baptizing people, witnessing for peace, and having (or not having) relations with the state. The question, "Does this matter so long as the baptizing, witnessing and relating are somehow done?" is one of those "simple" questions from which theologians sometimes shrink because they are so difficult. This one is difficult not least because, as MacRae points out, it raises in turn the question of the locus of authority in the Church. Dr. Sinclair-Faulkner's references to Calvin, Warfield, and West underline the importance and the slipperiness of this matter. Finally, we may hope that Sinclair-Faulkner's implied question, "How are Reformed and Mennonites to face up to the shadow side of their stories?" has been at least partially answered by the repudiation of the anathemas which preceded this and the former consultation, and by the consultations themselves. Of course, since the empirical Church comprises sinners it will ever be an "earthen vessel." This is a fact; it is not an excuse, and still less something of which to be proud.

Having, we trust, whetted the reader's appetite for the papers to follow, it remains only to add that those who participated in the consultation were unanimously of the opinion that the work begun in Zurich and continued in Strasbourg and Calgary must go forward.

Notes

1. This paragraph and the next two are drawn from my article in the *Calgary Herald* of 14 October 1989.

2. See the *Proceedings* and *Handbooks* of the Mennonite World Conference, Carol Stream, Illinois.

3. See Marcel Pradervand, *A Century of Service: A History of the World Alliance of Reformed Churches, 1875-1975* (Edinburgh: The Saint Andrew Press, 1975); Alan P. F. Sell, *A Reformed, Evangelical, Catholic Theology: The Contributions of the World Alliance of Reformed Churches, 1875-1982* (Grand Rapids: Eerdmans, 1991).

4. *The Scots Confession of Faith*, Article XXIII: "itaque damnamus errorem Anabaptistarum, qui ante fidem et rationis usum negant ad pueros pertinere baptismum." For the Reformed Confessions as here quoted, see *The Creeds of Christendom*, ed. Philip Schaff, rev. David S. Schaff (Grand Rapids: Baker Book House, 1985 reprint), III.

5. *The Belgic Confession*, Article XVIII: "C'est pourquoi nous confessons — contre l'hérésie des Anabaptistes, niant que Christ a pris chair humaine de sa mère — que Christ a participé à la même chair et sang des enfants."

6. Ibid., Article XXXIV: "Sur ceci nous détestons l'erreur des Anabaptistes, qui ne se contentent pas d'un seul baptême une fois reñu, et en outre condamnent le baptême des petits enfants des fidèles, lesquels nous crayons devoir être baptisés et scellés du signe de l'alliance."

7. Ibid., Article XXXVI: "Et sur ceci nous détestons l'erreur des Anabaptistes et autres mutins, et en général de tous ceux qui veuient rejeter les autorités et Magistrats, en renverser le justice, établissant communautés de biens, et confondant l'honnêteté que Dieu a mise entre les hommes."

8. *The Second Helvetic Confession*, Article XX: "Damnamus Anabaptistas, qui negant baptizandos esse infantulos recens natos a fidelibus."

9. Ibid., Article XXX: "Damnamus Anabaptistas, qui, ut Christianum negant fungi posse officio magistratus, ita etiam negant, quemquam a magistratu juste occidi, aut magistratum bellum genere posse, aut juramenta magistratui praesanda esse, etc."

10. Quoted in *From Ottawa to Seoul* (Geneva: World Alliance of Reformed Churches, 1989), p. 67.

11. H. Fast, "A Mennonite View on the Reformed Condemnations," in *Mennonites and Reformed in Dialogue*, eds. Hans Georg vom Berg, Henk Kossen, Larry Miller and Lukas Vischer (Geneva: World Alliance of Reformed Churches, 1986), p. 57.

12. See Alan P. F. Sell, "Anabaptist-Congregational Relations and Reformed-Mennonite Dialogue," *The Mennonite Quarterly Review* LXI no. 3 (July 1987): 321-34; idem, "Dubious Establishment? A Neglected Ecclesiological Testimony," *Mid-Stream* XXIV (1985): 1-28. These papers are reprinted in idem, *Dissenting Thought and the Life of the Churches: Studies in an English Tradition* (Lewiston, N.Y.: Mellen Research University Press, 1990).

PART ONE:

THE INITIAL PAPERS

Chapter II

BAPTISM IN THE REFORMED TRADITION

Charles C. West

The Equipment of the Church:

Jesus Christ has given the church preaching and teaching, praise and prayer, and Baptism and the Lord's Supper as means of fulfilling its service of God among men.

(Confession of 1967, Presbyterian Church, USA)

Q. 65. Since then faith alone makes us share in Christ and all his benefits, where does such faith originate?

A. The Holy Spirit creates it in our hearts by the preaching of the Holy Gospel and confirms it by the use of the Holy Sacraments.

Q. 66. What are the Sacraments?

A. They are visible holy signs and seals instituted by God in order that by their use he may more fully disclose and seal to us the promise of the Gospel.

(The Heidelberg Catechism)

Baptism:

By humble submission to John's baptism, Christ joined himself to men in their need and entered upon his ministry of reconciliation in the power of the Spirit. Christian baptism marks the receiving of the same Spirit by all his people. Baptism with water represents not only cleansing from sin but a dying with Christ and the joyful rising with him to new life. It commits all Christians to die each day to sin and to live for righteousness. In baptism, the church celebrates the renewal of the covenant by which God has bound his people to himself. By baptism, individuals are publicly received into the church to share in its life and ministry and the church becomes responsible for their training and support in Christian discipleship.

(The Confession of 1967, Presbyterian Church, USA)

Q. 74. Are infants also to be baptized?

A. Yes, because they as well as their parents are included in the covenant and belong to the people of God. Since both redemption from sin through the blood of Christ and the gift of faith from the Holy Spirit are promised to these children no less than to their parents, infants are also by baptism, as a sign of the covenant, to be incorporated into the Christian church and distinguished from the children of unbelievers. This was done in the Old Covenant by circumcision. In the New Covenant, baptism has been instituted to take its place.

(The Heidelberg Catechism)

I. Introduction

Let me begin with an illustrative story. Years ago, in the third decade of this century, a boy was baptized in a Presbyterian Church. At the age of four he was just old enough to remember it. His brother, aged one, who shared the experience, did not. The memory was of church in the formal external sense — black-robed minister, baptismal font, Gothic columns, and organ music. It may be that his parents promised "to bring him up in the nurture and admonition of the Lord" as the service prescribed. If so, they did not keep that promise. Four years later they moved from town, left the church, and never joined another. The boy learned liberal idealist humanism from teachers in school. Then, in college, a remarkable humanities course introduced him to the intellectual-spiritual searching of the Western world, from Plato to Goethe. At the same time, he experienced the betrayal of a socialist vision by the terror of Stalin and the crumbling of the peace movement faced with Nazi power. Only then did he begin seriously to ask about the ultimate power, the underlying reality, which could govern and give hope to human life.

The place where he began to find answers was not the local church, but the Student Christian Movement, opening out into the ecumenical movement worldwide. The tough, compassionate realism of Reinhold Niebuhr, the vigorous intellectual challenge of W. A. Visser 't Hooft, and Christian witness in the resistance out of China, Germany, and elsewhere — these were the channels through which, for him, the Word was preached and the Spirit moved.

There was, of course, a personal dimension to this experience. A young man with little sense of self-worth, struggling to find God and himself, was accepted into a community who valued him despite his failures and challenged him despite his weakness to share their mission. There was a moment of decision. It was simultaneously to join the church by confession of faith, to study theology, to become a minister, and to be a missionary, God willing to a non-Christian society. Since one must always be a denominational as well as an ecumenical Christian, the church chosen was Presbyterian, not by some childhood memory but because it was at that time and place the least self-conscious, most ecumenically open expression of the Holy Catholic Church available.

What did baptism at the age of four have to do with all of this? I take this to be not a rhetorical question but a real one. When, only a few years later, in a small congregation of the Church of Christ in China (which included the British Baptist Mission in its membership), within days of the arrival of communist armies, this same young man instructed and baptized twenty-one new Christians into the Church, he wished with all his heart that this sacrament could have been his at the moment of his commitment. Yet still later, not with reasoned theology but with a deep sense of the guidance of the Spirit, he and his wife brought their own children, still babies, to be baptized.

This is the man who now presumes to write about the Reformed understanding of baptism.

II. Perspective

What could a Reformed understanding of baptism be? There is no easy answer to this question, for two reasons. First, there is within the Reformed tradition a sharp difference both of practice and of theology concerning the question whether baptism is a sacrament and when it should be performed. John Calvin's view was firm and clear, as was the testimony of most Reformed confessions of the sixteenth and seventeenth centuries. The English Baptist tradition, however, in both its General and Particular forms, grew out of the Congregational wing of Reformed Christianity. To this day, except for the issue of believers' baptism and church government, there is as much Calvinism among Baptists as among Presbyterians. At the same time, the question of infant versus believers' baptism is fiercely debated among theologians in the Reformed tradition itself, led by that tradition's greatest twentieth-century exponent, Karl Barth.

Second, and more fundamentally, the Reformed tradition is not at heart concerned about its own identity, either in theology or in churchmanship. It seeks to respond in faithful witness to the living God whom the Bible reveals, in each time and place, in faithful dialogue with the whole tradition—past and present—of the Holy Catholic Church. Reformed churches seek unity with other communions in service to the common mission of the Church and are content to lose themselves in that unity when they find it. Reformed theology is content to be nothing more than ecumenical theology and claims to be nothing less. It is always being reformed in the ecumenical encounter.

In this context, then, let me offer two affirmations. They are, I believe, both Reformed and ecumenical. They are more in the nature of perceptions than of doctrines. They reflect an underlying awareness of where we are when we begin to reflect upon the work of God in the life of this world, especially in baptism.

First, God's omnipotence is the sovereignty of sanctifying grace in Jesus Christ. I mean by that what was expressed in both the Reformation slogans, *sola gratia* and *soli Deo gloria*. The character and purpose of God, the creator of the heavens and the earth, the sovereign Lord in the natural universe and in human affairs, is revealed in the life, death, and resurrection of Jesus Christ through the witness of the prophets and apostles. The power at the heart of the universe is the power of this love. Christian theology and church life have tried for centuries to come to grips with this inspiring, outrageous claim. Luther lived with it as paradox. Eastern Orthodoxy has tried to embrace the powers of history, the world, and nature in the church's drama of salvation. Roman Catholics have been tempted to turn grace itself into a sacramental power transaction. A large segment of modern Protestant Christianity has restricted grace to the personal, family, and local community life leaving the world to fend for itself with or without a prediction of its imminent destruction. Calvinists have too often drawn from their mentor a separation between the God of power and the God of grace. All of these have had their effect upon the understanding and practice of baptism. None of them has been adequate to the truth which the church confesses or to the redeeming power by which the world lives and is given hope. Yet we continue to celebrate this truth at Christmas, at Easter, and whenever the church gathers to pray. We continue to hope in, and to live by, this power even when we are unfaithful to its claim. We do so, among other ways, in baptism.

Second, human response to the gift and promise of God is participation in the reality of Christ in this world, that is, in the work and witness of the body of Christ, the pilgrim people of God, in and for this world. In this participation, Christ is present through the Holy Spirit, closer to the believer than the believer is to him or herself, judging, transforming, and calling from within. Yet in this relationship God the Father, Son, and Holy Spirit remains free and sovereign in love. The

Church and its sacraments are never sacred. Sanctification is always a judging and changing relationship, never an achieved status. Bound in this covenant of grace and promise to God, the Church is always being reformed through its mission to the world, seeking to become by faithful living that which by grace in the forgiveness of its sings, it already is. I am expressing here that which Reformed theologians in the sixteenth century tried so inadequately to express in the philosophical term *finitum non capax infiniti*. The real presence of Christ is always at the same time the presence of a mystery. The saving reality of God is a reality of calling and promise.

III. The History

This, too, has its implications for the meaning of baptism. Among them it raises the historical question, "How did baptism arise as an act of the Church initiating believers into its life, and as a response to the sanctifying grace of God in Christ?"

Evidence from the New Testament seems to show that baptism, in contrast to the Lord's Supper, was first of all a practice in the earliest church. Theological explanation was fragmentary and followed later. The concept was well known in New Testament times, both in metaphor and in practice. It signified immersion, repeated or intensive, originally in water but by extension in wine, sleep, debts, troubles, or miseries. Jesus' reference to "the baptism with which I am baptized" (Mark 10:38-39) was generally understandable in this metaphorical sense. Markus Barth lists three baptismal practices in pagan rituals of the time which may have influenced Christian understanding and practice: (a) as an act of purification, hygienic, moral, or social whereby the member is cleansed and restored to full membership in community; (b) sprinkling with water (semen of a god), or lifting out of water (the womb of a goddess) as being born into participation in deity; (c) water baptism accompanying rites of passage such as birth, name-giving, marriage, recovered health, victory in war, or even death, to indicate that they are swallowed up by a supra-temporal realm. [1] Of more direct influence, however, was Jewish practice which was not, Barth emphasizes, the actualization of the presence of God (sacramental) but the use of clean, pure water—a sign of God's sovereignty over primeval floods and chaos—to cleanse and to consecrate. Proselytes, especially women, were often baptized on reception into the Jewish community, as men were circumcised.

This is the context of John the Baptist and the baptism of Jesus. John's baptism was an insult to the Jewish establishment because it was not a rite of initiation. It assumed that active members of the Jewish community needed to be cleansed like proselytes, confessing their sins in anticipation of the judgment to come. Jesus' baptism in this context is not explained. Mark and Luke do not even raise the question. For Matthew, "Thus it is fitting for us to fulfill all righteousness" (4:15) sufficed as an answer. Despite the Baptist's strong prediction that "he will baptize you with the Holy Spirit and with fire" (Matt. 3:11; Lk. 3:16), there is no evidence that Jesus himself accepted this supersession of water by the Spirit and very little on the other hand that he instituted water baptism among believers. John 3:22 indicates that he did; John 4:2 says that his disciples baptized but that he did not. Mark 16:16, making baptism an absolute requirement for salvation, is probably a second-century addition.

The inclusion of a reference to baptism in the risen Christ's great commission, "Go therefore and make disciples of all nations, baptizing them in the name of the Father, and of the Son, and of the Holy Spirit" (Matt. 28:19), does not remove this uncertainty. Some commentators see it as a very late insertion, noting that Eusebius and other fourth-century writers quote the great commission text without it. Others suggest that it may have been a part of the Gospel of Matthew from the beginning. Few, however, (among them Karl Barth[2]), think that the command to baptize may have been part of the original commission. Whether at the end of the first century or in the fourth, it was probably added to reflect the practice of the Church.

Even if the text is the original words of Jesus, however, a question arises concerning its interpretation. The imperative verbs are "go — and make disciples." "Baptizing" and "teaching" are participles. They accompany and serve the primary commission. The assumption is that they happen; the instruction concerns how: for example, "when baptizing, do so in the name of the Father and of the Son and of the Holy Spirit."

The rest of the New Testament carries the practice forward with the same subordinate function. Peter commands baptism "in the name of Jesus Christ for the forgiveness of your sins" (Acts 2:38) in the mass conversion following the "baptism with the Holy Spirit" (Acts 1:5;2:4) of Pentecost. The Book of Acts records many cases of baptism as the first response of the Christian to the Gospel (2:41; 8:12; 8:38; 9:18 [Paul]; 10:48; 16:15; 16:33; 18:8). There is no evidence as to how the ceremony was performed except that water was used, that the Holy Spirit was received (Acts 19:2-6), and that the act was done in the name of the Lord Jesus, or Jesus Christ. There are also other conversions in Acts (9:35; 11:21; 13:12; 13:48; 17:34) where baptism is not mentioned. It may have been assumed, or it may not have taken place. There is no evidence that the apostles themselves, except for Paul, were baptized. The primitive Church was probably a mixture of baptized and unbaptized believers in which the custom of baptism as the act of initiating the believer into the Church was growing.

The Pauline and deutero-Pauline letters confirm this trend and give it theological depth. Paul leaves no doubt (I Cor. 1:13-17) that the Word of God in Christ and not baptism is the first effective saving reality. At the same time, he builds upon the fact of baptism to dramatize the new reality in which, by the grace of God, the Church finds itself. "As many as you as were baptized into Christ have put on Christ" (Gal. 3.27). There is "one Lord, one faith, one baptism, one God and Father of us all" (Eph. 4:5-6). "For by one Spirit we were all baptized into one body – Jews or Greeks, slaves or free – and all were made to drink of one Spirit" (I Cor. 12:13). There is also the classic text which clearly links the baptismal act with the events of the incarnation: "all of us who have been baptized into Christ Jesus were baptized into his death. We were buried therefore with him by baptism into death so that as Christ was raised from the dead by the glory of the Father, we too might walk in newness of life" (Rom. 6:3-4).

Here, despite the paucity of references, a theology of baptism begins to develop. It has, as I see it, two basic themes. (1) It is God through the Gospel who saves. Baptism is a significant form of participation by the Church and the believer in this new reality, so the Spirit is at work in it, but it is not part of the Gospel itself. The first letter of Peter draws a parallel to the obedience of Noah in building the ark which saved him and his family "through water." "Baptism, which corresponds to this, now saves you, not as a removal of dirt from the body, but as an appeal to God for a clear conscience through the resurrection of Jesus Christ, who has gone into heaven and is at the right hand of God, with angels, authorities, and powers subject to him" (I Peter 3:21-22).

(2) Baptism is an act of incorporation, not an individual transaction with God. It is parallel to the baptism of the people of Israel into Moses (I Cor. 10:2), or to Old Testament circumcision which it replaces (Col. 2:11-12). The faith of the one who comes to baptism

clearly plays a role, but this "one" may be an individual, a household, a throng of 3000 people swept by one spirit, or a whole *ethnos*.

So far and no further we can go with the New Testament. The rest is the history of a tradition. Scholars differ as to when infant baptism became common practice in the Church. It may have been a response to the fact that growing numbers of children were being born to Christian parents. It is clear that every New Testament example of baptism involves the decision of a person or a group to present themselves as believers for the ceremony. Unclear is whether or not baptized households (Acts 10:2; 16:15; 16:33; 18:8) were deemed as having a collective faith which included those not (yet) ready for personal decision. In any case, as children were born into the Christian community, the custom grew of baptizing them, even though such Church fathers as Tertullian objected to the practice. At the same time, the baptismal service did not accommodate itself to the fact that the one being received into the church was not capable of personal response. All the symbolism of the confession and renunciation of sin, of dying and rising with Christ, remained and is still present in full form today in the Eastern Orthodox baptismal liturgy. The paradox continues and we still wrestle with it. How we do so depends considerably on our understanding of the sacramental reality of the Church.

IV. The Question of Sacrament

Baptism has been called for centuries a sacrament. What does this mean? Here again theory follows practice. "Sacramental doctrine," Jaroslav Pelikan points out, "emerged from the concrete teaching and practice of the church."[3] The word *sacramentum* has New Testament roots as the Latin Vulgate translation of *mysterion*. The word appears in only one context in the gospels as the hidden message of the parable of the sower, revealed to the faithful (Mark 4:11 and parallels). In the Pauline and deutero-Pauline letters, however, it is prominent and refers, with a few exceptions, to the whole purpose and wisdom of God in Christ "manifested in the flesh, vindicated in the Spirit, seen by angels, preached among the nations, believed on in the world, taken up in glory" (I Timothy 3:16). This mystery is "hidden for ages and generations, but now made manifest to the saints" (Col. 1:26). It is "an economy for the fullness of time to unite all things in him, things in heaven and things on earth" (Eph. 1:10). It is a mystery finally to be fulfilled in the conquest of death (I Cor. 15:51). Mystery is a dimension of revelation, ever to be explored, never to be mastered, in the life of faith. It is the inexhaustible depth and breadth of the wisdom and love of God in Christ transforming and uniting all things. To the eye of faith, all reality is mysterious or, if one prefers the Latin word, sacramental. There is evidence that the term was used in this sense in the early centuries by both Latin and Greek fathers of the Church.

Sacrament had also, however, another root. *Sacramentum* was the pledge of money which a litigant in Roman law laid upon the altar of a god, prepared to forfeit it if he lost the case. By extension it came to mean any act of consecration which binds the performer to a relationship. Tertullian understood baptism as a sacrament in this sense: the self-offering of a believer for the gifts of remission of sins, deliverance from death, regeneration, and reception of the Holy Spirit. Augustine built on this. He placed it in the context of prevenient grace prior to human will, faith or decision, thereby legitimating infant baptism. His doctrine of sovereign grace confirmed the unbridgeable distance between the counsels of God gathering the saved community and the actions of the Church on earth. Nevertheless this same grace, he believed, worked through the sacraments of the Church, primarily baptism and the Lord's Supper. Baptism is effective in all the ways Tertullian described. It places the believer, or in the case of infants the potential believer, in the context of the salvific life of the Church.

This heritage has dominated the concept of sacrament ever since. The focus has shifted from the sacramental reality of God's purpose for all things in Christ, of which believers in all their acts are stewards (I Cor. 4:1; Eph. 3:2-3), to particular acts of the Church by which divine grace is effectively communicated. As is well known, the list of such acts expanded in the Middle Ages, in one case up to 30, before being codified at ten by the Council of Trent.

It is also well known that the Reformers took basic issue with this attribution of effective saving grace to acts of the Church in and of themselves (*ex opere operato*). They reinstated the primacy of the Word both in the sense that the Gospel should be proclaimed and in the sense that Christ the Word in Scripture is prior to and conditions all human acts. They reduced the number of sacraments to two, baptism and the Lord's Supper, on the grounds (questionable in the case of baptism) that they were commanded by the Lord. Without questioning the objective sovereignty of divine grace, they restored the faith of the believer to its role as effective recipient of the sacrament in place of the "work" of performing the sacrament properly in itself.

Nevertheless, the Reformers, with the exception of Zwingli and the Anabaptists, upheld the concept of sacrament as a particular act of the Church and devoted considerable thought to the question how and under what circumstances this act was a special vehicle of divine grace. Calvin moved from expounding the word *mysterion* in its broad New Testament sense directly to particular sacraments,[4] a move to which Karl Barth in the twentieth century takes vigorous and detailed exception.[5] Reformed theologians, especially, were careful to assert the priority of the Word. An agreement between Calvin and the pastors in Zurich (despite Zwingli?) reads as follows:

> The ends of the sacraments are to be marks and badges of Christian profession and fellowship or fraternity, to be incitements to gratitude and exercises of faith and a godly life; in short, to be contracts binding us to this. But among other ends the principal one is, that God may, by means of them, testify, represent, and seal his grace to us. For although they signify nothing else than is announced to us by the word itself, yet it is a great matter, *first*, that there is submitted to our eye a kind of living image which makes a deeper impression on the senses, by bringing the object in a manner directly before them, while they bring the death of Christ and all his benefits to our remembrance, that faith may be the better exercised; and, *secondly*, that what the mouth of God had announced is, as it were, confirmed and ratified by seals.[6]

The sacraments, the agreement goes on to affirm, effect nothing by themselves. They are instruments of God. It is Christ alone in the Holy Spirit who works through them. They do not confer grace by themselves. Unbelievers do not benefit from them, but only those to whom the Spirit gives faith. The sacraments confirm and bear witness to the work of God; the work, however, transcends the sacraments.

Nevertheless, for Calvin and the Reformed tradition, the sacraments are essential to the life of the Church. They are, to quote Calvin quoting Augustine, "testimon(ies) of divine grace toward us, confirmed by an outward sign" or "visible form(s) of an invisible grace." They are signs which confirm and instruct our faith. "Not", writes Calvin, "that I suppose there is some secret force or other perpetually seated in them by which they are able to promote or confirm faith by themselves. Rather I consider that they have been instituted by the Lord to the end that they may serve to establish and increase faith." (*Institute* IV.xiv.9) Or, as he puts it in another place, citing Chrysostom, they are "covenants by which God links himself with us and we pledge ourselves to purity and holiness in life since there is interposed here a mutual agreement between God and ourselves" (*Institute* IV.xiv.19).

Of what value is the concept "sacrament" to all of this, especially to baptism? The Reformed tradition, in answer to this question, has tended to move in two directions.

1. The first movement is toward a modified Augustinian Catholic position wherein baptism, despite its subordination and validation in the one work of God in the Gospel, is nevertheless a necessary and effective instrument of this work in the initiation of the Christian life through entry into the Church. The right celebration of Word *and* sacrament constitute the Church. A special work of the Holy Spirit is here performed, confirming and sealing for the church member the whole work of sovereign redeeming grace for him or herself and the world, which he or she perceives by faith, hears in the message of the Church, and reads in the Bible. From this position arise both questions and convictions about the validity of the baptismal sacrament: its priority over and determination of the faith of the recipient, hence infant baptism; its independence of the character of the officiant, given only the intention to baptize in the triune name; its once-for-allness, regardless of the ecclesial or personal context of its celebration. What is preserved here is the witness of the Church's tradition to the effective sovereignty of the grace of God constituting and maintaining its common life above and beyond the pride, the failures, and the unfaithfulness of Church and believer in this sinful world. Although the New Testament does not link the word mystery/sacrament with either baptism or the Lord's Supper, there is an inherent logic of faith in their having become sacramental acts. In the Eucharist this is based upon the invitation of Christ himself. In baptism, it arose naturally as a celebration of the moment of commitment and initiation. In a sense, the other Roman Catholic sacraments of confirmation, ordination, and marriage are reaffirmations and extensions of the baptismal event. To call baptism a sacrament is a reminder that the whole mystery of God's purpose for the believer and the world is both the cause and the goal, the subject and the object, of this determining moment in the life of the believer and the Church.

2. Karl Barth, joined by others,[7] takes vigorous issue with this direction. "Faith," he writes, "as a human action is nowhere called a mystery (in the New Testament), nor is Christian obedience, nor love, nor hope, nor the existence and function of the *ecclesia*, nor its proclamation of the Gospel, nor its tradition as such, nor baptism, nor the Lord's Supper." The one New Testament mystery/sacrament is the purpose and work of God in history incarnate in Jesus Christ. The line must be drawn clearly between this reality, present and active in our midst, and all human responses,

however blessed, fruitful and faithful they may be (*Church Dogmatics* IV.4, p. 109). Otherwise the Church moves toward salvation by participation in specific acts which assure them a share in salvation and eternal life. This is the pattern of pagan mystery religions of the ancient Hellenistic world. Cultic representations of the incarnate grace of God in Christ move in to take the place of the incarnation itself. What happens then is that cultic acts replace what should be the response of the believer in his or her whole Christian life to the gift, presence, and promise of God. Baptism belongs, in Barth's view, to ethics as the first response of human beings to God's gracious work: the response of commitment, self-giving, repentance, and participation in the life, death, and resurrection of Christ for this world. It is entry into the community which shares this obedience and this hope.

It follows that for Barth and others who share his view, there is no problem of the objectivity of grace and therefore validity in the sacrament over against the subjective faith of the believer. Grace is objectively active in the whole presence of God in the world, in the life of the Church which despite its faults bears faithful witness, and in the inclusion of all humanity in the mystery of God's gracious purpose in Christ. Baptism is a human act, a faithful response, the initiation of the Christian life in the world and in the church. It also follows that Barth has no place for the baptism of those who are not personally able or ready to make this commitment.

Barth has picked up the Baptist side of the Reformed tradition and given it fresh twentieth-century expression. He has done so without delivering the ceremony of baptism into subjectivism. The whole objective power of the grace of God in Jesus Christ is present in believers' baptism as in all that the Church does in worship and in witness. Barth has taken the transcendent sovereignty of God's grace over all human acts and the primary effectiveness of the word of God in human history, which are Reformation themes, and has carried them consistently through. All that is said positively by Calvin in the Reformed confessions about the sacraments as signs and seals, as covenants, and as means for making the saving work of God more vividly present to the minds and hearts of believers, still has its place.

Still, something is missing. Does it lie in the space between the whole claim of God in Christ on human life, the whole stewardship which is given us of the mysteries of God for the world, and the particular acts in which this is expressed? The Christian life is full of ambiguities, of relative choices made in faithful obedience yet more corrupted by the institutional powers in which we work, or by our own unclear motives, than we often realize. We live by the forgiving grace of God for our failure to be proper stewards of God's will and purpose. In worship we confess this and hear the word of forgiveness and new life. We baptize to place the beginning of life in the context of that grace. Is there something in the continuity of this ceremony from the first century to now which in itself refers us to that assured context? Can the great mystery of which the New Testament speaks become here objectively concrete? Can *a* sacrament reflect *the* sacrament without, as Barth fears, replacing it?

V. Baptism and the Church

Questions like these are questions about our understanding of the Church. Here we can start with at least one nearly universal agreement: the Church is prior to the sacraments. It is the context of baptism and an actor, with the believing person or family, in receiving the baptized into the Church. "All baptism," says the World Council of Churches document *Baptism, Eucharist, and Ministry*, "is rooted in and declares Christ's faithfulness unto death. It has its setting within the life and faith of the church and, through the witness of the whole church, points to the faithfulness of God, the ground of all life in faith." (IV,12) The Baptist-Reformed consensus of 1977 is even more explicit. "With regard to Baptism, there is no vicarious faith, and yet the faith of the church, which precedes that of the individual, is the soil in which the faith of the individual is rooted, because the work of the Holy Spirit pervades the whole life of the church. We propose to regard the children of believers — Baptist and Reformed — as being involved in a process of preparation for the full privileges and responsibilities of membership in the church of Christ: they are already within the operational sphere of the Holy Spirit."[8]

These statements conceal, however, a deeper question. What is the relation between the work of God in Christ through the life of the Church and the work of human beings in the Church responding in faith to God? Geoffrey Wainwright puts the issue with irenic precision. "On fundamental matters of the christological, ecclesiological, eschatological and ethical meaning of baptism, there has been widespread agreement among recent New Testament scholars, whatever their denominational allegiance. Discord arises when the discussion turns into the question of grace and faith, to the working of God and man, in relation to baptism."[9] Let me suggest three answers to this question, not mutually exclusive, but different in emphasis and in the implications they bear for the place of baptism in the life of the Christian and the community.

1. For the first emphasis, let me quote an Anglican contributor to the ecumenical discussion:

> The church is the extension in time and space of the Incarnate Word of God, crucified, ascended, glorified, operating among men through the indwelling in them of His Holy Spirit, Who mediates to it His Victorious Life. Thus, although the church is visible and tangible, it is a supernatural corporation. Its life is on earth, but its citizenship is in heaven. Its habitat is this globe and the affairs of men are its concern, but the dwelling place of its spirit is the eternal world. It has here no continuing city; it seeks the city which lies beyond.[10]

This testimony admirably expresses a sense of the corporate reality of the church through the ages prior to and embracing its members in a sacramental unity which is widespread across the spectrum of the ecumenical movement. It is an emphasis which the Amsterdam Assembly of the World Council of Churches in 1948 described as Catholic over against Protestant or evangelical, but it finds expression also in the confessions of the Reformation in the sixteenth and seventeenth century. The Scots Confession of 1560 declares roundly:

> As we believe in one God, Father, Son and Holy Ghost, so we firmly believe that from the beginning there has been, now is, and to the end of the world shall be, one Kirk, that is to say, one company and multitude of men chosen by God, who rightly worship and embrace him by true faith in Jesus Christ who is the only Head of the Kirk, even as it is the body and spouse of Christ Jesus. This Kirk is catholic, that is, universal, because it contains the chosen of all ages, of all realms, nations and tongues, be they of the Jews or be they of the Gentiles, who have communion with God the Father and with His Son Christ Jesus, through the sanctification of His Holy Spirit.

In such expressions as these, there is no ambivalence, no *simul justus et peccator*, no reliance on the quality of a relationship in defining the Church and its sacraments. Whether constituted by divine election or by apostolic succession through a corporate body, the Church is present in the world and beyond it as an objective structure of judgment and grace. The individual believer finds him or herself participating in this structure by faith and subject to its discipline, but the emphasis is on the divine-human whole rather than on the individual.

The implications of this ecclesiology are clearly sacramental, in the catholic sense described above, with all the dangers of *ex opere operato* which beset the Roman and Orthodox traditions. That even the Reformation churches have had to express some form of this perspective, however, is evidence that it cannot be ignored without undermining the full meaning of the Gospel. The church universal—Protestant, Catholic and Orthodox—confesses, in the words of the Nicene Creed, one, holy, catholic, and apostolic Church through all the ages. The objective continuity of this Church from its beginnings with the apostles to its role in the final judgment must constantly be understood anew, liberated from distortion by human religious organization and philosophy, but it cannot be reduced to a form of contemporary experience with no more history than that of the participating families who stand in for their children at baptism. How can we so baptized as to celebrate the entry of the baptized into a community of faith that transcends our generation and our culture?

2. The Church is a community in which God acts through Word and sacrament among sinful human beings justifying them by grace through their faith and guiding their lives in the Spirit. The Barmen Declaration of 1934 puts this most eloquently:

> The Christian church is the congregation of the brethren in which Jesus Christ acts presently as the Lord in Word and Sacrament through the Holy Spirit. As the church pardoned sinners, it has to testify in the midst of a sinful world, with its faith and obedience, with its message as with its order, that it is solely his property, and that it lives and wants to live solely from his comfort and from his direction in the expectation of his appearance (Article III).

The emphasis here is on what happens to the believer in the community. The Church is holy in the sense that the holiness of God pervades it in the Spirit, forgiving and transforming its members and calling them to obedience in a sinful world.

For the church fathers at Barmen, facing Nazism, this confidence was a declaration of independence: "We reject the false doctrine, as though the church were permitted to abandon the form of its message and order to its own pleasure or to changes in prevailing ideological and political conviction." It was the context of the church's resistance to an alien ideology which had taken over the world around it. In its Reformed and Lutheran roots, it was not inconsistent with active service in the world, with all the moral compromises this might involve, depending upon divine forgiveness as well as being guided by divine command. It was based on a firm understanding of positive interaction between Church and world until the time of the final judgment.

The implications of the Barmen Declaration as it stands, however, taken out of context, could easily be accepted by another ecclesiology—that of nineteenth-century Anglo-Saxon revivalism. Here the emphasis is far more strongly on the Church against the world, the community of those who have been saved by grace, who live by the experience of this grace, continually renewed in the worship and community of the Church. This ecclesiology is also in its way missionary, but concerned for the salvation of individuals out of the world rather than for the reconciliation of the world in Christ. The emphasis is on individual decision and individual experience finding salvation in the community experience of the church itself. Here baptism must follow upon conversion. It results from an experience of divine grace grasping the individual life and leads to commitment of that life to the love of God in Christ. Children grow up expecting that they will move from the realm of law to guidance of the Spirit when they have this experience and make this decision.

Is this also the implication of the Barmen Declaration? Many have thought so and this has given rise to a serious questioning of infant baptism in the Reformed and Lutheran churches of Europe following the Second World War. Karl Barth, from 1943 on, took a strong stand in this controversy. His ecclesiology, however, is more various in its implications. For Barth, the church is the area in which the subjective realization of reconciliation in human life by the action of the Holy Spirit takes place. It is not "the outcome of a free undertaking to analyze and come to terms with the self-revealing God by gathering together a community which confesses Him by setting up a doctrine which expounds and proclaims his truth in the way that seems most appropriate to these men."[11] Neither is the Church in itself the source of divine reconciliation. "All ecclesiology is grounded, critically limited, but also positively determined by christology; and this applies in respect of the particular statement which here concerns us, namely that the Church exists for the world. The community neither can nor should believe in itself. Even in this particular respect, there can be no *credo in ecclesiam*."[12] The reality of the Church is rooted in the mystery of Pentecost. It is a relational reality, a continuing event of interaction between God in Christ through the Holy Spirit and sinful self-willed humanity wherein God gathers and upbuilds his community and sends it into the world with the message of reconciliation. No institution, tradition, or even reformation of the Church can itself guarantee its faithfulness, but always and only the divine word judging and transforming it.

Early in the *Church Dogmatics*, Barth links this dynamic reality of Church to the two sacraments of baptism and the Lord's Supper. We cannot, of course, call them absolutely necessary to salvation "for to tie us to the divine sign giving would also be to tie God." But, the authority of the prophets and apostles and through it the grace of the incarnate Word of God is set at the beginning of the Christian church and therefore at the beginning of our existence as the children of God, just as baptism is put at the beginning of our Christian life as an objective testimony pronounced upon us.... We are bound to baptism and the Lord's Supper in token of this ordering and maintenance of life, by the word mediated through the prophetic and apostolic word. For this ordering, this maintenance of life is inseparable from this life, the life of the children of God. For that reason and in that sense, we have to say in all seriousness that sacraments are an indispensable "means of grace."[13]

The later Barth repudiated the concept of particular sacraments because he came to believe that the concept cannot be separated from its abuse. His ecclesiology, however, has remained constant: the Church is the community whose reality is the action of God in Christ through the Holy Spirit among believers who are gathered, nurtured, and sent into the world as witnesses. It is the place where the sinful world meets its judge and redeemer and is sanctified without ever becoming in itself sacred. This sanctification takes place first through the community and second in the individual life. Baptism is an act of initiation in this Church and a part of this sanctification.

3. Third, the Church is participation in the mission of God to all humanity.

To be reconciled to God is to be sent into the world as his reconciling community. This community, the church universal, is entrusted with God's mission of reconciliation and shares his labor of healing the enmities which separate men from God and from each other. Christ has called the church to this mission and given it the gift of the Holy Spirit. The church maintains continuity with the apostles and with Israel by faithful obedience to this call (The Confession of 1967, Presbyterian Church, USA, Part II, Section A, 1).

In other words, the apostolate defines the Church, and the activities of the Church as it gathers, including baptism, serve to equip the community for its missionary service. The radical missiologist Hans Hoekendijk put it more sharply:

Where in this context does the church stand? Certainly not at the starting point nor at the end. The church has no fixed place at all in this context; it *happens* insofar as it actually proclaims the Kingdom to the world. The church has no other existence than in *actu Christi*, that is in *actu apostoli*.... The real autochthony of the church, the soil in which it should be rooted, is the foundation of the apostles and the prophets. Only insofar as the church shares in the mission of the apostles, only insofar as it is on the way toward the ends of the earth and the end of time, does it remain "autochonous."[14]

Not all who affirm the missionary nature of the Church—and certainly not the Presbyterian Church USA!—would go so far as Hoekendijk, but the emphasis is clear. The Church is the covenant community of those who have been called to make disciples of all nations, to announce and serve the coming of the Kingdom of God. It is thoroughly and completely worldly. It is that portion of the world which has been qualified by knowing and believing in God's reconciling purpose for the whole world in Christ. It lives by and in this mission.

One might expect that the consequences of this ecclesiology would lead toward a strong affirmation of believers' baptism, and indeed in the Confession of 1967 and elsewhere, it does so. Baptism is the first consequence of hearing and believing the missionary message. However, there are two reasons why this affirmation is not exclusive. The first is the absolute priority of divine action and divine grace over human response. This truth, expressed in the doctrine of election going back to Augustine, comes out strongly in Calvin and in most of the Reformed confessions. It has been rescued from its anti-missionary implications by the evangelical movements of the nineteenth century,[15] and finally by Karl Barth's celebration of the victorious determination of all human existence by divine grace, working in the life, death, and resurrection of Jesus Christ. Who can be understood as outside the redeeming work of this grace? Who in the community of faith can be called a non-participant because he or she, for whatever reason, is not (yet) in a position to make the affirmation of faith which the Church calls for?

Second, the mission of the Church is directed toward the whole world. Not only individuals but families, local communities, cultures, and structures of economic and political life are objects of mission. Furthermore, as we have come to realize more and more in the past twenty years, but which we should have known from reading the Psalms and the prophets long ago, the whole of God's creation participates in human history for good or ill and therefore in the new reality which is given and promised in Christ. People, however, are born into earthly communities, cultures, and orders. Their growth and development is determined by these, and if perchance an immigrant chooses a new nation, an entrepreneur organizes a new business, or a child become adult finds him or herself cut off from a family, they are still within the context of the forces and attachments which were there before them. Mission is discerning the form of Christ's redeeming presence in the midst of the principalities and powers of this world. When does this process start? When does a member of the Christian community begin to believe? When does he or she being to take responsibility for his or her response in faith to the reality of the world as the reality of God determines its? In the context of these questions and realities, the time and the meaning of baptism, also within a mission-centred understanding of the Church, belong.

VI. Personal Conclusion

Such an account as the above cries out for some resolution. The Reformed tradition as such, however, is too ecumenical, too dynamic, too creative of new theological insights to provide it. The point of view which draws this essay together must therefore be personal. Let me express it in five propositions.

1. The fundamental reality of the Church into which baptism is the initiation is covenantal. It is the community of human beings who participate in and are stewards of the mysteries of God's economy for all things, revealed in the life, death, and resurrection of Jesus Christ. Barth is right that Christ himself is the one true sacrament. Because this is so, the whole life of the Christian is in a sense sacramental. The whole of reality experienced in faith is sacramentally perceived. Sacrament/ mystery, however, does not in this context mean the general presence of the divine in the human or the natural, but human participation in the historical action of God, reconciling the world to himself and making us ambassadors of reconciliation. Baptism is the act which brings us into the sphere of this reality.

2. Baptism, like the Lord's Supper, is not *a* sacrament alongside the Word which is Christ's whole mysterious presence with us in the church, but it can be understood in a secondary and derivative sense as sacramental. This is what I understand Calvin and the ministers of Zurich to be saying. As an act of the Church rooted in its earliest history, this ceremony is an expression of the initiating moment in the life of faith, placed in the context of God's redeeming purpose for that life and for the whole world. It is not only, as Barth would have it, the first act of human response, the beginning of the Christian life and therefore of Christian ethics. The Holy Spirit is present in the response of the Christian life to the commands of God, in judgment, forgiveness, and sanctification, of course. However, baptism is a sacramental reality in another sense than this. It is the ceremony of pure recognition and commitment. It is the first embrace, the act of strength and of love whereby the relationship is acknowledged and accepted which will later bear fruit in a life.

This initial ceremony stands by itself in having this character. There will be later acts which build upon it: the decision of the believer to affirm membership in the church on a more mature level (confirmation), the decision of a man and woman to commit themselves to each other in life-long marriage, the decision of a person to pursue one calling and not another. These are also beginnings in a way. They all take place, however, in a context already acknowledged: the covenant claim of God on the life in question. They define spheres in which the promise of that covenant will be realized. Baptism can be called in a special sense sacramental as an act of the Church setting this context.

3. Baptism is an act which takes place in an ongoing community into which some enter by birth and others by conversion. The Christian Church is not a collection of individuals, each of whom has made a decision or had an experience on the basis of which he or she acknowledges and accepts membership. The reverse is true. Christ in his Church calls people who are enslaved in both body and mind to other social powers and forces out of that bondage into the freedom of communion with him. The convert moves from one socially determined context into another, to become a slave to Christ rather than to the elemental forces of the universe. This is liberation.

This has, I think, two implications for baptism. First, it need not always be an individual ceremony. As we have seen above, households were baptized in New Testament times, in one case a crowd of 3000 people, and in the recorded command of Jesus, even nations. Our modern sensitivities recoil at the story of Clovis, the sixth-century king of the Franks, baptizing his army by command in a local river, or the modern Chinese warlord Feng Yu-Hsiang doing the same with a fire hose.[16] But these stories make the point that under some circumstances the faith of an individual is not different from the faith of a whole community, and that the forces which bring about conversion may be social as well as personal. Individuality is the fruit of love in the covenant relation which God has established with his people and into which he brings others through the witness of the Church in various ways.

Second, children of believers participate in the believing community from the moment of their birth. They are also self-centred sinners, like the rest of us, from the beginning. The baptism of infants, therefore, is a proper recognition of the social determinants operating upon a developing child's life and of the context of faith into which he or she grows. One cannot trace a moment of beginning for a child's faith, or for its passage from death to new life in Christ. Awareness of being in this context grows as the child grows. The faith not only of the parents but of the Church, both the local congregation and the church universal, both the Church now and the Church from the beginning to the end of time, are part of the context of this growth. Not to baptize an infant who lives and develops in such a context is to create a false dichotomy between faith and unfaith, between inside and outside the Church.

This would not be so if Pilgram Marpeck, an early Anabaptist writer, were correct:

> In the new covenant, the children are pronounced holy without baptism, without sacrifice, without faith or unfaith; they are simply received by Christ, although Paul says "without faith no man can please God." Children and the retarded are not required to believe or disbelieve these words, but those who are born from the knowledge of good and evil into the innocence and simplicity of faith are required to believe. The witness of God and Christ belongs to the process of becoming like children; but human understanding, all fleshly pretension, deceit, and desires are to be crucified with Christ through baptism and confidence in the future life, they are buried into the death of Christ.[17]

The insight in this passage is that children — and, one should note, the retarded, that is, all those who will never reach a condition of mature, independent judgment — are part of the Church, present and blessed by Christ along with the rest of us. The errors, it seems to me, are two: (1) that children and the retarded are innocent, that is, without participation in the sin of the rest of the human race, and (2) that baptism is not really a ceremony of initiation into the life of the Church with Christ but rather a purgative ritual which makes us again like children. Both, I submit, fail to grasp the character of that society called the Church which gives us our humanity in Christ's sacrifice, calling, and risen presence.

4. Nevertheless, the act of baptism in the Church retains and should retain the tension which underlies the controversy between infant and adult baptism. It is an act of initiation, the beginning of new life in Christ; it is also an act of dying to the old self and rising again with Christ. It sets the context for the growth of the believer in faith and in the Church for many from the earliest moments of consciousness. It also involves a decision of faith to move from the old life to the new. The Eastern Orthodox Church expresses this tension in its baptismal liturgy which embodies all the theology of Romans 6, including questions to the bapitzee, even when an infant is being baptized. It is recognized in some Reformed churches which accept both believers' and infant baptism in the confidence that they will witness to each other. The family whose baby is baptized, the church in which this baptism is practised, must never forget the question which the opposing practice poses: will the

child be nurtured so as to realize with increasing depth the meaning of dying and rising with Christ and of living by the promise of the new creation in the midst of the old? Those who postpone baptism, and the church which follows this practice, are never free from the counterquestion: how is this child being included in the body of Christ, in the communion of believers, while waiting for the moment of mature decision? In the mutual questioning on both sides, the way in which the grace of God in Christ works through the Church to include and nourish its children is the reality we seek to discern.

5. Baptism is the beginning of ethics. I have said above that it is more than this, but without this it would be an empty ritual. It is the beginning of a new perspective which sees Christ in the world and the world in Christ and which therefore judges no one any longer "according to the flesh" (II Cor. 5:16). For the adult convert, this is clear; it will have been part of his or her struggle from the moment of serious listening to the Word. But for the parents of the baptized infant, also, baptism is a moment of self-examination and new direction. The sacrifices of time and freedom, the changes in life's habits and direction, and all the other joys and burdens which a baby brings, are placed in perspective as these parents become the nurturers of this child's faith in God as part of their parental responsibilities. Baptism is in a way a paradigm of the Christian life: "I appeal to you therefore, brethren, by the mercies of God, to present your bodies as a living sacrifice, holy and acceptable to God which is your spiritual worship. Do not be conformed to this world, but be transformed by the renewal of your mind, that you may prove what is the will of God, what is good and acceptable and perfect" (Rom. 12:1-2). In this presentation, in this transformation, we become "servants of Christ and stewards of the mysteries of God" (I Cor. 4:1). These mysteries may be expressed in the conversion of a culture, in the liberation of a people from oppression and injustice, in the cultivation of the land, or in the raising of a child. Baptism sets the stage for them all.

Notes

1. Markus Barth, "Baptism," in *The Interpreter's Dictionary of the Bible*, supplementary volume (Nashville: Abingdon, 1962).

2. Karl Barth, *Church Dogmatics* (Edinburgh: T. & T. Clark, 1969), IV, Part 4, p. 95.

3. Jaroslav Pelikan, *The Christian Tradition* (Chicago: University of Chicago Press, 1972) I, p. 162.

4. J. Calvin, *Institute*, Book IV.xiv. 2-3.

5. Karl Barth, *Church Dogmatics*, IV, pt. 4, pp. 101-28.

6. "Mutual consent in regard to the sacraments between the ministers of the church of Zurich and John Calvin, minister of the church of Geneva, 1554," John Calvin, *Tracts*, vol. 2 (Edinburgh, 1849).

7. Notably Hendrikus Berkhof, *Christian Faith* (Grand Rapids: Eerdmans, 1986), p. 348.

8. *Baptists and Reformed in Dialogue*, Studies from the World Alliance of Reformed Churches, No. 4, pp. 23-24.

9. Geoffrey Wainwright, *Christian Initiation*, 1969, (Richmond: John Knox Press), p. 11.

10. John A.F. Gregg, Archbishop of Armagh and Primate of all Ireland, in *The Universal Church in God's Design* (Amsterdam: Assembly Series, I, London: S.C.M. Press, 1948), p. 59.

11. Karl Barth, *Church Dogmatics* I, pt. 2, p. 213.

12. Karl Barth, *Church Dogmatics* (1962) IV, pt. 3, p. 786.

13. Karl Barth, *Church Dogmatics* (1939), I, pt. 2, pp. 231-32.

14. Hans Hoekendijk, *The Church Inside Out* (Philadelphia: Westminster, 1966), p. 42.

15. Cf. The Declaratory Statement to the Westminster Confession, adopted by the Presbyterian Church, USA in 1903.

16. Feng Yu-Hsiang said it wasn't true, pointing out that in his part of the country there wasn't that much water pressure.

17. Pilgram Marpeck, "Confession," 1532, quoted from *Anabaptism in Outline* Walter Klaassen, ed. (Kitchener, Ontario: Herald Press, 1981), p. 176.

Chapter III

BAPTISM IN THE MENNONITE TRADITION

Marlin E. Miller

I. Introduction

The topic of this chapter is misleading if taken at a simple and straightforward surface reading. The title refers to *"baptism* in the Mennonite tradition" as if baptism were a univocal and coherent concept among Mennonites. The topic further implies that *"the Mennonite tradition"* with respect to baptism is like a single river that has remained within the same well-worn riverbed and flowed continuously in one direction through the surrounding ecclesial and theological landscapes for the past four-and-a-half centuries. Neither apparent implication is correct. There have been and continue to be *several* Mennonite traditions with regard to baptism. And both the understanding and practice of baptism have *varied*, not insignificantly, among Mennonites in North America, and even more among Mennonites around the world.[1]

Both differing theological understandings and various practices of baptism itself have comprised the somewhat diverse Mennonite traditions of baptism. The understandings include but are not necessarily limited to: variations in focusing upon the divine initiative or upon the believer's response as decisive for baptism; the ways in which the "internal" baptism of the Holy Spirit and the "external" baptism with water relate to each other; the relative emphasis placed upon the individual believer's or the Christian community's role and significance in baptism; whether baptism is by the Holy Spirit, water, and "blood," or primarily by the Holy Spirit and water; the theological connection between baptism and church discipline; and both varied and changing interpretations of "rebirth" or "regeneration" or "conversion" as the presupposition of baptism in Mennonite history. In addition, influences from the contemporary charismatic movement and by occasional and scattered tendencies to distinguish between being baptized and becoming a member of the Church have further varied understandings of baptism.

The practices among Mennonites with regard to baptism have also varied. Such differences have included: whether the preferred or even normative mode of baptism should be by immersion or by pouring or by sprinkling; the average age at which children born into and nurtured in Christian families may be expected to come to faith and receive baptism;[2] whether being "baptized upon confession of faith" means publicly affirming one's faith in Jesus Christ as Lord and Saviour or giving public assent to the faith of the Church as articulated in a corporate confessional statement, or writing out one's own faith statement; and the specific content of baptismal liturgies and vows (for example, whether the baptismal vow includes a commitment to participate in church discipline, the readiness to serve in pastoral ministry if called by the church, etc.). To this list could be added the differing degrees of routinization among some Mennonite groups during different periods of their history, of "instruction" (catechism) of children of the church during their early teen years with the expectation that they would more or less automatically request baptism upon completion of instruction. In other settings, such classes have not been formalized but are convened only when young people express personal interest in beginning such instruction with a view toward being baptized.

Reasons for the varieties in baptismal understanding and practice are doubtless multiple. Simple biblicism, the lack of an explicit dogmatic tradition, the consistent ambivalence toward formally binding corporate confessions of faith, the congregationalist oriented polity, and influences from numerous revival and church renewal movements among Mennonites in several religious, cultural, and national settings have doubtless contributed to these differences. For whatever reason, there are more differences and variations among Mennonites on this presumably distinguishing cardinal practice and doctrine than might be expected on first glance. The closer one looks at varieties of baptism in Mennonite traditions, the more problematic the assumption becomes that *the* Mennonite *tradition* on *baptism* has been passed on without spot or wrinkle and can easily be located and summarized for the purposes of ecumenical and theological conversation. These variations would only increase if their implications for other doctrines such as original sin and free will were listed in the catalogue already assembled.

Nevertheless, Mennonites over the centuries and in many countries have shared a set of common convictions about Christian baptism. These common convictions regarding baptism have in fact counted as a distinguishing doctrine and practice for Mennonites, particularly when compared to many, if not most, major Christian traditions. These common convictions have focused on several central understandings and practices. They particularly include both the acceptance of believers' baptism as the only valid Christian baptism and the consequent rejection of infant baptism, either fundamental reinterpretation of or a rejection of a sacramental view of baptism (and the implications of such a view), and the close connection between baptism and beginning of life of Christian discipleship.

In addition, Mennonites in one way or another have also usually emphasized "regeneration" as a presupposition of baptism. The several Mennonite traditions have further agreed that unbaptized infants are saved rather than eternally condemned and have frequently commended some pattern of child and/or parent dedication as an alternative to infant baptism for children of Christian parents. At least until rather recently, Mennonites have generally insisted that persons baptized as infants may become members of a congregation only by being "baptized upon confession of faith" (commonly called "rebaptism" by most major Christian traditions).[3] Finally, Mennonites, as most Christian groups, have traditionally grounded water baptism in the ordinance and institution of Jesus Christ. Simultaneously they have understood its significance in ways which have undergirded believers' baptist rather than pedobaptist convictions.

In light of the convictions broadly shared by most Mennonites regarding baptism and in view of the not insignificant variations in baptismal understandings and practices among them, this presentation will attempt to represent *"the best"* regarding baptism in the Mennonite tradition(s). I have selected the major cues from several six-teenth-century Anabaptist writers, from a few Anabaptist and Mennonite confessional statements ranging from the sixteenth to the twentieth century, from the results of contemporary "neo-Anabaptist" thought and scholarship, and from some formal as well as informal discussions regarding baptism among Mennonites. Because of the context of conversation between Reformed and Mennonite traditions for which it has been prepared, this attempt will in addition seek to address several issues which have arisen either in the traditional controversies and disputations as well as in more recent ecumenical dialogue between spokespersons of these two ecclesiastical and theological streams.[4]

I consider Balthasar Hübmaier, Pilgram Marpeck, and Dirk Philips the most helpful sixteenth-century Anabaptist and Mennonite writers on baptism. The first book-length treatment on Anabaptist baptism was Rollin S. Armour's *Anabaptist Baptism: A Representative Study*, in 1966. Others, including A.J. Beachy, Christof Windhorst, and

Wayne Pipkin, have since provided insightful interpretations of Anabaptist thought and practice. Further, among the many Mennonite confessional statements, this article gives primary attention to the traditions represented by the Schleitheim Articles of 1527, the Dordrecht Confession of 1632, the Mennonite Articles of Faith (Ris) of 1766, the Mennonite Confession of Faith of 1963, the Mennonite Brethren Confession of Faith of 1975, and the Confession of Faith in a Mennonite Perspective currently being drafted.[5] Finally, other than several article, or essay-length treatments, Marlin Jeschke's *Believers' Baptism for Children of the Church* provides the most comprehensive constructive interpretation of baptism in a "neo-Anabaptist" vein among contemporary North American Mennonites.

Even within this selective reading of baptism in Mennonite traditions, I have limited the scope of this article to several specific themes, namely the Scriptural order of baptism, baptism as "sign" or "sacrament" (and in what sense), the relation between baptism and the church, the relation between baptism and discipleship or ethics, and the recipients of baptism. These topics are either of foundational significance for baptism in the Mennonite traditions or of particular relevance for conversation between the Reformed and the Mennonite traditions.

II. The Scriptural Order of Christian Baptism

In his *On the Christian Baptism of Believers* completed on June 11, 1525, Balthasar Hübmaier sounded a theme which has recurred with variations throughout Anabaptist and Mennonite annals of baptismal thought and practice.[6] Written in part as a response to Zwingli's *On Baptism, Rebaptism, and Infant Baptism*, Hübmaier's booklet underscored a specific biblical order of Christian baptism "both in regard to the words and the meaning...," namely: "(1) word, (2) hearing, (3) faith, (4) baptism, (5) work."[7] Hübmaier contends that this order of baptism appears consistently both in Jesus Christ, institution of baptism according to Matthew 28:18ff. and Mark 16:15ff. as well as in apostolic teaching and practice according to the book of Acts and the Epistles. Baptism follows the proclamation of the Gospel, the hearing of the Gospel, and the response to it in faith. Baptism is, moreover, to be followed by a life of Christian discipleship sustained and encouraged by the community of believers.

This understanding of the Scriptural order of baptism from the very beginnings of the Anabaptist movement subsequently gained the broad consensus of Anabaptist and Mennonite groups. Its normative significance is echoed also by Marpeck and Philips in the third and fifth decades of the Anabaptist movement. After commenting on Matthew 28:18ff., Marpeck summarizes this view as follows:

> Thus, briefly concerning the order: first, to learn; we are instructed to know the will of God and to believe Christ. When we have been taught that we can know Christ and believe in Him, then it is time to be baptized, to take off our old fleshly lusts and to put on Christ, a new spiritual life. After that, just as we have agreed, in being baptized, to complete the will of God, we learn, or are instructed, to be obedient in all things, and not again return to sin, as a dog does to his vomit or as a washed sow again to its dirt (2 Pet. 2:22). Let each Christian judge what we say, and especially consider Romans 6, Galatians 3, Ephesians 5, Hebrews 6, I Peter 4, 2 Peter 2, John 3, I John 5, and other passages of Scripture.[8]

Although the nuances of Marpeck's terminology ("teaching" or "instruction") may differ somewhat from Hübmaier's vocabulary ("proclamation of gospel" and "teaching"), the foundational order remains the same. In both cases one kind of "teaching" (or preaching) precedes baptism and another kind of "teaching" follows it. Baptism properly comes in the "middle" between the initial proclamation of the gospel and the instruction in Christian discipleship.

Philips similarly bases the order of baptism particularly upon the "ordinance and institution" of Jesus Christ as recorded in Matthew 28 and Mark 16 and confirmed and maintained by the apostles. In his *Concerning the Baptism of Our Lord Jesus Christ* from 1564, he asserts:

> This is the true unalterable ordinance and institution of the Lord with respect to baptism just as the words of Christ above, quoted out of both gospels (Matt. 28:19; Mark 16:15) clearly bring together and testify. The teaching of the gospel before and after baptism must be pursued, so that everyone may come to a genuine faith through the grace of God and may be baptized, manifest his remorse over sin and prove his faith therewith (Acts 2:38; 3:19). Thereafter, he must still hear God's word at all times and dedicate himself to maintain all the commandments of Jesus Christ.[9]

As did Marpeck, Philips thus emphasizes that the biblical order of baptism includes the initial preaching of the Gospel, a faith response to it, the reception of baptism, and continuing instruction in the Christian life within the context of the believing community.

In grounding their understanding of baptism on the ordinance and institution of Jesus Christ, these early Anabaptist and Mennonite writers agreed with the Roman Catholic and Protestant theologians who taught that Christian baptism had been instituted by the resurrected Lord on the basis on Matthew 28 and Mark 16. The Anabaptist and Mennonite teachers, however, interpreted the term "making disciples" in Matthew 28:19, as meaning "preaching" the Gospel (and synonymous with "preach" in Mark 16:15) or "teaching" salvation through Jesus Christ to non-believers, as the necessary precondition to their hearing the word of salvation and responding to it in faith (or rejecting it). The word in Matthew 28: 20, "teaching," was then interpreted to mean the ongoing and comprehensive instruction in all of Jesus' teachings and commandments within the context of the Christian Church for those who respond in faith to the Gospel and are baptized and thus incorporated into the believing community. This particular passage, broadly adopted as a classical baptismal text in the mainstream Christian traditions, thus provided the incipient Mennonite traditions not only with a major building block in the theological foundation for baptism but also with an essential component of the brief for an order of baptism which considers believers' baptism to be the normative and only Scriptural pattern of valid Christian baptism.

This order of baptism, in which the proclamation of the Gospel and a faith response issue in the request for and the reception of baptism as incorporation into the Church and the beginning of a life of Christian discipleship, represents the foundational consensus of the Mennonite traditions from their origins in the sixteenth century to the present.[10] To be sure, this consensus has been articulated in various ways and has been made more or less explicit in churchly statements and theological writings.

The diversity of formulation has doubtless been conditioned in part by somewhat differing theological perspectives among the Mennonite traditions as well as by the varieties of polemical situations which have contributed to the shaping of these traditions. For example, the importance of having come to faith in Jesus Christ as the prior condition of baptism has at times been emphasized to such a degree that it has overshadowed other dimensions of the biblical order of baptism. Such overstatements have frequently arisen as attempted correctives to what have been perceived to be unacceptable understandings and practices of baptism in the pedobaptist traditions. Furthermore, the influences of pietist, revivalist, and charismatic renewal movements, as well as of more recent cultural influences, have frequently contributed to what sometimes amounts to an overemphasis on the subjective and individual dimensions of Christian baptism in Mennonite teaching and practice.[11] Nor should one rule out the possibility of an occasional lack of theological balance among Mennonites. The foundational consensus of the Mennonite traditions regarding the normative Scriptural order of Christian baptism thus remains at least as much a challenge to many contemporary Mennonites as to other Christian traditions and communities.

The basis for the above pattern of baptism does not depend only on a particular reading of an isolated text but is the most clearly attested view generally in the New Testament.[12] Both the current ecumenical consensus as reflected in the *Baptism, Eucharist, and Ministry* document of the World Council of Churches, and the conclusions of the Mennonite-Reformed Dialogue in the Netherlands either agree with or are compatible with the view that this order of baptism comes closest to the Scriptural pattern.[13]

I would, however, like to make several additional comments on the concept of a normative biblical "order of baptism" and its potential significance for the understanding and practice of Christian baptism.

First, the emphasis upon a normative order of baptism means that *a specific temporal* sequence of events, decisions, and actions belongs to a correct understanding and practice of Christian baptism. The proclamation of and the hearing of the Gospel precede water baptism. The baptizand's having come to faith and requesting baptism precede that individual's baptism and incorporation into the Christian Church. Participation in the life of the church and walking in the way of Jesus Christ are to follow the commitment made in that direction during the ceremony of baptism.[14]

Second, the emphasis upon a specific order of baptism includes the claim that this order is *normative* because it is *the New Testament order*. According to the New Testament, this order has been established and commanded by Jesus Christ and maintained by the apostles. Hübmaier, Marpeck, and Philips as well as more recent representatives of this tradition have based this "order" on the "ordinance" and "command" of the risen Lord and apostolic practice. "Order" thus connotes not only temporal sequence but also the authoritative pattern. Varieties of experience and diversity of traditions outside and beyond the New Testament Scriptures should therefore be judged by this pattern rather than fundamentally modifying or supplanting it. This claim should not be construed to mean that every instance of baptism in the Scriptures explicitly reflects precisely the same experience of baptism or an identical sequence of events in all accompanying details. However, the claim does contend that the variations in individual cases tend to reinforce rather than significantly modify or contradict the normative scriptural order.

Third, this emphasis upon the biblical order of baptism presupposes what may be called *the structure of baptismal reality*. This emphasis thus assumes that the various "images" of baptism in the New Testament are posited upon and reflect this pattern of baptism.[15] Any theological interpretation of Christian baptism should therefore correspond to the baptismal reality embedded in this order rather than seek to provide the rationale for a significantly different order of baptism.

For example, a theological understanding of the priority of divine grace issuing in an order of baptism where water baptism may precede the baptizand's faith response to the proclamation of the Gospel would, from this perspective, reflect both a different baptismal reality and a qualitatively different interpretation of divine grace than those reflected in the New Testament. Similarly, an interpretation of baptism as the incorporation of persons into the Christian Church in such a way that baptism may precede the baptizand's declared intention to begin a life of discipleship and to begin participation in the Church as the body of Christ would imply both a fundamentally different baptismal reality and a qualitatively different ecclesiology and understanding of Christian life and ethics than those presupposed and articulated in the New Testament. In either case, theological interpretations of the priority of divine grace, the nature of the Christian Church, and Christian ethics which may claim Scriptural foundations should also be consistent with the biblical order of baptism as the normative structure of baptismal reality.

Fourth, and finally, the biblical order of baptism points to an *appropriate relation between the "objective" and "subjective" dimensions* of Christian baptism.[16] Mennonite traditions have frequently given considerable – and most likely excessive – attention to the subjective aspects of baptism. This emphasis has sought to maintain the biblical order of baptism and to correct what have been seen as the deviant and excessive emphases upon the so-called objective side of baptism by the mainstream traditions since the fourth and fifth centuries. However, the influences of Zwingli and some mystic traditions upon sixteenth-century Anabaptists and Mennonites, the traditional believers' baptist insistence upon personally coming to faith and confessing faith prior to being baptized, the reactions to and suspicions of sacramentalism in all its forms, and the subsequent influence of pietism, revivalism, and modern Western individualism have doubtless contributed to an all too frequently exaggerated preoccupation with the subjective, and an all too frequent neglect of the objective aspects of baptism. The concept of a normative biblical order of baptism, however, is here meant to connote a certain "objectivity" and to include both objective and subjective as well as both individual and corporate dimensions.

III. Baptism as Sacrament or Sign

Although the various Mennonite traditions have frequently differed on the theological categories which they have used to speak about baptism, they have shared a common rejection of *traditional sacramental* understandings and practice. During the last three centuries this common stance has usually included a strong preference for an alternative theological vocabulary as well. Terms such as "ordinance" or "sign" or "symbol" have become commonplace and have almost entirely replaced the concept of "sacrament." Particularly the concept "mystery" in the theological sense remains an almost incomprehensible and unknown "mystery" in the ordinary sense among Mennonite and broader believers' church groups.

In the early decades of the Anabaptist and Mennonite movements, however, the term "sacrament" was sometimes reinterpreted as well as avoided. The early reinterpretation of "sacrament" is instructive for understanding the core convictions regarding baptism in the Mennonite traditions and for evaluating the theological validity of their formulations.

The early Anabaptist and Mennonite teachers and groups who did refer to baptism as a "sacrament" explicitly rejected the understanding of sacrament as a means of grace *ex opere operato* which can take place quite independently of faith. Rather, they interpreted "sacrament" in the sense of a covenant or a solemn pledge of loyalty on the basis of the term's classical meaning in Latin.[17] Thus understood, the term sacrament underscored their view of the biblical order of baptism, which includes a public commitment to follow Jesus Christ in life as a consequence of having come to and confessed faith in him. In addition they found confirmation for this concept of sacrament as a pledge or covenant in the words of a widely used baptismal text among them, namely I Peter 3:21 which refers to baptism as the "pledge of a good conscience to God."

Among those who reinterpreted the traditional concept of baptism as a sacrament, Pilgram Marpeck was perhaps the one who gave it the most substantive theological meaning. He also sought to incorporate both the "subjective" and the "objective" dimensions of Christian baptism into his reinterpretation of sacrament.[18]

Marpeck acknowledged that the term is never used in Scripture to refer to baptism. However, he proposed that it could be used correctly in relation to baptism if taken in its ancient and natural meaning, namely as an oath or pledge "that refers to an event that is special or holy or a work that has that kind of connotation."

The relation between the perceptible expression of the pledge and that to which it refers can be illustrated by the example of a knight who commits himself to serve his lord in battle and raises his finger in making this oath. The raising of the finger is neither the fighting, nor the endurance during the battle, nor the victorious outcome of the battle. The "action" is rather the "covenant, made in the firm hope that, according to the command and desire of his Lord, he will diligently attack the enemy of his Lord, even risking his life until death." Marpeck thus suggested that baptism is a sacrament in the sense that it is the visible expression of the believer's pledge or covenant of faithfulness to Jesus Christ in life.

Baptism as a sacrament refers not only to the believer's part in this covenant of faith. Baptism also refers to the divine initiative of grace which initiates and establishes this covenant. Marpeck illustrated this aspect of baptism with an analogy between the convenantal transaction of which baptism is a sign and the way in which friends give and receive gifts. When this happens,

> all that is done thereby is to indicate the friendliness, love, and faithfulness of those who give them toward those who receive them. In the same way, love and faithfulness are not the gifts themselves but are, rather, the heart which the gifts indicate. Unity and trust are indicated to the receiver of the gifts, and all goodness, love, friendliness, and faithfulness to the one who gives it. Similarly, the word sacrament has no meaning.... He who receives the gift receives that for which it was given: sanctification.... The gift must come spontaneously [*auss freier herligkeyt*] as an act of love and an inclined will, and it must come from one who could very well neglect it without any shame or disrespect.... He who receives the gift reciprocates in turn with his whole heart and being, and that is called sanctification.[19]

The "covenant of a good conscience with God" is thus established by the grace of God which is grounded purely in itself. The believer's commitment and pledge is the grateful acceptance of this divine gift and the desire to use it according to the intention for which it has been given. Water baptism as a sign of the believer's commitment to this covenantal transaction thus presupposes the action of divine grace in initiating the covenant, forgiving the sinner, and in enabling the believer to respond by committing himself or herself to the purpose for which God has given the covenant.

This emphasis upon *both* the prior action of divine grace and the necessity of a personal faith commitment in relation to the baptismal covenant has generally been shared in the Anabaptist and Mennonite traditions. To be sure, the usual insistence upon repentance, confession, and the commitment of faith has not infrequently overshadowed the emphasis upon the priority of grace. Sometimes repentance, as the beginning of the saving process, and discipleship, as its continuance, were stressed so much that it sounded to Protestant ears as if repentance and good works were being made the necessary means for meriting God's grace.

Nevertheless, contemporary scholarship has shown that the early Mennonite and Anabaptist traditions usually acknowledged that the ability and the will to turn to God in faith are a gift of God in Christ rather than an ability resident in human beings apart from divine grace.[20] This traditional view has continued to be affirmed by Mennonite teachers and theologians. For example, Marlin Jeschke reiterates the point in his recent *Believers' Baptism for Children of the Church*:

In the New Testament baptism is...always considered the work of divine grace. Baptism represents the activity of God's Word and Spirit in creating spiritual life. And baptism is the church's overt recognition of this prior work of God, this act of prevenient grace.[21]

Even though both the Mennonite and Protestant traditions can therefore generally agree on the priority and the gift-quality of divine grace in the relationship between grace and the response of faith, the *nature* of God's grace and its *effects* in the lives of Christian believers have usually been understood differently by these traditions.

The preceding quotation from Jeschke reflects the understanding broadly shared by the Anabaptist and Mennonite traditions that God's grace is expressed not only in a declaration of forgiveness but primarily as a creative and transforming power which regenerates and renews sinful human beings (and will one day issue in the "creation of a new heaven and a new earth"). This view has provided the basis for expecting grace to produce a significant and even visible transformation of character, conduct, and relationships in the believers and in the church as a community in the midst of the unbelieving world. In this regard, the Anabaptist and Mennonite traditions have differed from the Protestant traditions that have understood grace primarily in terms of God's forgiveness and acceptance, granted through justification, which restores fallen human nature.

The interpretation of baptism as a sacrament in the Anabaptist tradition thus shares with the majority Protestant traditions the assumption that God's graceful initiative precedes and calls forth the believer's faith and commitment. Because divine grace is primarily a power which restores fallen human nature and enables the response of obedient faith, the sacramental significance of baptism focuses upon the believer's confession of faith and pledge. Any understanding of baptism which can be enacted not only independently of the believing response of faith and commitment, but even without emphasizing that the believing response and commitment is an *essential* part of the *divinely initiated* covenantal transaction of which baptism is the sign, represents both a different understanding of divine grace and of sacramental reality. Baptism is thus a sign of God's new creation and new order, not only of God's restoration of a fallen creation and a fallen order. Because baptism witnesses to the renewal of human nature through divine grace, the concept of baptism as a "sacrament" focuses on the believer's commitment and pledge to live according to God's new creation in Christ as the effect of divine grace.[22]

The Anabaptist/Mennonite rejection of sacraments in the traditional sense and the reinterpretation of sacrament has led to somewhat diverse ways of theologically understanding and formulating how the grace made available in Jesus Christ is communicated to the believers. Sometimes this communication has been formulated primarily in terms of the believers being baptized by Christ "inwardly" with the Holy Spirit. Sometimes it has been couched primarily in terms of the believers hearing the Word of God which was made incarnate in Jesus and is proclaimed to us.[23]

In either case, however, the Anabaptist and Mennonite traditions did not intend to separate Word and Spirit any more than the mainstream Protestant traditions, even though there have doubtless been differences of emphases between them. According to the Reformed tradition, the Spirit is understood particularly as the interpreter of the Word. This orientation accordingly stresses the relation of baptism to the proclaimed Word of forgiveness as the means of communicating divine grace to the believer which is confirmed by the Holy Spirit. According to the Mennonite and Anabaptist traditions, the Spirit above all "makes the Word become reality in the life of the believer and in that of the congregation."[24] This emphasis is quite consistent with their concept of grace as a creative and transforming power at work in the lives of the believers and the believing community. This emphasis accordingly focuses—after presupposing the dimension of forgiveness—on the relation of baptism to the transforming action of the Holy Spirit in the believing community and in the believer in both the community's and believer's response to the grace of God incarnate in Jesus Christ the Word as known in the Scriptures.

Baptism may thus be understood as the visible sign and witness of that covenantal transaction which is initiated and established by God's grace in Jesus Christ and issues in the believer's confession of faith in and commitment to Jesus Christ and incorporation into the Christian Church. Baptism does not effect the communication of this covenantal transaction apart from the individual's faith and commitment. However, baptism does witness to, correspond to, and participate in this covenantal transaction when the baptismal candidate's faith and commitment are expressed and confirmed by the baptizing church.[25]

IV. Baptism as Incorporation and Entry into the Church

As the visible mark of entry and incorporation into the Christian community, baptism can be properly understood only in relation to the reality of the Christian Church. In other words, the theology and practice of baptism should be consistent with a corresponding ecclesiology, and a given ecclesiology implies and brings with it a corresponding practice and view of baptism. The believers' baptist tradition in a Mennonite perspective corresponds to an identifiable understanding of the Church and proposes that this understanding of the Church is consistent with the order and reality of baptism as summarized in the two previous sections of this essay.

In particular, believers' baptism corresponds to an understanding of the Church in which the Church is by definition a missionary community in the midst of a still unbelieving world. Furthermore, by virtue of its existence as a missionary community, the Church is grounded upon the work of the Holy Spirit who has called it into being and sustains it, rather than built upon the continuities of familial or ethnic or national peoplehood. This means that baptism signals the incorporation and entry into the society of those who are being redeemed through the power of the Holy Spirit and through faith in Christ, where the divisions of family, race, gender, and class are relativized and reconciled in him. The churchly reality which coincides with the normative order and reality of baptism therefore represents a qualitatively different society than the communities which extend and reinforce familial, national, class, and other such bonds.

In contemporary ecumenical theology, it has become more or less commonplace to refer to the Church as a missionary community. This emphasis doubtless both derives from the renewal of a biblical vision of God's people and the rise of the modern missionary movement as well as from the dechristianization of the West and the legal disengagement of church and state in post-Enlightenment Western societies.

With respect to the question of Christian baptism, the broader ecumenical emphasis upon the Church as a missionary community has meant a growing awareness and theological articulation of the missionary dimension of baptism in the sense that baptism marks the boundaries of the faith community in distinction to those of *the entire society or national body* and in the sense that the continuing existence of the Christian Church depends upon inviting non-believers to faith in Jesus Christ. This emphasis has also meant a growing awareness and appreciation of the minority and missionary stance of the Christian churches in many countries which have never been nominally Christian and in some cases are avowedly non- or even anti-Christian.   Traces of this growing appreciation for the Church as a missionary community have shown up in ecumenical conversations on baptism and contributed to some measure of convergence between believers' baptist and pedobaptist perspectives.[26]

The sociological referent for baptism which remains controversial between the pedobaptist and believers' baptist traditions, however, is the situation of the Christian *family* in relation to the Church as community of believers.   The current practice of infant baptism finds a major theological justification in the argument that a child of Christian parents is surrounded by the faith of the parents (and that of the Christian community) in a way which significantly differs from the situation of a child born to non-Christian parents. Up to this point, the believers' baptist traditions would doubtless agree. From the latter perspective, however, the move from acknowledging a significant difference in the two situations to justifying infant baptism on the basis of that difference amounts to the shift from one concept of the Christian Church to a qualitatively different ecclesiology, namely from the Church as faith community to the Church as an ethnic community (or at best a confusing mixture of the two).   Even the commendable reservations about the frequent "apparently indiscriminate" baptismal practice of many large majority churches in North America and Europe and the laudable call to "rediscover" the "continuing call of Christian nurture" do not fundamentally alter this ecclesiological issue.[27] The missionary character of the Church necessarily implies that the Church is a faith community rather than an ethnic community and calls for an ecclesiology and an accompanying baptismal practice that witnesses to and reinforces rather than undermines this reality.[28]

In addition to signalling the missionary character of the Christian community, baptism marks the candidate's entry and incorporation into the Christian church. As Jeschke observes:

> The believer is baptized by the church, not self-baptized. To begin with he receives the invitation of the gospel from someone who is already a member of the body of Christ. And then it is the church that hears and recognizes the authenticity of the confession of faith. And finally baptism according to biblical thought entails binding oneself to the regenerate assembly.[29]

Baptism as the sign of the covenantal transaction which issues in the identification of a believer with Christ necessarily includes entry and incorporation into the Christian community as the concrete and visible expression of the body of Christ.

Although generally agreeing on the linking of baptism with church membership, Mennonite traditions have differed in the emphasis they have placed upon this connection and the ways in which it has been theologically articulated. One line of thought has emphasized the spiritual and individual aspects of the connection between baptism and the Church by stressing the fundamental significance of the believer's identification with Christ. Another has stressed the visible and corporate dimensions of this connection by emphasizing the incorporation of the believer into the Christian community as the visible Church.

Dirk Philips is an early representative voice of the first view. Although he assumes, and occasionally explicitly asserts, that entry into the visible Church is through baptism, he loosens this connection to some degree by repeatedly emphasizing the importance of the individual and spiritual dimensions in the relation of the believer to the body of Christ. In his *Concerning the Baptism of our Lord Jesus Christ*, for example, he stresses that:

> faith is a gift of the Holy Spirit through which all believers are gathered into one body, and thereupon they are baptized as a sign and proof of the true inner being and the spiritual fellowship they have with Christ and all the holy ones.[30]

This orientation has been at home primarily in the Dutch Mennonite tradition and extensions of it into other Mennonite groups over the centuries. Within the North American and European contexts, it has been reinforced and at times distorted by the influences of revivalism and pietism as well as Western individualism.[31]

Pilgram Marpeck is a representative early spokesperson for the line of thought which stresses the corporate and visible aspects of the connection between baptism and becoming a member of the Church. In his *Admonition of 1542* he concludes his summary of baptism as follows:

> Therefore, whoever wants to be a member of Christ's church must first enter through baptism, through faith in Christ, and must lead a new life in obedience to the Word, shunning and avoiding all evil through the true ban of Christ. This, summarized, is the true church of Christ, no matter where it is in the world. They lead an external life, that is in baptism, teaching, the ban, and the communion of Christ, and they walk in righteousness and truth.[32]

Similar understandings have been at home primarily among the Swiss and South German traditions and their extensions into other Mennonite groups. In the North American context, this orientation has been aided and abetted by the use of the Dordrecht Confession of 1632 (Dutch!) among these groups. In its articles on baptism and the church, Dordrecht also underscores the significance of baptism as incorporation into the visible church. This stance has doubtless been both reinforced and distorted by the frequently strong ethnic character of European and North American Mennonite groups.

Neither of these traditional emphases has intended to divorce the individual from the corporate, nor the spiritual from the visible aspects of the connection between baptism and church membership. Even though the link between church membership and baptism has been couched in different theological terms and weighted differently by the various Mennonite traditions, the primary concerns in this regard are to affirm baptism as the sign of the believer's becoming a member of the Church and to strike a proper theological and practical balance between the individual and corporate aspects of baptism. In any case, baptism as incorporation and entry into the Church upon the baptizand's confession of faith remains a constitutive dimension of baptism in a believers' baptist perspective as represented, however well or poorly, by the Mennonite traditions.[33]

In addition to marking the entry and incorporation of believers into the Church and corresponding to the missionary character of the Church as a faith community, baptism in a believers' baptist perspective focuses on the constitutive importance of the individual believer's faith in relation to the faith of the believing community. For this reason, Mennonites and others have consistently emphasized that the "faith of the Church" should be interpreted in ways which invite, encourage, and support the individual's coming to faith and requesting baptism rather than in ways which amount to having the "faith of the Church" stand in for an individual's baptism prior to his or her coming to faith.

The *Baptism* section of the *Baptism, Eucharist, and Ministry* document states that the "practice of infant baptism emphasizes the corporate faith and the faith which the child shares with its parents."[34] From a believers' baptist perspective, the justification of this practice on the grounds that the faith of the Church surrounds the child of Christian parents obscures beyond recognition how it is that the child may come to "share" the faith of the Church and the faith of its parents. Furthermore, this rationale appears not to acknowledge, other than by default, that the baptized child may not come to actually "share" the faith of the Church and its parents.[35] Simultaneously, the *Baptism* document's emphasis on the Christian nurture of children born to Christian parents in both the home and the Church and on the "constant requirement of a continuing growth of personal response in faith" can only be affirmed from a Mennonite perspective. However, the Christian nurture of children takes place in the hope that they will themselves *appropriate* the faith of the believing community and receive baptism on that basis. In this sense, the faith of Church precedes and encourages the faith of the individual but cannot substitute for it.[36]

The emphasis upon the faith of the individual believer in contrast to the faith of the Church has sometimes been exaggerated among believers' baptist groups. This happens when a believer's confession of faith is taken to be almost exclusively a confession of individual faith rather than including, at least in significant measure, the appropriation of the faith stance of the believing community.

Mennonites sometimes have also been susceptible to emphasizing the individual's faith at the cost of the faith of the Church in relation to baptism. Among the Dutch Mennonites this has taken the form of individuals writing and making their own personal confession of faith on the occasion of being baptized. Among some North American Mennonite groups, there are currently some tendencies for baptismal candidates to "say something about" their faith during the ceremony without necessarily including any explicit references to the corporate faith of the believing community. Such tendencies should, however, hardly be considered endemic to a believers' baptist orientation rightly understood and practised. They do not correspond well either to the missionary character of the Church or to becoming a member of the faith community. They also tend to replace a personal confession of faith which the believing community *also acknowledges* as an appropriation of its corporate faith with a predominantly individual expression of faith the community is asked to ratify.

The theology and practice of valid Christian baptism thus corresponds to an ecclesiology which includes the understanding of the Church as a missionary community, according to which baptism marks the entry and incorporation into the Church and in which the individual believer's coming to faith includes an appropriation of the faith of the Church.

V. Baptism and the Pledge to Mutual Support and Discipline

By now it will have become evident that the various Anabaptist and Mennonite understandings of baptism have consistently included an ethical orientation. The normative order of baptism concludes with the believer's declared intention to begin a life of discipleship as enabled by the Holy Spirit. The reinterpretation of "sacrament" sees baptism as the sign in which the believer makes a holy commitment in response to God's transforming grace in Jesus Christ. The view of baptism as entry and incorporation into the Christian Church as a faith community in which believers are called to live out their new humanity in Christ implies an ethical orientation in which the divisions of ethnic, racial, and national bonds lose the status of primary moral obligations. As we have seen, this ethical orientation is certainly not the entire story of baptism. However, the commitment to "follow Christ in life" has been linked with baptism among Mennonites since the beginnings of the Anabaptist movement in the sixteenth century.

In his paper on "The Baptismal Theology of Balthasar Hubmaier," Wayne Pipkin suggests that the Anabaptist "emphasis on discipleship may well be the distinctive element in believers' baptism."[37] Whether or not it is *the* distinctive element, discipleship certainly constitutes a significant dimension of Christian baptism in a believers' baptist perspective. Indeed, any attempt to describe and evaluate the common convictions of the Anabaptist and Mennonite traditions on Christian baptism without attention to discipleship as *foundational* for both the understanding and practice of baptism is seriously remiss. Discipleship presupposes the forgiveness of sin and the transforming power of grace in the believers.   Discipleship unfolds the ethical implications of baptism as a sign of new life in Christ and links both of these dimensions with an understanding of the Church as the community of mutual support and discipline for those whose sins have been forgiven and who have committed themselves to walk in newness of life.[38]

Of the ways in which baptism is linked to Christian ethical concerns, perhaps the most significant is the connection between baptism and discipline. The early Anabaptist and Mennonite vocabularies referred to congregational discipline as "fraternal admonition" or "the ban" on the basis of Matthew 18:15ff., a classical text for church discipline. The practical and theological connection between baptism and mutual discipline goes back to the origins (and even "pre-origins") of the Anabaptist movement.

Several months before the first believers' baptisms took place in Zurich, Conrad Grebel and his associates contended in their letter to Thomas Müntzer that:

> without Christ's rule of binding and loosing, even an adult should not be baptized. The Scriptures describe baptism for us, that it signifies the washing away of sins by faith and the blood of Christ (that the nature of the baptized and believing one is changing before and after), that it signifies one has died and shall (die) to sin and walks in newness of life and Spirit and one will surely be saved if one through the inward baptism lives the faith according to this meaning.[39]

By "Christ's rule of binding and loosing," Grebel meant the procedure outlined in Matthew 18:15-18 for accountability and mutual discipline among the followers of Christ. He had doubtless learned from Zwingli to understand this "rule of binding and loosing" as the basis for the congregation's authority to make binding decisions in doctrinal and ethical matters. Making, or at least maintaining, the connection between baptism and discipline appears however to have arisen among the "radical reformers" like Grebel and his circle.

For the early Anabaptist and Mennonite movements, congregational discipline became an essential means of renewing the church and encouraging a life of Christian discipleship in both its corporate and individual expressions. Furthermore, the "rule of Christ" was understood as the alternative to the rule of "the sword" used to maintain and to enforce the standards of the "world." As the rule of Christ's love, congregational discipline constitutes among believers the alternative to the rule of coercion and violence in the civil community.[40]

For these reasons, mutual address and discipline constituted a key mark of the true Church and took on an importance equal to or at least similar to baptism and the Lord's Supper. The Schleitheim Articles of 1527 exemplify this significance of discipline and its relation to baptism as well as to the Lord's Supper. The first three articles record consensus on baptism, congregational discipline, and the Lord's Supper, in that order. Using the term "ban" for congregational discipline, Article Two states:

> The ban shall be employed with all those who have given themselves over to the Lord, to walk after [Him] in His commandments; those who have been baptized into the one body of Christ, and let themselves be called brothers or sisters, and still somehow slip and fall into error and sin.... The same [shall] be warned twice privately and the third time be publicly admonished before the entire congregation according to the command of Christ (Mt. 18).[41]

Balthasar Hübmaier was the first to give the relationship between baptism and mutual discipline liturgical shape by including a pledge to participate in mutual accountability and support in the actual baptismal ceremony. According to his "A Form for Water Baptism," the minister first asks the baptismal candidate to confess his or her faith in question and answer form and in terms of the Apostles' Creed. After the candidate has responded affirmatively to each of the three articles in the creed, the minister asks whether he or she renounces the devil. After an affirmative response to this question, the minister inquires about the candidate's commitments to walk in newness of life and to give and receive counsel:

> Q. Will you henceforth lead your life and walk according to the Word of Christ, as he gives you grace, if so speak;
> A. I will
> Q. If now you should sin and your brother knows it, will you let him admonish you once, twice, and the third time before the church, and willingly and obediently accept fraternal admonition, if so speak;
> A. I will
> Q. Do you desire now upon this faith and pledge to be baptized in water according to the institution of Christ, incorporated and thereby counted in the visible Christian church, for the forgiveness of your sins, if so speak;
> A. I desire it in the power of God.[42]

Although Mennonites have never adopted a uniform liturgical order, traces of a pledge to walk in Christian obedience and to participate in mutual discipline have persisted in their understandings and practice of baptism. In a recent *Minister's Manual* jointly published and recommended by the two largest North American Mennonite groups, two of the three suggested forms of baptism solicit, among other things, a response to the question whether the believer is "willing to give and receive counsel" in the congregation.[43] In both cases, the candidate is baptized after his or her affirmative response to this question.

According to Hübmaier, the theological rationale for linking the commitment to participate in mutual discipline and support to baptism is related both to the nature of the Church and to sin. The church is the body of those who have been forgiven and who have committed themselves to live as disciples of Christ. Living according to the way of Christ includes adopting his "rule" for mutual correction in the body of believers. Baptism as the sign of entering into and being incorporated into the body of believers therefore includes declaring one's intention to accept this "rule." The "authority" of one member to "admonish another" comes from the "baptismal commitment" in which a person "subject[s]" himself or herself "to the church and all her members."[44] In this sense, the entering into mutual support and discipline shares in the voluntary character of believers' baptism in response to the divine initiative of grace which creates the Church as the new community of the redeemed. In addition to this ecclesiological basis for connecting discipline and baptism, discipline is an essential means by which sin is addressed, ongoing forgiveness and reconciliation are experienced, and mutual support and correction are implemented in the community of believers.

Although congregational discipline in one form or another has remained a major concern for Mennonite understandings and practice among most groups, at least until recent decades, relatively little attention has been given to its theological and liturgical significance for baptism and to baptism's connection to it beyond what had already been articulated by Hübmaier.[45] As a consequence, baptism and discipline have not infrequently been understood and practised as two basic, but separate, characteristics of the Church. In such instances, the loss of a substantive theological vision for including the commitment to participate in a process of mutual discipline and support in the congregation has most likely contributed either to excessively individualistic understandings of baptism or to legalistic practices of discipline or to both.

Regaining and elaborating something of this vision could be crucial for the churches in today's world. The encroachments of individualism and secularism are making their inroads among Mennonite and other believers' church groups where baptism is not explicitly linked to mutual support and address. In addition to facing similar challenges, the majority churches can no longer assume an identity distinguishing them from the surrounding society. If our churches are to be characterized by a missionary and an ethical orientation in today's pluralistic societies, they may very well need to rediscover and regain a theology and practice of supportive congregational accountability and discipline, including its connection to Christian baptism.

VI. The Recipients of Baptism

To say that believers' baptism and the rejection of infant baptism have been common tenets of Anabaptist and Mennonite baptismal understandings and practice is to state the obvious. However, to assume that the justification for this twofold consensus hinges *only* upon a narrowly defined understanding of baptizing those who can make "a personal confession of faith" should, by now, be considerably less obvious.

According to the biblical order, valid baptism follows the response of faith to the proclamation of the gospel and the renewing work of the Holy Spirit in the person who requests baptism. The biblical order is grounded in the reality of the convenantal transaction which issues in the beginning of Christian life. This covenantal transaction has been initiated and established by the grace of God which in turn enables the free response of the person coming to faith. Moreover, divine grace is expressed not only by God's forgiving and accepting the person for Christ's sake, but also by God's transforming the person into a member of Christ's body and enabling the person to live as a follower of Christ. For that reason, baptism includes both the believer's confession of faith and a commitment to a life of discipleship.

The confession of faith and the commitment to a life of discipleship include both individual and corporate dimensions. Baptism is therefore the sign of entry and incorporation into the Church as the body of Christ. The character of the Church as a missionary and faith community rather than an ethnic or national community means that the Church baptizes those who have come to faith in Jesus Christ irrespective of their familial or social or national adherence. The nature of the Church as the community which is called to extend forgiveness and reconciliation as well as to provide mutual address and discipline in the name of Christ means that baptism includes the readiness and commitment to participate in that calling. The acceptance of believers' baptism and the rejection of infant baptism in the Mennonite traditions has been based upon several foundational characteristics of the Christian Church as well as upon the reality of God's grace and the human response of obedient faith.

The issue of who may receive baptism has been answered among Mennonites primarily on the basis of the foregoing considerations. The question of what constitutes valid or spurious Christian baptism has therefore not usually been answered by stipulating criteria having to do with ministerial office or mode of water baptism or baptismal liturgy.[46]

Whether to acknowledge the baptism of infants as a valid baptism has been raised among contemporary Mennonites primarily in the practical terms of whether to accept persons baptized as infants by other churches into the membership of Mennonite congregations. North American Mennonite congregations, at least until recently, have generally assumed the resolution of this matter to be an open and shut case: because infant baptism does not meet the normative biblical and theological criteria for Christian baptism, the candidate may become a member only upon "confession of faith" *and baptism*. Strictly speaking, this has not been understood as amounting to requiring "rebaptism" because infant baptism by definition would not be considered a valid baptism.

More recently a number of congregations have begun to differentiate between persons who were baptized as infants but did not subsequently confess their faith in a public way and persons who, though baptized as infants, have at some point publicly confessed their faith and continued to lead a Christian life. Some congregations have left it to individuals in the latter category to decide whether they wish to request baptism in becoming members or whether they desire to become members without baptism by publicly acknowledging that they are in harmony with Mennonite teachings and church practices.[47]

The present draft for a new Confession of Faith in Mennonite Perspective also suggests that congregation "may consider transfer of membership without rebaptism" for persons in this category.[48] This suggestion has thus far proven to be quite controversial. Some pastors and church leaders see in the proposal an unwelcome compromise of a foundational principle for which many early Anabaptists and Mennonites suffered persecution and death. Others have expressed support for the proposal on the basis of both historical and theological reasons. In any case, from a Mennonite perspective the major problem amounts to breaking apart the various elements of baptism which belong together in a particular way. Neither baptizing infants fifteen years *before* they come to faith and begin to participate in the life and work of the Church nor baptizing believers ten years *after* they have appropriated the Christian faith and continued to participate in the witness and service of the Church clearly puts together all the pieces of Christian baptism which belong together.

This brokenness may itself suggest that the baptismal issue is no longer *as* divisive as it was when it contributed to divisions in the sixteenth-century reformation movements that have persisted until the present time. Nevertheless, this brokenness will doubtless remain until the further reformation of the churches' baptismal traditions has again brought them into agreement with the apostolic tradition. Karl Barth was most likely correct in not expecting "the full healing of the Church from advances in the matter of infant baptism." Simultaneously, he was most likely also correct with what appear to be a series of rhetorical questions in the Preface to his volume on baptism:

> How can the Church be or become again...an essentially missionary and mature rather than immature Church, so long as it...continues to dispense the water of baptism with the same undiscriminating generosity as it has now done for centuries? How can it be credible to the rest of the world so long as it persists in thinking that it can pacify its concern for recruitment of personnel in this way which is responsible neither to God, to its own message, nor to those who live either externally or internally *extra muros?* Of what help will the best ecclesiology be to us so long as there is obstinate evasion of long overdue reform at this small but practically decisive point?[49]

Notes

1. See, for example, "Baptism," in *The Mennonite Encyclopedia*, (Scottdale: Mennonite Publishing House, 1956), vol. I, pp. 224-28; my article "The Mennonites," in Merle D. Strege, *Baptism and Church: A Believers' Church Vision* (Grand Rapids: Sagamore Books, 1986), pp. 15ff.; *A Bibliography of Anabaptism 1520-1630*, compiled by Hans J. Hillerbrand (Elkhart: Institute of Mennonite Studies, 1962); and *Mennonite Bibliography 1631-1961*, compiled by Nelson P. Springer and A. J. Klassen (Scottdale: Herald Press, 1977), vols. I and II, list approximately 280 entries on baptism.

2. This age has varied from 5 or 6 years old among some North American Mennonites influenced by the "child evangelism" movement prior to the mid-twentieth century, to persons in their 30s and 40s among the Dutch Mennonites. For the most part, ages of those baptized in their youth in North American congregations have gone up during the last few decades. The median age of baptism in the major North American Mennonite groups in the early 1970s was 14.9; see J. Howard Kauffman and Leland Harder, *Anabaptists Four Centuries Later* (Scottdale and Kitchener: Herald Press, 1975), pp. 70-72.

3. Because of its significance for ecumenical conversation and inter-church relations, I will return to this issue later in section VI of this presentation. A few congregations and church leaders have either made exceptions to this general rule, left the matter up to the candidate for baptism, or proposed reconsideration of the traditional practice. A preliminary draft of a

commentary to the article on "baptism" in a confession of faith being developed co-operatively by the General Conference Mennonite Church and the Mennonite Church in North America suggests: "If applicants for membership who were baptized as infants have since publicly confessed or confirmed faith in Jesus Christ, have long been living a life of faith and Christian witness, have been actively participating in a Christian congregation, and commit themselves henceforth to teach and practise baptism for those of an age of accountability who freely request it, churches may consider the transfer of membership without rebaptism." These exceptions tend, however, to confirm the current status of this expectation as a "common conviction" among most Mennonites.

4. See *Mennonites and Reformed in Dialogue*, Studies from the World Alliance of Reformed Churches #7 (Geneva and Lombard, 1986).

5. These statements, except the confession currently being drafted, are reprinted in Howard John Loewen, *One Lord, One Church, One Hope, and One God, Mennonite Confessions of Faith* (Elkhart: Institute of Mennonite Studies, 1985). Schleitheim and Dordrecht are also included in: John Leith, ed., *Creeds of the Church*, 3rd ed. (Atlanta: John Knox Press, 1982), pp. 281ff.

6. In H. Wayne Pipkin and John H. Yoder, trans. and ed., *Balthasar Hubmaier: Theologian of Anabaptism* (Scottdale and Kitchener: Herald Press, 1989), pp. 95-145. See also Rollin Stely Armour, *Anabaptist Baptism: A Representative Study* (Scottdale: Herald Press, 1966), pp. 19-57; Christof Windhorst, *Täuferisches Taufverständnis: Balthasar Hubmaiers Lehre Zwischen Traditioneller und Reformatorischer Theologie* (Leiden: E. J. Brill, 1976); and H. Wayne Pipkin, "The Baptismal Theology of Balthasar Hubmaier," unpublished essay available from the author, 1989, at the Associated Mennonite Biblical Seminaries, Elkhart, Indiana.

7. *On the Christian Baptism of Believers*, in Pipkin and Yoder, *Balthasar Hubmaier*, p. 129.

8. *The Admonition of 1542*, in William Klassen and Walter Klaassen, *The Writings of Pilgram Marpeck* (Scottdale and Kitchener: Herald Press, 1978), p. 183.

9. *Concerning the Baptism of Our Lord Jesus Christ*, Biblitheca Reformatoria Neerlandica (The Hague: Martinus Nijhoff), vol. X, 1914, pp. 69ff., translation according to an unpublished, but forthcoming, manuscript by C. J. Dyck, Associated Mennonite Biblical Seminaries, p. 3.

10. See, for example, the Schleitheim Articles of 1527, Article I; the Dordrecht Confession of 1632, Articles V and VII; the Mennonite Articles of Faith (Ris) of 1766, Article XXV; the Glaubensbekenntnis der Mennoniten in Canada of 1930, Artikel IX; the Mennonite Confession of Faith of 1963, Articles 8 and 11; and the Mennonite Brethren Confession of Faith of 1975, Articles VII and IX, all in Loewen, *One Lord*, pp. 79, 64f., 97f., 306, 175f., and 176f. The same order is reflected in Marlin Jeschke, *Believers' Baptism for Children of the Church* (Scottdale: Herald Press, 1983), chapter 2, "The New Testament Pattern and Meaning of Baptism," pp. 41ff.

11. The Reformed expressions of concern for giving the "faith of the Church" its appropriate weight and for avoiding an excessively "individualistic faith" merit the serious attention of believers' baptist traditions, *Mennonites and Reformed in Dialogue*, p. 69. See *Baptists and Reformed in Dialogue* (Geneva: World Alliance of Reformed Churches, 1986), pp. 18f., and section IV of this essay.

12. Contemporary biblical scholarship, however, suggests that some aspects of traditional Roman Catholic, Protestant, and Mennonite interpretations of Matthew 28: 18f. may require revision and even correction. Karl Barth, among others, notes the reservations which should be brought to bear upon the traditional interpretations of the passage, *Church Dogmatics*, IV.4, pp. 51f. The 1982 *Baptism, Eucharist, and Ministry* document of the World Council of Churches presupposes some modification of traditional interpretations, §1. With respect to the Mennonite traditions in particular, the participial forms of "going," "baptizing," "teaching," in verses 19 and 20, together with the imperative form of "make disciples," do not unambiguously reinforce the simple sequence of preaching, hearing, responding in faith, receiving baptism. Nor do they, depending on the meaning of "make disciples" and "baptizing," necessarily contradict that order.

13. *Baptism, Eucharist, and Ministry*, §11: "...baptism upon personal profession of faith is the most clearly attested pattern in the New Testament documents." See also *Mennonites and Reformed in Dialogue*, pp. 67ff.

14. Alan P. F. Sell suggests that the "process of Christian initiation as comprising several moments – baptism, nurture, conversion, confession of faith, reception as a member – be reexamined with a view to determining whether baptism need any longer be a church-dividing issue" between Reformed and Mennonites: "Anabaptists and English Independents," *The Mennonite Quarterly Review*, LXI, 1987: 333. If Sell's initial phrasing were to follow the sequence "preaching and/or nurture, conversion, confession of faith – baptism – reception as a member, continuing nurture and instruction, it would be recognized as synonomous with a believers' baptist perspective.

15. The term "images" is borrowed from *Baptism, Eucharist, and Ministry*, §2 in the Baptism section. These "images" include participation in Christ's death and resurrection, a washing away of sin, a new birth, an enlightenment by Christ, a reclothing in Christ, a renewal by the Spirit, the experience of salvation from the flood, an exodus from bondage, and a liberation into a new humanity.

16. Rollin S. Armour, *Anabaptist Baptism: A Representative Study* (Scottdale: Herald Press, 1966), pp. 139f. correctly notes that "there were objective elements in Anabaptist baptism as well as subjective elements."

17. See Hübmaier, "A Form for Water Baptism," in Pipkin and Yoder, *Balthasar Hubmaier* p. 391; Marpeck *The Writings of Pilgram Marpeck*, pp. 168ff.; Armour, *Anabaptist Baptism*, p. 56 and 185 n. 132. On sacraments among sixteenth-century Anabaptists and Mennonites, see Alvin J. Beachy, *The Concept of Grace in the Radical Reformation* (Nieuwkoop: B. de Graaf, 1977), pp. 99ff. Karl Barth refers to this possible interpretation in a passing note on Zwingli, *Church Dogmatics*, IV.4, p. 109, but does not employ it constructively

in his rejection of the sacramentalist theological traditions and for his interpretation of water baptism in ethical terms.

18. Armour has demonstrated that there were objective as well as subjective elements in Anabaptist baptism. This objective character was, however, not located simply in the ordinance of baptism, "for behind the baptismal action stood the church of the regenerate, which administered the ordinance. The action, therefore...was the testimony of the very people of God, which people would give the signs of Christ only to those in whom they recognized His Spirit." *Anabaptist Baptism*, p. 140.

19. In Pipkin and Yoder, *Balthasar Hubmaier*, pp. 169f. Although Marpeck's *Admonition of 1542* borrows heavily from B. Rothmann's *Bekenntnisse van beyden Sacramenten*, the citation comes almost entirely from Marpeck and his circle.

20. See Beachy, *Concept of Grace*; J. A. Oosterbaan, "Grace in Dutch Mennonite Theology," in *A Legacy of Faith*, ed., C. J. Dyck (Newton: Faith and Life Press, 1962), pp. 69-85; John R. Loeschen, *The Divine Community: Trinity, Church, and Ethics in Reformation Theologies* (Kirksville: The Sixteenth Century Journal Publishers, Inc., 1981), pp. 79ff. "On Menno Simons"; *Mennonites and Reformed in Dialogue*, p. 69; and Thomas N. Finger, "Grace," in *The Mennonite Encyclopedia*, vol. V, forthcoming. In Anabaptist and Mennonite traditions, this prevenient grace has sometimes been grounded more in Christ's atonement, sometimes more in God's original creative activity. Marpeck and Hübmaier tended toward the latter, Menno Simons and Dirk Philips toward the former view. Contemporary Mennonite theologians have not yet devoted major attention to clarifying this issue or to working toward theological consensus on it.

21. P. 54.

22. Karl Barth's rejection of baptism as "sacrament" also seeks to emphasize both the priority of divine grace and the free and obedient response of the believer. As a consequence, Barth limits "sacramental" reality to Jesus Christ, i.e., interprets sacrament in strictly Christological terms. "Baptism takes place in active recognition of the grace of God which justifies, sanctifies and calls. It is not itself, however the bearer, means, or instrument of grace. Baptism responds to a mystery, the sacrament of the history of Jesus Christ, of His resurrection, of the outpouring of the Holy Spirit. It is not itself, however, a mystery or a sacrament." *Church Dogmatics* IV.4, 102. Similar formulations may be found among some early Anabaptist writers, for example, Philips: "Jesus Christ alone...is the only and true sign of grace...Christ is and remains the true and only sign of grace, and all external signs direct us from themselves to him." *Concerning the Baptism of our Lord Jesus Christ*, C. J. Dyck trans. pp. 45f. However, the reinterpretation of "sacrament" in the Anabaptist and Mennonite traditions has apparently included ecclesiological and anthropological/soteriological dimensions rather than being limited strictly to a Christological reference, as in Barth's case.

23. For example, Menno Simons and Dirk Philips strongly emphasized the role of the Holy Spirit in this regard; Hübmaier, on the other hand, spoke more in terms of the proclaimed Word. See also Christof Windhorst, *Täuferisches Taufverständnis*, pp. 185ff. The quotation from Jeschke on p. 49 above simply refers to the activity of both God's Word and Spirit in creating spiritual life.

24. *Mennonites and Reformed in Dialogue*, p. 63.

25. Within the limits of this essay, I shall not seek to summarize—or to constructively formulate—more precisely the relation between baptism and the "covenantal transaction" (my term) of which it is the sign or sacrament in a way consistent with the Anabaptist and Mennonite traditions. Here, again, attempts to counter and correct the majority churches' sacramentalist views, the Mennonites' lack of a consistent teaching tradition, and various church renewal and cultural influences have all contributed to some diversity and most likely to some confusing and theologically problematic views which tend either toward making arbitrary the relation between baptism and that to which it refers, or toward over-emphasizing the individual believer's confession as the referent of baptism at the expense of divine grace and the confirming testimony of the Church.

26. For example, the Dutch Reformed-Mennonite Dialogue notes that "The period of the 'nation-church' and of the Christian society is past." *Mennonites and Reformed in Dialogue*, p. 69. See also: Faith and Order Paper #97 on the 1979 Louisville Consultation on Believers' Baptism, reprinted as the Winter 1980 issue of *Review and Expositor; A Baptist Theological Journal*, vol. LXXVII, 1:103, 106, 108; and *Baptists and Reformed in Dialogue* (Geneva: World Alliance of Reformed Churches, 1984), pp. 16, 32.

27. In the *Baptism* section of *Baptism, Eucharist, and Ministry*, the commentaries to paragraphs 13 and 14. Marlin Jeschke, *Believers' Baptism for Children of the Church* (Scottdale and Kitchener: Herald Press, 1983), pp. 27ff. agrees that children of believers "have always had the best exposure to the appeal of the covenant of faith." Nonetheless this does not theologically and practically justify a baptismal practice which cannot avoid an ecclesiology that mixes—or confuses—ethnic community and faith community. Jeschke notes that two conceptions of the people of God (Israel), namely as ethnic nation versus community of faith, came into tension long before the rise of the Church. This tension was resolved in the New Testament in favour of the faith community.

28. Franklin H. Littell underscored the significance of the "Great Commission" and missionary witness for the early Anabaptist and Mennonite understanding of the Church: *The Origins of Sectarian Protestantism: A Study of the Anabaptist View of the Church* (New York: The Macmillan Company, 1964, originally 1952), pp. 109ff. See also Donald F. Durnbaugh, "Mission and Evangelism," in *The Believers' Church: The History and Character of Radical Protestantism* (Scottdale and Kitchener: Herald Press, 1985, originally 1968), pp. 226ff. Later Mennonites have unfortunately all too frequently and in their own ways undermined the missionary nature of the Church by adopting an understanding of the Church and a routinization of catechetical and baptismal

practice which have in effect reinforced the notion of the Church as an ethnic group at the expense of the Church as a faith community.

29. Jeschke, *Believers' Baptism*, p. 47.

30. Translation by C. J. Dyck, p. 43.

31. The Ris Confession, for example, in the very lengthy article XXV "Of Water Baptism," notes only in passing that believers were "added to the church" according to the book of Acts, but does not further develop this observation (Loewen, *One Lord*, pp. 97 ff.). The bilateral conversations between the Reformed and the Mennonites in the Netherlands during the 1970s reflect this orientation among the Mennonites see *Mennonites and Reformed in Dialogue*, pp. 64ff. In the North American context, similar emphases have — perhaps oddly — found expression, not only among the groups which derive from the Dutch stream, but also among some groups whose traditions originated with the other major strand, namely the Swiss and German movements. In such cases, such as the 1963 Mennonite Confession of Faith, revivalism has presumably played a major role. This confessional statement omits any reference to baptism as entry/incorporation into the Church in its article on baptism: "We regard water baptism as an ordinance of Christ which symbolizes the baptism of the Holy Spirit, divine cleansing from sin and its guilt, identification with Christ in his death and resurrection, and the commitment to follow him in a life of faithful discipleship." Nor does it make any such reference in its article on the Church, in Loewen, *One Lord*, pp. 75 and 76.

32. In Pipkin and Yoder, *Balthsar Hubmaier*, p. 300. The entire paragraph is original to Marpeck and his circle rather than having been adopted or adapted from Rothmann.

33. Morris West observes that "there would be a number of Baptists who would also say that it [the point at which a person is brought into the community of the Church] is really at the point of a believing response to the fact of the Gospel by the individual." *Review and Expositor* (Winter, 1980):19, (Faith and Order Paper #97). There may also be individual Mennonites who would entertain a similar view. But this would be in conflict with the generally strong emphasis upon becoming a member of the Church with baptism in the Mennonite traditions.

34. In the commentary to paragraph 12.

35. To be sure, the document assumes that "the personal response will be offered at a later moment in life" when an infant is baptized (paragraph 12). And it also suggests that "the personal faith of the recipient" is essential for "the full fruit of baptism" (commentary on paragraph 12). For these assumptions regarding the relation between the individual's and the Church's faith to be credible and theologically consistent, at least from the position represented by this essay, they would, however minimally, seem to require a practice and theological justification for something like a ceremony of "disavowal" as well as of "confirmation." Note also the measure of convergence as well as basic

divergence on this matter in the "Reformed-Mennonite dialogue in the Netherlands," p. 69.

36. See especially Jeschke's "The Discipline and the Instruction of the Lord," chapter 3 in *Believers' Baptism for Children of the Church*, pp. 66-80. In both the "baptism of an adult convert from paganism and of someone nurtured within the church," the common denominator is that baptism calls for the "appropriation of faith."

37. Pipkin, "Baptismal Theology," p. 12.

38. Larry Miller has noted that the theme of mutual support and congregational discipline was "most conspicuous by its absence" in reports of the Reformed-Baptist bilateral conversations, in spite of the presumption that such concerns were historically an important element in both the Reformed and Baptist traditions (*Baptists and Reformed in Dialogue*, p. 53). Nor did the relation between baptism and discipleship, including mutual support and discipline, apparently figure prominently in the dialogues between the Mennonites and the Reformed in the Netherlands (cf. pp. 65-71), even though discipline was mentioned as one of the distinguishing marks of the Church. Miller suggested that Mennonites and Reformed (and Baptists) might, in future exchanges, do well to listen to Schleitheim and Hübmaier, and to Bucer and Calvin on communitarian discernment and congregational discipline. I have accepted that "fraternal admonition" with respect to Schleitheim and Hübmaier in the hope that others will do the same with regard to Bucer and Calvin.

39. In Leland Harder, ed., *The Sources of Swiss Anabaptism, The Grebel Letters and Related Documents* (Scottdale: Herald Press, 1985), p. 290.

40. For further information on congregational discipline among Mennonites in general, see: "Discipline," in *The Mennonite Encyclopedia* (Scottdale: Mennonite Publishing House, 1956), vol. II, pp. 69f; Walter Klaassen, ed., *Anabaptism in Outline, Selected Primary Sources* (Scottdale and Kitchener: Herald Press, 1981), pp. 211-31. Contemporary interpretations have been developed primarily by John Howard Yoder and Marlin Jeschke: John H. Yoder, "Binding and Loosing," *The Concern Pamphlet Series*, #14 (February 1967); Marlin Jeschke, *Disciplining the Brother: Congregational Discipline According to the Gospel* (Scottdale and Kitchener: Herald Press, 1972).

41. In Loewen, *One Lord*, p. 79. The Schleitheim Articles are also included in *Creeds of the Churches*, John H. Leith, ed. (Atlanta: John Knox Press, 1983).

42. In Pipkin and Yoder, *Balthasar Hubmaier*, p. 389. See also Hübmaier's "On Fraternal Admonition," ibid., pp. 386ff.

43. *Minister's Manual*, Heinz Dorothea Janzen, ed. (Newton and Scottdale: Faith and Life Press and Mennonite Publishing House, 1983), pp. 22f.

44. "On Fraternal Admonition," in Pipkin and Yoder, *Balthasar Hubmaier*, p. 383.

45. In their interpretations of discipline neither Jeschke nor Yoder make constructive use of this connection, which has ecclesiological and ethical as well as liturgical dimensions.

46. This statement would need to be qualified with respect to the mode of baptism. The Mennonite Brethren consider baptism by immersion to be normative and have historically not considered other modes of baptism to constitute valid baptism. According to the 1975 Confession, however: "Local congregations may receive into fellowship those who have been baptized by another mode on their confession of faith." That means that decisions on the matter have been left in the hands of the congregations rather than being binding on the entire group of Mennonite Brethren congregations. Loewen, *One Lord*, p. 177.

47. Jeschke argues for this position: "On the cardinal principle that baptism signifies the act of accountable entrance upon the way of faith, we must decide that baptism is out of place here, for the individual in question is not now coming to faith but has been a practicing Christian for possibly many years and is merely transferring church membership." *Believers' Baptism*, p. 139.

48. See note 3 of this essay.

49. Karl Barth, *Church Dogmatics*, IV.4, p. xi.

Chapter IV

PEACE IN CHURCH, FAMILY, AND STATE:

A REFORMED VIEW

Max L. Stackhouse

In one sense, the debates between the Reformed tradition deriving from John Calvin and the "Magisterial Reformation" on one side and the Anabaptist tradition deriving from Menno Simons and the "Radical Reformation" on the other are over. It was once doubted by each whether the other was genuinely Christian and had a place in the true community of faith or in the same society. Each repudiated the other. When the Mennonites said that baptism was not valid if performed on children, the authenticity of the convictions, sacraments, and membership in the people of God of the Calvinists was denied. When the Calvinists persecuted Mennonites who refused to participate in civil activities such as military service, they denied the Mennonites a place in the common life.

Today, each of these two heirs of Christian catholicity tends to recognize that the other may well have an authentic faith, a genuine morality, and a valid ministry—indeed, a grace that comes from the one God whom both traditions know in Jesus Christ. The Holy Spirit blows where it wills; we find it possible to suggest today that these two traditions represent distinct kinds of "orders" in the *ecumene* of God, each of which may have a distinct vocation and witness.

I. Conflict Still

And yet, in another sense, the debates are not at all at an end. Tensions remain *between* the two traditions and they have parallels *within* each of the two traditions. They live in modern Protestantism. They show up in the divided minds of faithful believers precisely because the chief issues that once divided our forebears so dramatically, and which we have come here to discuss, are not fully and finally resolved anywhere. When we practise pedobaptism, we must take special care in regard to confirmation, for the mature Christian must not only have received the prevenient grace given undeservedly to all the saints, but must also "believe in his heart," and "confess with his lips." When we practise only the baptism of adult believers, we must take special care in regard to both the Church's inclusive nurture of children and the cultivation of the capacity to discern the grace of God where it occurs outside the consciousness of the convicted. This double accent is surely of great concern to God; which one we call baptism and mark with water may be less so. It could be that the absence of one is what hardens the lines of dispute. Similarly, while neither tradition doubts that Christians must be witnesses for peace, neither one is able to avoid dispute about the proper means, and the limits of means, that may be used to protect the innocent neighbour under threat—specifically if this appears to require the legitimate restraint of evil by the use of coercive force.

Such debates appear in all ecumenically open communions, including the one to which I belong, The United Church of Christ (USA). The Pilgrim and Puritan Congregationalists who came to the New World seeking freedom of religion (and many of the separatist Christian churches who later joined them) extended the fierce independence of the Free Church heritage anticipated in the "sects" of the European "Radical Reformation." Indeed, before they arrived at Plymouth Rock, they had sought refuge in Holland where Dutch Anabaptists had already helped engender a measure of religious freedom. However, desire for independence was also wedded to establishmentarian tendencies. The forebears who fought for religious freedom on theological grounds in Scotland, France, Switzerland, Hungary, and England also used the state to resist Anabaptism in New England. The tradition that established a democratic polity and fostered the freedom of conscience within the community of faith, and allied with "liberal" political theorists to demand it in the modern, constitutional state, also hanged Quakers on Boston Common—echoing the persecution of Mennonites on the continent.

When Evangelical and Reformed congregations came to the USA two centuries later, largely to avoid the Prussian draft, the tendency to form congregations held together by a deep piety, a distrust of magisterial Christianity, *and* a German regard for authority, set these communities of faith on a trajectory of development that would bring about their eventual merger with the heirs of Puritan Congregationalism. In that development, the theological heirs of the Augustana Confession and the Heidelberg Catechism joined those of the Cambridge Platform (the New England version of Westminster), and all were linked in a covenantal polity. Thus was formed the tradition that linked the heirs of

Jonathan Edwards and Washington Gladden to the traditions that shaped Paul Tillich and the Niebuhrs.

What also stamped the soul of the United Church of Christ was, and is, a "pietist-pacifist" streak that simultaneously presses against all temptations to become a magisterial church. Yet, this heritage attempts constantly to shape the common life through social involvements and to believe that grace is sometimes mediated by "secular" social institutions. The strong emphasis on Free Church, congregational authority meant that adult members had a special status and special responsibilities in the discernment of God's will and way for the community, but that discernment was to reach beyond the congregation, for God was sovereign over the whole of society.

If we may rehearse the history from which I speak for one more moment, we should remember that these various deeper ecclesial streams were united at the time of the American civil rights and anti-Vietnam movements. The denomination's historic tensions were reinforced by these developments. Indeed, the civil rights movement itself was in part born of the Free Church tradition that understood its roots to be in the prophetic side of the biblical message, especially as it was incarnated afresh in the black churches. Not a few Baptist, Methodist, and Presbyterian blacks, sometimes prompted by New England carpetbaggers and educators, had formed new churches with a congregational polity and joined this communion. The grandchildren of slaves and their Yankee supporters sought both a freedom for people to shape their own lives *and* a principled justice to order society — with the understanding that this freedom would be allowed and this justice would be enforced with the help of federal troops, if necessary, as a part of God's grace.

Shortly thereafter, the anti-Vietnam movement prompted many morally sensitive church leaders to retreat from all that smacked of an enforcement of freedom and justice. Many embraced themes from the heritage of Christian pacifism. Yet, not a few embraced the idea that Christians could, in good conscience, join in efforts to overthrow colonial imperialism by force — the "righteous revolution" became the modern form of the ancient notion of "holy war." Indeed, many expressed contempt for any who claimed the benefits of freedom and justice but would try to protect their own pious purity in oppressive and revolutionary situations by refusing to sin bravely so that grace could abound for all. World-denying forms of piety and pacifism are linked to world-affirming forms of prophetic judgment and political action. (The attempts at synthesis, with their considerable internal tensions, can be seen in such UCC official pronouncements as *"Just Peace,"* a widely used policy guide and study document.)

These conflicting tendencies in the United Church of Christ have parallels in the paradoxical emphases of many ecumenically oriented churches today. Indeed, they may be rooted in deep tensions within the Christian tradition itself. H. Richard Niebuhr reminded us some time ago that it has been possible to find warrants in Holy Scripture and our common classic traditions for Christ against Culture, Christ Above Culture, Christ and Culture in Paradox, Christ in Culture, or Christ Transforming Culture. If this is so, then the best we might do in a discussion such as this is to seek the most faithful, most honest, most just, and most fitting ways of inviting our churches to think through the issues again as we face the twenty-first century together, praying that we may approximate to the kinds of wisdom our forebears exemplified and at least make no greater errors.

II. An Approach

One way of taking up the issues today is to recognize the modern ambiguities in the relationship of the Church to two decisive institutions of civilization: family and state. The questions could be put this way: do we believe that these institutions are possible and proper channels of grace? Are they pertinent to human salvation? Ought the church to affirm these structures of the common life and become intertwined at any points with them? Do we, ought we, trust them although we know them to be feeble reeds? And if so, under what conditions? What parts of "the world," seen in institutional terms, shall we affirm and what parts shall we deny, if the traditions that brought Christ to us and us to Christ are to be edified by dialogue with other parts of the people of God?

This approach ought not be seen in isolation. Indeed, it should be seen in the context of a great number of matters already wisely discussed in ecumenical dialogues, such as the substantive findings and the pointed footnotes that appear in the World Council of Churches document, *Baptism, Eucharist, and Ministry.* Much of the Reformed tradition is in deep agreement with the findings on baptism. Similarly, we could turn to the discussions of the propriety of Christian participation in wars of liberation as they have appeared, for instance, in regard to South Africa. Because the dominant ideology of the policy of *apartheid* is cast in the language of an heretical form of Reformed thinking, most of the world's Reformed Christians are morally outraged and have easily allied with

Catholic, Anglican, Lutheran, and Methodist communions in supporting radical political action as a mark of faith in that setting. All the hard issues about the Christian understanding of peace and political force are present there.

Others will properly raise again the biblical and exegetical questions in regard either to *Baptism, Eucharist, and Ministry* or to the use of force in establishing actual peace. We might inquire as to whether the findings of modern research have contributed fresh data or insight to our understanding of the biblical texts on these matters. We might ask further as to whether Calvin or Menno best understood the Scriptures when it comes to understanding the basic issues of sin and grace in regard to either issue. Did either of the two better grasp the deepest, widest, most enduring, most orthodox understanding of the issues that now appear before us in new forms?

Implicit in our dialogical context and this particular approach to it is also the question of whether each side has properly understood what the other has been trying to say all these years. Are we now at a place in ecumenical understanding where we can recognize the special contribution of each of these two giants of faith to the larger totality of world Christianity? In fact, in the face of contemporary secularisms, the rise of neo-pagan spiritualities, and the new and wider encounter with the world's religions, it could be that some of the tensions between these traditions now have to be seen as now so intramural as to be trivial, although we know that family disputes are often the most difficult to reconcile.

It is in the context of these possibilities that we can ask how a theologically grounded social ethics might offer an interpretation of key institutional and ethical issues that are decisive for our ministries in the twenty-first century. For if these issues are not before us, it is possible that hidden, conflicting hermeneutical principles will reign in exegetical, historical, or systematic efforts, and conflicts between and within our churches, and in our hearts, will simply be perpetuated in the future. A great presumption of the Reformed heritage, that all concretions of Christian faith and order must constantly be reformed because they are ever in need of reform, would be betrayed.

If we approach the matter this way, it turns out that a chief question is "membership." Membership is simultaneously a matter of institutional affiliation, personal identity, and social relationship. It requires a theology of institution. It is subject to ethical and social as well as theological analysis. From this point of view we can ask whether common patterns of social relationship outside the Church that also demand moral responsibilities are, can be, or should be in our time, recognized by the Church as proper channels for the mediation of grace. It is a question that, in the past, was posed in terms of the "Orders of Creation (more often of Preservation, and sometimes of Redemption)," or the "Mandates of Human Relationships," or "Spheres of Relative Sovereignty in Society," or "Covenants of Civilization."

The issues appear today in three areas: (1) How shall we understand the relationship between membership in the family and membership in the Church, especially in those stages of life when we are utterly dependent on others to make life decisions for us? (2) How shall we understand the relationship of membership in the Church to membership in the state — especially if the latter involves (as it ever must in history) the use of coercive violence to maintain a modicum of peace? (3) How shall we organize our contemporary witness on these questions today — especially as we face new patterns of family and political life, and new religious and theological interpretations of their significance, on the brink of a new century that demands a new cosmopolitan Christian awareness? In each of these areas, we must ask whether, in any regard, the finite and temporal is capable of bearing and mediating the infinite and eternal?

To speak of membership in the context of a theology of institutions allows us to become more refined about the issues before us than general remarks about "Christ and Culture" might allow. Indeed, the differences exposed by this approach should be seen in the context of similarities in other areas. For instance, both traditions have embraced an ethic of hard work and economic prudence and been cautious about some of the "high" arts. The Calvinist heritage may have been much more prone to accept — indeed to promote and value — technological innovation than has the Mennonite, but they share a doctrine of fallen nature and a conviction that it is a proper human vocation to intervene in the bio-physical order to restore it to the order God intended in creation through disciplined, stewardly activity.

Both traditions have been suspicious of the graphic, plastic, and kinetic arts while cultivating music, poetry, and rhetoric, *the* characteristic art forms of Protestants. These traditions are, after all, more orally than visually oriented due to their accent on the Word of God with its aniconic, ascetic, and oratorical tendencies. The drama, theatre, dance, costume, painting, and sculpture smack too much of the heathen festival, the pagan idol, or of the merely esthetic mass for both these traditions.

Both long presumed these led to decadence. In sum, the faithful in our churches tend to embrace technology, with cautious reservations, and to distrust the fine arts, with selective exceptions.

In such areas, thus, we find that Calvinists and Mennonites might have considerable convergence and marginal divergence in a theology of institutions. However, in the areas of baptism and peace, when we view them as issues of membership on the boundaries of church and family and church and state, tensions remain, primarily because the Reformed heritage tends, penultimately, to affirm these "secular" arenas and yet ultimately to deny their capacity to flourish rightly outside of theological guidance and support. It may be that if we are to understand one another on these issues, and understand the tensions within our own traditions, we shall have to think through these questions again in somewhat new terms both in intentional continuity with our biblical and theological traditions and with a recognition that new issues today confront us.

III. Baptism

In baptism, one becomes a member of the community of faith wherein one is nurtured to engage in the worship of the God made known through Jesus Christ. Through membership, persons are prompted to holy living, to the loving service of the neighbour, and to seek the formation of just and peaceful communities in the world.

We need to note three aspects of church membership from the beginning. First, we are not born into it. There is no such thing as a born and bred Christian. Getting born is not religiously distinctive, and no one is saved by being born, or by being born into a Christian family. Wherever a branch of Christianity has become simply an ethnic group, the faith is threatened. Insofar as the practice of believers' baptism protests baptism as a ritual celebration of birth, its advocates have a valid point. The family is not the Church. One may, in tribal religions, be born into a totemic clan; one may, in Hinduism, be born into a religious caste; one may, in feudal societies, be born into a sanctified status, peasant or noble; and we are each born into a specific gene-pool, family, class, gender, nation, and cultural-linguistic group. About these "ascriptive ties" in "communities of origin," as some sociologists call them, no choice exists. We may have a "membership of sorts," but it is not a Christian membership. From the early Church on, Christians have held that redemption is not brought by family or genealogical connections.

Christianity differs with Judaism on these matters. It also differs with the Unification Church, in which the holy family is indistinguishable from the redemptive community, and with the Latter Day Saints (Mormons) who baptize genealogical ancestors. Instead, Christianity understands church membership in terms of a "community of orientation," based on ties of will, trust, belief, or conviction. The involuntary facts of genetics and social ecology are not sufficient, and yet, membership of the deepest kind is not entirely a voluntary matter either.

Thus, second, we need to note that we humans do not make ourselves Church members. Becoming a member involves an element that can only be captured in the passive voice. We are called, invited, drawn into the Church by a power beyond human control—one which, theologically, we may call grace, election, or providence and which no one fully chooses. Of course, we can analyze, through the use of the social sciences, the channels and dynamics by which grace frequently flows. We can study the processes of formation, nurture, persuasion, education, initiation, induction, acculturation, and socialization and we can use these in evangelism in hopes that God will see fit to use these channels to manifest grace. Indeed, we can argue that the Church has a duty to see that these possible channels of grace are available to the next generation of potential believers even if we know that church membership is not finally determined by any initiative we might take on this front.

Third, the signs that symbolize the transition into member-ship—water and the trinitarian invocation—are neither magic nor epiphenomenal expressions. That is, they are neither incantations that themselves actualized the presence of grace, nor are they merely public announcements of something that was already accomplished without baptism. Were that so, any kind of a notice or celebration would do. Rather, baptism involves the outward and visible sign of the inward and spiritual grace that signals and evokes the binding together of the person and the community under God. It involves a covenantal affirmation that the community is enlarged and that the person may participate in the community and the community will participate in the life of the person in order to actualize in the heart of each and the lives of all, so far as possible, the righteousness, purposes, and mercies of God.

Now if these three things are so—if baptism involves a membership of orientation beyond communities or origin, but is partially involuntary because of the power of grace that may operate through institutionalized structures and processes, and simultaneously bonds participants together under God — it would seem that it would be possible for baptism to take place either for adults at the time of conversion or for children at the time when the family of origin, in the presence of the community of faith, is prompted to transcend its procreative role and to agree to serve as the present agent, representative, and instrument of the Church, to make available the channels of grace for the new person. Not only is the child symbolically cleansed of any pre-conscious alienation from the love of God and bound to the community of faith and recognized as a new member of the people of God, but those parents who are members of the Church and members of the child's family are commissioned to be the church elders in the home until the child is able to deal directly and personally with non-parental church elders.

The key question, of course, is whether one holds that the family can properly serve as a community of orientation as well as a community of origin, as a channel of grace, as resident elders of the church as well as parents in the nurture of the next generation. Can the family be, as the Puritan forebears believed it could be, "a little church," a covenantal community of faith as well as a sexual and social community with legal, political, economic, and cultural significance? Can this very worldly and temporal institution (there is no marriage in heaven, and we pledge fidelity to a spouse only until death) be affirmed as a potential channel of grace, and ought it be commissioned to do so in a rite that focuses direct and immediate attention on the primary spiritual and moral fact of life — children are to be seen first of all as children of God, part of the people of God; and parents have a holy vocation in regard to them, one the Church commissions them to accept as a ministry for a time.

If this is at least one of the theologically valid social and ethical meanings of baptism, then it involves the pledge of the parent or parents to be the arm of the community of faith in the spiritual and moral formation, in the Christian socialization, acculturation and education of a child, even if the opportunity is given, at the time of confirmation, for the child to decide against this influence. In the meantime, the family would be charged to recognize that its functions involve a ministry. When parents raise a child, when they discipline, guide or teach it by precept or example, the child is not only theirs but the Church's because the child is first of all God's.

Viewing the issues this way also clarifies the nature and character of family life in a day when it has become increasingly confused and when it is in grave moral and spiritual danger. Inevitably, aspects of family life centre in sexuality. Economic, political, and legal understandings of the family change, as do cultural images and sex-role stereotypes, but some things are constant: were humans not created male and female it is doubtful that we would have families at all. It is unlikely that sexuality will ever go entirely out of style, but the blessed bonds that tie lover to beloved, and the ecstasies that bring new generations to being, are very much in need of a deep theological, ethical, spiritual renewal. The family has a high vocation.

Christians have doubted this high role of the family at times in the past. Some traditions have held that celibacy is spiritually higher or morally purer or ecclesiastically superior than family and sexuality. To be sure, we can understand that, in certain periods, the Church was about to be absorbed into clan, tribal, or *potestas patria* patterns of family life, or the Church was about to be swallowed into feudal patterns of succession. We may even, in retrospect, applaud the decisions of Christians to cut the nerve of the temptation and to separate clearly the institution of the Church from that of the family.

At other times, sectarian emphases from the Gnostics through the Catharii, the Muensterites, the Shakers and the contemporary Metropolitan Community Churches have denied the theological significance of the family with its emphasis on procreation for various reasons — some having to do with libertine denial of its constraints, others with ascetic denials of the holiness of sexual vitality, eschatological denials of its continued necessity, or denials of the normativity of dual sexuality as a feature of God's design for human physical intimacy.

Even in the mainstreams of modern, Western Christianity, divorce is so widely accepted as a practice that the family as an order of preservation, as a mandate of God, as a covenantal sphere with a redemptive vocation is functionally doubted. Who is not aware of struggling single-parent families, abandoned mothers, or abused women and children — prime population sources of the new homeless and poverty underclass? Such realities are a social and moral scandal; they reveal failures both of public policy and of the communities of faith to cultivate the proper vocation of the family in all its responsibilities.

We can recognize, to be sure, the propriety of a number of contemporary protests against "the family." The family is about ordering the relationships of males and females and parents and children, and some common ways of ordering these relationships have been oppressive. Not a few of the current critiques of the family by feminist Christians properly protest against the false and exploitative forms of the family that have occurred from time to time, even within the history of

Christianity. Further, they recognize that the fundamental *raison d'être* of the Church is not about specific forms of sexuality at all. The Church's one foundation in Jesus Christ has to do with a reconciled relationship of the self to God and neighbour and the doing of God's will in the midst of life.

It may be that in a context such as our own, we may have to affirm, as our forebears did before us when faced with other challenges, that doing God's will means today that we can, we should, we must articulate in fresh ways the constitutive meanings of baptism as they bear on membership in the institution of the family as a loving, coarchic, covenantal extension of the community of faith with a calling to become a possible channel of God's grace in the midst of sexuality, procreation, and the sustained responsibilities of nurture; and that practices followed in the community of the family should actualize and honour the primary membership of the child in the community of faith and the people of God.

In brief, infant baptism viewed from the standpoint of social ethics with a focus on membership and institutional relations invites the question of whether the Church can and should entrust the Christian members of the Church who live together as a family with the challenge and opportunity to extend the care of the Church to a new member, while acknowledging that other channels of grace that bring people to conviction and membership as adults are equally valid.

IV. Peace

Parallel issues may well be present in issues of peace as they bear on membership and the relationship of Church and state. The Church is not a state any more than the church is a family. Great havoc is wrought when people begin to treat any regime as holy, as the primary community of devotion or spiritual identity, or as the decisive instrument to define, enhance, or enforce proper faith. The Anabaptist traditions have known for centuries that princes, rulers, states, and governments are not competent in such matters and that coerced confessions of faith lead to a lie in the soul, to the persecution of conscience, and to the easy idolatries of nationalism and imperialism. So do politically enforced ideologies that oppose religion and abuse people for holding to their faith or practising their religion.

It is for such reasons as these that our traditions have converged in holding that there should be an institutional separation of Church and state. The early leaders of the Magisterial Reformation knew that a distinction had to be maintained even if some were, for a time, diverted in their thinking by the medieval notion that the Church consisted essentially of the clergy who were paid by state-enforced taxation. Nevertheless, they established, properly, an organizational distinction between the *ministerium* and the *magisterium* much as earlier traditions had distinguished between the *sacerdotum* and *imperium*, between pope and emperor, bishop and king, and priest and knight.

Followers of Christ have always been aware of the fact that the kingdoms of the earth are not the same as the kingdom of heaven, and they have ever tried to implement that distinction in social history—for leaders. However, many presumed that, for the people, membership in a political realm implied membership in a common religion, and that one would fall if it were not supported by the other. In this they failed to apply their own awareness to the whole people of God. Only under the compelling theological arguments of the "sectarians" (reinforced by the ideals of "tolerance" of the humanists and the Enlightenment) was the wider meaning of the "priesthood of all believers" applied to all members. Slowly the pernicious principle of *cuius regio, eius religio* was overcome.

In consequence, we know that membership in one of these two organizations, Church and state, must not be determined by membership in the other. The finances, officers, and discipline of one should not be confused with the finances, officers, and discipline of the other. The common life is not a single ellipse with two centres—Church and state. Rather, it is two circles that may only partly overlap at the organizational level. The centre points and the horizons of the two spheres are distinct. The worship of God and the cultivation of genuine piety among the people is not the same as the establishment of a secure social order or the serving of the common good. For one thing, the state's sense of what is "common" is always bounded geographically by borders and legally by citizenship, while the church's sense of "the people" reaches to all parts of the world and includes, in principle, all those of whatever legal status called by God to partake in the community of faith. Further, sin, repentance, and forgiveness are different from crime, punishment, and rehabilitation, even if they overlap.

Moreover, and rather decisive for our discussions, the means that Church and state use to deal with questions of peace are notably distinct. Any church or state that does not enhance peace will soon get lost in conflict or self-destruction, but the Church pursues peace in terms of love and justice by the powers of word and spirit. It seeks to actualize these by the disciplines of liturgy, example, service, and sacrifice. The state pursues peace in terms of law and order, tempered by mercy, which it seeks to actualize by the powers of authority, command, and regulation—enforced, when necessary, by the power of the sword and the arts of negotiated compromise which we call statecraft.

We should have no illusion about this. Anyone who thinks that it is possible to be politically involved or relevant or responsible without engaging in coercion and compromise simply does not have a firm grip of the nature of political life. Nor does it help to argue that Christian non-violence is both uncompromisingly moral *and* can be proven pragmatically to be the best sort of political prudence, for when it turns out not to work politically—and it sooner or later inevitably does fail in a world of sin—what has been held to be "Christ's way" is discredited.

It is better to say that, given the reality of sin, unredeemed humanity (which in some measure is within each of us and among every group—including pacifist ones—as well as around us all) requires states because we are always beset by the threats of violence from within or without and believe with considerable justification that these threats can only be constrained by granting the state a relative monopoly on the legitimate use of violence, and then putting that authority under just law and counterbalancing coercive power with other forms of power in a pluralistic society.

Both Church and state may seek to establish peace; but one proceeds from word and heart to exterior behaviour—including the clarification of those ethical principles by which we can recognize the difference between just and unjust laws—while the other proceeds from the efforts to establish a legitimate order that is more or less just, in which word and heart may find expression without violent disruption.

For all these reasons, almost all Christian traditions increasingly recognize that Church and state are to be institutionally separated. This, of course, leads us to two issues much debated in our past. One is at the level of individual membership: can a Christian, remaining a faithful part of the believing community, have a vocation to serve the people and the cause of peace by assuming also the duties to exercise the powers of the state with its law, authority, and the sword? We can put it this way: can the means of coercion ever be also means of grace? It is close to, but not the same as, the question that Luther raised when he asked whether soldiers also could be saved.

The Reformed tradition has generally argued in the affirmative, that "magistracy" can be a high calling, indeed one of the very highest from which someone whom God calls to such tasks may not shrink. Putting on the whole armour of God, one is to risk purity of soul to serve God's purposes. That has led this tradition to adopt and adapt the classic categories of *jus ad bellum* and *jus in bello*, to articulate and to try to follow the ethical criteria that ought properly to be applied when taking up the power of the sword. The attention given to these modes of moral reasoning, of course, reveals both that Christians must live with a presumption of pacifism and that in certain circumstances one may be called by God to set the presumption aside for the sake of a just peace. It is only this presumption that could allow the idea of a righteous revolution in any circumstance.

This tradition has been constantly aware that the "Peace Churches" doubt such arguments. The sting of this doubt has sometimes been sharply felt, in part because travesties have been done in the name of "just war." Wars obviously unjust have been called just by those wanting to draw the mantle of spiritual legitimacy around brutishness.

Besides, several parts of the gospel seem to have little patience for such concerns; those who do take up the sword know how easy it is to become preoccupied with the merely external ways of the world to the neglect of the Word. Nevertheless, in times of crisis when the freedom of the gospel has to be defended, when the innocent neighbour has to be defended from rape, murder, mayhem, or systemic oppression, and when faithful Christians feel called to overthrow naked evil and establish the relative justice, peace, and order possible in human affairs, this tradition fears that its critics may lead the Church to irresponsibility. In the name of faithfulness, the narrow-souled may fail to see how God can use all sorts of means to bring about the New Jerusalem; they may stay quietly in their lands of Ur rather than, like Abraham and Sarah, going out in faith to seek the city that has foundations as a part of the full meaning of peace.

An important distinction must be introduced at this point. The separation of Church and state is not the same as the separation of religion and politics. No civil order exists that is not influenced by religion in its basic definitions of what is just order and legitimate authority. For Reformed Christians this is not only a social and historical fact. This tradition has argued that it is the duty of Christian leadership to draw on biblical and ethical insights to shape a public theology and to help define the normative shape of the common polity, and that it is an intellectual and moral error to try to construct government on purely humanistic grounds alone. That is because human reason, one of the greatest gifts of God, is still a feeble reed when the tides of wealth and power flow. Although no viable political order can be established without reason, humanistic political orders are inclined to rot from within when they do not have a rootage in the most profound religious awareness. More importantly, God is sovereign over all spheres of life and administers grace through many and varied channels, including public affairs of a distinctly political, even a coercive, kind.

Those who know something about the truth and justice of God must equip the people generally, and political leaders specifically, to discern whether morally legitimate coercion can and should be used in specific circumstances, for example, in the protection of the freedom of religion, in the defence of an innocent child against molestation, in the dismantling of a racist tyranny, or in the establishment of human rights or democracy. This is the view that some believers who are actively engaged in the life of the Church as laity may be called to use constrained coercion (in fear and trembling) as a means of grace, in the service of the neighbour and to the greater glory of God.

It may be that our traditions will continue to disagree about many aspects of these questions. However, new conditions are inviting new alignments in our traditions on the key questions. For one thing, the modern structures of political democracy which were generated out of the confluence of the Reformed and "sectarian" traditions (as reinforced by aspects of the Enlightenment), mean that everyone is a magistrate, at least episodically. Whoever casts a ballot is one of many "rulers" deciding the future of the regime. The citizen who casts the ballot is often also the believer who uses theology and Christian ethics to guide political judgments. Religious and political values get blurred in democracies at the level of the individuals who are members of both church and state, even if the institutions of church and state are increasingly separate. On the whole, both the faith and the civilization is best served if an integration, not a separation, takes place in the moral life of the person. Judgments of integrity will include not only realistic assessments of the situation but normative visions of how we are to deal with them in terms of the justice and love of God.

At another level entirely, we have to recognize that although East/West hostility is much reduced today due to the collapse of Communism as both a viable ideology and a workable system, the world still has, and will have as long as we can see into the future, nuclear weaponry. The nations now compete in proposals for disarmament, yet many in our churches have lived through world wars, tyrannies, arms races, and the threats of nuclear destruction. They know in their bones that we shall have to live with the prospect that these can be revived at any time from now until the end of history.

Not a few have developed a moral repugnance against all means of coercive violence like that which other generations had against human sexuality. Others remember the victory over Fascism and see the present moves toward disarmament as partly due to strong defence policies in the Cold War days. They have been convinced that force, or the threat of it, had to be used, and in principle morally ought to have been used, to resist the militarisms of Hitler and of Stalin.

Still, many Reformed believers have become suspicious of any doctrine that views the use of coercion as a proper vocation, while others become more convinced than ever that Christian responsibility may entail picking up the sword on behalf of social justice. Many features of the "Peace Church" traditions are being incorporated in Reformed communions as moral "orthodoxy." Conscientious objection to all military service is honoured equally with government service, selective conscientious objection and selective conscientious combatance, and this is the position implicit in all "just war" teachings and doctrines about the high, Godly vocation of magistracy.

At the same time, a decided moral preference is given to church members who refuse to work for any company engaged in the design, manufacture, or sale of military weaponry. The sense of obedience to Christ in this area brings about new forms of disengagement from or opposition to society, just as one hears of Mennonites entering government service, running for political office, working in defence industries, or even becoming career officers in the armed forces, patterns long present and selectively approved in Calvinist history.

What shall we say in such a context? What of the state with its inevitable potential for coercion? Even if the whole pattern of governance becomes increasingly democratic, shall the church cultivate an appreciation of the high calling of political leadership? It would be morally precious to suggest that one may, in a legislature, vote for laws that are enforced coercively, but that one may not participate in the enforcement itself, and remain a faithful believer. What in the world shall we affirm and what shall we deny as we try to be obedient to God, faithful to the whole Gospel, and both loving and just to the neighbour?

Implicit in all that has been suggested here is the question already encountered in the discussion of baptism. Is it possible that we can, under conditions of democracy and separation of Church and state, trust, affirm, and thereby strengthen and guide political leaders, policies, and structures as possible channels of grace in the actualization of God's purposes of peace?

If so, it is also likely that we will continue to need voices who remind us of the all-too human tendencies to idolatrize the state and to repair too quickly to the power of the sword when the power of the Word would be more graceful. Yet, frankly, few authentic Christians want the Mennonites to run the Pentagon. Fortunately, few wish to. We may have to lift up again the biblical notion of a plurality of gifts and vocations. The Christian pacifist, the Christian magistrate, and the Christian arms-manufacturer may all have temporal and worldly vocations from God that are to be recognized and honoured by our communities of faith, even if the communities edify and guide these members by constantly demanding that they repeatedly engage each other and maintain a common reference to the eternal and transcendental source of all genuine and just peace.

If that is possible, we may in the future affirm the vocation of the family in a new way and the vocation to the state in a new way, while preserving the insight that neither membership in the family nor in the state may be confused with membership in the Church. If a vision of plural memberships with multiple vocations becomes central to the theology of institutions, our memberships in these three "covenants" of civilization may be clarified and our two traditions may become increasingly aware of our common membership in the body of Christ that surpasses, after all, any identity that we might find in those communities from which we come, including those deriving from John Calvin or Menno Simons. We may even find ourselves to have been by the grace of God members of one another, in Christ, falsely contending against ourselves.

Bibliography

Baltzell, E. Digby. *Puritan Boston and Quaker Philadelphia*. Boston: Beacon Press, 1979.

Gunnemann, Louis H. *United and Uniting*. New York: United Church Press, 1987.

Gustafson, James. *Ethics from a Theocentric Perspective*, 2 Vol. Chicago: University of Chicago Press, 1981-84.

Johnson, James T. *The Just War Tradition and the Restraint of War*. Princeton: Princeton University Press, 1981.

_____. *The Quest for Peace: Three Moral Traditions in Western Cultural History*. Princeton: Princeton University Press, 1987.

Kuyper, Abraham. *Lectures on Calvinism.* Grand Rapids: Wm. B. Eerdmans Publishing Co., 1931.

Leites, Edmund. *The Puritan Conscience and Modern Sexuality.* New Haven: Yale University Press, 1986.

Niebuhr, H. Richard. *Christ and Culture.* New York: Harper & Bros., 1951.

Parsons, Talcott. *The System of Modern Societies.* Englewood Cliffs, NJ: Prentice-Hall, 1971.

Ramsey, Paul with S. Hauerwas. *Speak Up for Just War or Pacifism.* University Park, PA: Pennsylvania State University Press, 1988.

Reimer, A. James. "Anabaptist-Mennonite Systematic Theology," *The Ecumenist,* Vol. 21, No. 4 (May/June 1983): 68-72.

Smith, C. Henry. *The Story of the Mennonites.* 4th ed. Newton, Kansas: Mennonite Publication Office, 1957.

Stackhouse, Max L. *Ethics and the Urban Ethos.* Boston: Beacon Press, 1973.

_____. *Public Theology and Political Economy.* Grand Rapids: Eerdmans Publishing House, 1987.

_____. *Creeds, Society and Human Rights.* Grand Rapids: Eerdmans Publishing House, 1985.

Thistlethwaite, Susan. *Just Peace.* New York: Pilgrim Press, 1985.

Troeltsch, Ernst. *The Social Teachings of the Christian Churches.* Translated by Olive Wyon. New York: Macmillan, 1931.

Weber, Max. *Economy and Society.* Edited by G. Roth et al. New York: Bedminster Press, 1968.

White, Ron D. and E.J. Fisher, eds. *Partners in Peace and Education.* Grand Rapids: Eerdmans Publishing House, 1988.

Wright, Conrad, ed. *American Unitarianism 1805-1865.* Boston: Northeastern University Press, 1989.

Yoder, John Howard. *When War Is Unjust.* Minneapolis: Augsburg Publishing House, 1984.

Chapter V

PEACE IN THE MENNONITE TRADITION:

TOWARD A THEOLOGICAL UNDERSTANDING

OF A REGULATIVE CONCEPT

Howard John Loewen

I. Understanding the Issue Intra-Textually

A Grammar

To speak of peace in the Mennonite tradition is to move to its theological centre and become involved in a discussion of the internal structure of Mennonite theology. The language of peace has an important regulative function in the Mennonite tradition. The grammar of peace gives expression to the internal theological structure of the tradition. It is a way of talking about Mennonite theology as it is internally motivated.

The grammar of a tradition must always be ascertained in relation to its living context, the text of the contemporary world, in conversation with the text of tradition. Within this context the appropriate translation of a theological heritage can occur. In order to ascertain the current form of the grammar of peace in the Mennonite tradition we must necessarily read three critical texts: the text of Scripture, the text of history, and the text of the contemporary world.[1]

Our procedure, therefore, involves outlining and ascertaining an intra-textual understanding of the grammar of peace in the Mennonite tradition by exploring these three texts. Our task is to understand how the language of peace functions in a minority tradition currently in transition. To deal seriously with one's tradition is to take seriously the revisions which occur as transitional stages of the tradition. This is an Anabaptist-Mennonite view of how tradition is appropriated.

Such an approach is necessary, especially in the context of inter-confessional conversation because it has been a particular view of the Mennonite tradition, namely, the long stereotyped history of Mennonite separatism, which has provided the primary frame of reference for both Mennonites and those who have become their interlocutors to interpret the regulative concept of peace. The inadequacy of that frame of reference requires an approach which establishes a conceptually broad and methodologically adequate framework in which peace, as a regulative concept, can be understood for the purposes of constructive inter-confessional dialogue. (See "Excursus on Peace as a Regulative Concept" pp. 107-108.)

The Texts

From this perspective, the primary issue is not what Mennonites say about peace historically and how this differs or compares with other traditions. The central question is, "How does the language of peace function in the Mennonite tradition intra-textually[2] and how can this contribute to inter-confessional conversation?"

In the hermeneutical section ("Scripture as Text"), we deal with the anterior biblical history of the regulative concept of peace in order to show the hermeneutical groundwork for the concept of peace. The purpose here is to begin with the biblical data so as to establish the primacy of the biblical argument and to show how Mennonite theology tries to have its conceptual framework shaped by biblical reality.

In the historiographical section ("History as Text"), we focus on the interior history of the Mennonite tradition in order to show the historical context for the contemporary developments regarding the concept of peace and the major shift that has taken place.

In our heuristical section ("Contemporary World as Text"), we deal with the exterior history which has given shape to the concept of peace in order to show how theological developments relating to the contemporary church-world issue have impacted Mennonite peace theology.

Our thesis is that the Anabaptist-Mennonite peace tradition is not intrinsically separationist but transformationist. This claim is made on the basis of contemporary Mennonite theological self-understanding regarding the inter-related texts of Scripture, history, and the contemporary world. We have identified these texts as the sources for ascertaining the grammar of peace in the Mennonite tradition. What we propose to do next is to ascertain the shifts that have occurred in the development of the grammar of peace in each of these areas.

II. Scripture as Text: Hermeneutical Foundations
Scripture in Hermeneutical Perspective

In the context of inter-confessional dialogue, it is important first of all to identify a critical methodological issue that has important bearing on our hermeneutical considerations.[3] Methodologically, the Mennonite tradition does not begin with creedal, confessional, or systematic theology even though the purpose of this study is to move toward appropriating that norming process more self-consciously.

Rather, it begins with the biblical text and its *de facto* authority for faith and life as expressed in worship, ethics, and mission. Nor does it simply begin with how the text was read historically but, rather, how it is read hermeneutically, that is, how it is currently read out of contemporary experience and how contemporary readings "develop" beyond the traditional readings in the meanings they render.

Our intra-textual analysis begins with the hermeneutical orientation of a biblicist tradition regarding questions of war, peace, and the Church's relation to the world. It is important to note that there are continuing differences within the Mennonite tradition regarding the explanation of warfare in Israel, the extent to which Jesus' ministry is political in nature, and the degree to which (and how) the Church should be involved in society today. Yet in spite of those variations, there is agreement on the basic hermeneutical perspective in contemporary Mennonite scholarship.[4]

Exodus 15 and God the Warrior
In the Mennonite tradition, warfare has its roots in humanity's fall. Three variants exist as to how that theological point is translated. For some, Old Testament warfare expressed God's will for the people when kingdom and state were combined; for others, God allowed war as a concession to Israel's sin; more recently, there are those who see it primarily as the result of Israel's failure to trust God as warrior.[5]

Increasingly, Mennonite biblical scholarship sees the roots of pacifism in the Old Testament. It has come to consider more fully the development and context of the issue of war. It affirms that God is warrior in both testaments and that the change regarding the increase of violence and war is not in God's moral will but in the historical circumstances. God never intended violence. In the Old Testament, the "time" for a fuller revelation of a non-violent way had not yet come.[6]

The work of Millard Lind is a salient example of these hermeneutical observations, especially as they are brought to bear on the theological problem of God as warrior.[7] Lind seeks to identify and discuss the main aspects of ancient Israel's theology of violent political power. His thesis is that Yahweh as God of war fought for his people by miracle, not by sword and spear, nor through armies of his people.

He maintains that the Exodus rather than the Conquest or Judges provides the fundamental paradigm of holy war in the OT. Exodus 15, the Song of Moses, is the paradigmatic text portraying Israel's future passage through the sea of nations: "Yahweh I sing: he has covered himself in glory,/ horse and rider he has thrown into the sea./ Yahweh is my strength, my song,/ he is my salvation./ This is my God, I praise him;/ the God of my father, I extol him./ Yahweh is a warrior;/ Yahweh is his name." (15:1-3)

According to Lind, this text shows how God as warrior deals effectively with the enemy. What is distinct about Yahweh's war and kingship is not that he entered history, but the way in which he entered history. The difference between Israel and other nations was that she was to rely on Yahweh's miraculous power, a message echoed later by Jesus and the early church.

For Lind, this method of Yahweh's fighting affected Israel's theo-political structure in a fundamental way. Moreover, Yahweh's warfare was directed not only against Israel's enemies but at times against Israel herself through the armies of Israel's enemies. According to Lind, the human agent in the work of Yahweh was not so much the warrior as the prophet. The Exodus event, and the deliverance from Egypt through a prophetic leader, is the fundamental paradigm for Israel's holy war and for her "prophetic" political structure. Yahweh's rule as warrior king is mediated to Israel through her worship. The wars of Yahweh affected deeply the structure of Israel's cultic life.

Lind's work is instructive "not just because he has achieved certain significant exegetical and historical results, but because he has challenged the assumption that God the warrior is inevitably or even primarily a symbolic call to arms. ...He has called into question...the assumption that a particular symbolic pattern necessarily reflects, in a direct and predictable way, specific social norms and values."[8]

Thus Lind shows how the biblical symbol of God the warrior functions by observing how the texts use that symbol conceptually. Acknowledging that principle insight is to recognize God the warrior as a central theological issue for the contemporary Church.

Luke 4 and the Politics of Jesus

Contemporary Mennonite biblical scholarship has come to recognize more fully the complexity of God the warrior as a central theological problem and the diversity of interpretation that stems from the recognition of that problem. Accordingly, it can best deal with the apparent incompatibility between these diverse views in Scripture within a concept of biblical unity that affirms historical development in the canonical text. The principles that guide intra-canonical dialogue are best informed by a revelation in history approach rather than one that emphasizes rational coherence at the logical, propositional level.[9]

So that "while revelation in history suffers limitation from history it also creates a new history, a new economics, and a new politics: hence this view of biblical authority requires an understanding of divine revelation as dynamically interacting with history and culture."[10]

That emphasis in Mennonite peace theology has provided the basis for affirming two important methodological points. First, it represents an epistemological orientation which claims that the reign of God as manifested in Israel, Jesus, and the early Church is truly embodied in culture. Second, it represents a hermeneutical perspective which recognizes that one's economic, political, social, and religious locations in culture play powerful roles in determining how one reads the Bible.[11]

The work of John Howard Yoder is the premier example of the implementation of this epistemological and hermeneutical perspective, especially as it is brought to bear on the theological problem of "the politics of Jesus." In this work, Yoder sets forth the possibility of a messianic ethic by challenging mainstream ethics regarding the relevance of the NT Jesus for contemporary questions of social ethics. He "seeks to describe the connection which might relate New Testament studies with contemporary social ethics, especially as this latter discipline is currently preoccupied with the problems of power and revolution."[12] In developing his thesis, Yoder "concentrates largely on one document, on the canonical text of the Gospel according to Luke."[13] He uses the storyline of Luke to build a bridge from the canon to the present regarding the particular social-political-ethical option proffered by Jesus.

The inaugural address of Jesus in Luke 4:16-30 is the basis of the Gospel, and paradigmatic for Jesus' entire ministry: "The Spirit of the Lord is on me, / because he has anointed me / to preach good news to the poor. / He has sent me to proclaim freedom for the prisoners / and recovery of sight for the blind, / to release the oppressed, / to proclaim the year of the Lord's favor" (4:18-19).

This text shows Jesus inaugurating a new reign that contrasts with the positions of the first- and second-century freedom fighters. It focuses on the jubilee year and shows how Jesus is clearly inaugurating a new regime that has a new kind of power politic, a new understanding of economics, and a new social order that involves a restructuring of relationships between people, including opening of the new age to gentiles.[14]

In the end, "Jesus was traded for a Zealot leader and put to death as 'King of the Jews.'" Yoder insists that Jesus was indeed a threat to Roman and Jewish authorities and that one should not try to explain that away. His life and death is "proof of the political relevance of nonviolent tactics, and not proof Pilate and Caiaphas were exceptionally dull or dishonorable men." For Yoder "Jesus' threat was serious enough to warrant execution" and "the suffering martyrdom of the messiah is the inauguration of the kingdom."

Yoder concludes that "Jesus was, in his divinely mandated prophethood, priesthood, and kingship, the bearer of a new possibility of human, social, and therefore political relationships. His baptism is the inauguration and his cross is the culmination of that new regime in which his disciples are called to share." According to Yoder, we may choose to reject this option but "no longer may we come to this choice in the name of systematic theology or honest hermeneutics."[15]

Yoder has contributed significantly toward marking the politics of Jesus a central theological issue for the church today. He insists that counter to the prior assumptions of many modern interpreters Jesus' "deeds show a coherent, conscious socio-political character and direction, and that his words are inseparable therefrom."[16]

Romans 13 and the Powers That Be

The relevance of the way of Jesus for the disciple of Christ today and the degree to which the Church, as the body of Christ, should be involved in contemporary societal issues remains a major point of discussion for all Christians. Since historical and contemporary Mennonite peace theology holds that peace is at the heart of the Gospel and that the nature and mission of the Church leads to the way of non-violence, it has, in principle, if not always in practice, claimed the relevance of the way of Jesus for all spheres of life. What the implementation of that conviction means in the modern world has not always been clear to a tradition in transition. Yet it has attempted to forge an appropriate hermeneutical response to this theological problem.

Methodologically, the question of the applicability of Christian ethics to all spheres of life is a critical one. Central to this social-ethical move is understanding the relationship of the Church to broader society.

The fulcrum of the debate for Mennonite theology turns on the issue of Church-state relationships. This is one particular aspect of the larger, enduring problem of the relationship of Church to world, its mission to be "in" the world but not "of " it, and the moral tension resulting from the existence of Christian belief in the midst of other beliefs.

The *crux interpretum* for adjudicating the issue of the relationship of the Church to the state is Romans 13. As in the case of Exodus 15 and Luke 4 (and the hermeneutical developments they represent in the tradition), so Romans 13 has received careful scrutiny from contemporary Mennonite biblical scholarship. The purpose has been to understand its relevance for a consistent social ethic involving the Church's relationship to the state as one of the spheres within the larger context of culture which poses significant questions about violence and non-violence for the church. The Romans research of Mennonite biblical scholar John E. Toews has been instrumental in giving focus to this section.[17]

Romans 13 instructs Christians to submit to governing authorities and not rebel against a government which threatened to mistreat them. The text represents another exhortation within a whole series of exhortations given in Romans 12-15: "Everyone must submit to the governing authorities, for there is no authority except that which God has established" (13:1, 5a).[18]

Here Paul's concern is not with civil government *per se* but with Christian conduct which takes place inevitably within a civil sphere, in this case, the reality of the Roman empire. Here we have another instance of living the transformed life (cf. 12:1-2) for which the Church is presumed to be the basic context out of which such a life is lived (cf. 12:3-8).

Moreover, it is important to note that the state is defined as one of the "authorities" (*exousiai*). These authorities (*exousiai*) are not merely earthly rulers but spiritual powers of which earthly rulers are agents and over which Christ is supreme Lord.[19] Christians are to "be subject" (*hupotasso*) to these governing "powers."[20]

The task of the "governing authorities" is to carry out consistently the particular function of rewarding good and evil, in short to secure just governance. The obligation of the Christian is circumscribed by the rendering of taxes and honouring discerningly (cf. Mk. 12:17). The qualifying question here is, In what sense is the Christian subject to the state?

However, although Christians like all others are "ordered" by the state, they are to give their ultimate loyalty and obedience to God, who through Christ, is Lord also of the state. The "governing authorities" are the "powers" with a positive but clearly provisional role. The eschatological orientation of the entire section (cf. 12:1ff. and 13:11-14) is a salient reminder of this fact.

Thus Christians on the one hand are called away from violent revolution toward a non-violent way of life. There is a recognition that the Christian is provisionally ordered by Caesar. On the other hand, Christians cannot, under the Lordship of Christ, uncritically legitimate any form of government but are called to be discriminating in their assessment of all governments. There is a recognition that Christians are primarily ordered by Christ. Such a stance will place them into tension with governments.

For Mennonite theology, this reading of Romans 13 is consonant with God's message to Israel, the ministry of Jesus, and the mission of the early church. The example of the life of Paul, the other apostles, and the early Christians demonstrates such an understanding regarding the relationship of the Christian to the state (cf. Acts 16:35-39; 23:1-5; 25:10-12). [21]

Therefore, for Mennonite theology Romans 13, as an exemplar of the mission of the early Church in its meaning and manifestation, moves strongly in the same direction as Exodus 15 and Luke 4, the respective exemplars for God's message to Israel and the ministry of Jesus. It represents the enduring theological problem of the relationship of the Church to the world of the powers, particularly the state.

Scripture in Theological Perspective

In this section we have tried to provide several examples of how current Mennonite theology has self-consciously reflected on the concept of peace from its textual basis in Scripture. We have tried to portray how Scripture itself is conceptualized and functions in the norming process of the Mennonite tradition. Moreover, in showing how Mennonite biblical scholarship establishes the interpretive framework of three representative texts (Exodus 15, Luke 4, and Romans 13), we have attempted to give some indication regarding the development of the concept of peace during a transitional period for the Mennonite tradition.

We have, in the process, identified three central and related theological issues: the problem of God the warrior, the politics of Jesus the Messiah, and the powers that have been subjected to the Spirit of the risen Lord. Together they raise the fundamental question of the relationship of God and the people of God to the world, an issue which we will continue to explore below. The interpretive approach represented in our three samplings constitutes the hermeneutical foundation in Mennonite theology for a transformational theology of peace.

The Mennonite tradition has, by this kind of hermeneutical reflection, exemplified the primacy of Scripture in its constructive theological moves, reinforced the centrality of the regulative concept of peace, expanded its own understanding of the concept of peace, become more sensitive to the cultural context (biblical and contemporary) which gives relevance to a theology of peace, and occasioned opportunities for dialogue on hermeneutical rather than doctrinaire grounds.

III. History as Text: Historiographical Developments
Anabaptist Vision

Mennonite scholarship in the pre-WWII period participated in, and in fact gave impetus to, the broader reinterpretation of the story of the Radical Reformation. The conventional picture of the Anabaptist movement as created by mainline church historians over the centuries was increasingly being dismantled. The standard interpretations could no longer hold their ground against the new scholarly investigations of the primary sources which had received impetus from Troeltsch and Harnack's favourable assessments of the radicals.[22]

Through historical research, Mennonites have experienced a recovery of the sixteenth-century Anabaptist vision in the twentieth century. The centre of that vision affirmed the essence of Christianity as discipleship, the Church as a voluntary community, and the ethic of love and non-resistance.[23] The rediscovery of the roots of Mennonite theology and social ethics in the Radical Reformation has led to a refocusing of the peace ethic. Developments in the Mennonite tradition relative to the concept of peace must be understood from the interpretive standpoint of the rediscovery, the antecedent conditions for its emergence, and the subsequent response to it. (See "Excursus on Mennonite Historiography," pp. 108-111.)

Major Transition

J. Richard Burkholder, a Mennonite social ethicist, has chronicled these developments in an essay on Mennonites in ecumenical dialogue on peace and justice. According to Burkholder, there has been a "movement from the withdrawal stance of the 1920s to almost total social and cultural participation in the 1980s," a shift which has put "heavy strains on traditional theological and ethical formulations."[24]

Two major world wars, Vietnam, civil rights, and the general social turmoil of the 1960s pushed Mennonites "to re-examine and extend the traditional teachings as they sought to respond to events in light of biblical teachings."[25] Burkholder rightly contends that "since World War II, the peace testimony has been refocused as a primary theme in the identity of the Mennonite churches" and "Mennonite scholars began to create a more comprehensive peace theology and looked for opportunities to share their convictions with the wider Christian church."[26]

Burkholder convincingly shows that Mennonites are no longer "the quiet in the land." Although historically much of Mennonite theology and experience fits into Troeltsch's classical sectarian model, the twentieth-century reality of being catapulted into the modern world has changed. Burkholder states that "a new 'internal dynamic' in the life of the church—in particular its tremendously expanding global mission and service activity—has interacted with the cataclysmic events of 'external history'—world wars, revolutions and famine—to bring about significant change in the way Mennonites have come to think and act in the political realm."[27]

All of this spelled the need for rethinking Church-state and Church-world theology. For Burkholder the point is that modern Mennonites at their best have developed a style of political activity that transcends the classic church or sect options and provides a model worth further analysis and development as a distinct type.

He concludes that "a new day has dawned" in the North American churches. Quoting Daniel Smith, a Quaker, he observes that "Mennonite scholarship is the major source today of creative non-violent theology and Biblical analysis, read far more widely than among the Mennonite faithful themselves. This has not come without some painful introspection on the part of Mennonites themselves as they have moved from the farmlands to the world's capitals to express their growing activism in giving witness to Christian nonviolence and social justice."[28]

Burkholder has clearly demonstrated that there have been major developments in Mennonite social ethics in the post-WWII period, from a stance of withdrawal to one of involvement. He shows that "the Mennonite understanding of the gospel is growing and changing. With these social changes have come new theological developments and interaction on the ecumenical scene. Mennonite peace theology has matured significantly since the 1950s, as a result both of digging deeper into biblical and historical foundations and of creative interaction with the issues of the times."[29]

Mennonite Social Ethics

Considering the concept of peace in light of the social ethical developments in the Mennonite tradition brings into sharp relief the issue of social responsibility regarding the relationship of the Mennonite community to the world. How one is socially responsible in applying an ethic of peace and non-resistance has been a critical point of tension, for both those inside and those external to the tradition.

Here the critical analysis of J. Lawrence Burkholder is most timely.[30] According to him, the main impetus of social thought and action in the Mennonite tradition has been the endeavour to carve out a total way of life in accordance with the biblical doctrine of non-resistance. It has served as a regulative concept in a profound way. Burkholder maintains that "Mennonite social thought is avowedly an inference of nonresistance."[31] Accordingly, peace in the Mennonite tradition can be adequately understood only if we obtain some sense of how social ethical thinking has developed in the tradition. That can only be seen in conjunction with the recovery of the Anabaptist vision.

Burkholder contends that until the post-WWII period the Mennonite tradition had not been forced to face the issue of "social responsibility." For generations "the framework of Mennonite social ethics was restricted denominationally to the Mennonite church and to the Mennonite community." Thus "the social problems considered by Mennonites have been those which have emerged in the Mennonite community" and "they have addressed themselves to world problems only as they have become immediate problems to the Mennonites."[32] They have in the past refused to accept responsibility for the social order.

Burkholder maintains that through their emphasis upon the pure church, its perfectionistic ethic, and its primitivistic biblicism they have spent the major part of their energies perfecting ways of separation. Thus Mennonites did not work out the universal implications of the Lordship of Christ. The focus has been on the Church and not on culture and creation as whole.

Two closely related factors have contributed to re-evaluating the adequacy of this stance in the Mennonite tradition. The first is sociological. The social forces resident in the Mennonite tradition point to an accelerated rate of cultural accommodation. In every way—

intellectually, politically, culturally — Mennonites have entered the modern world. The second is theological. The discovery of and commitment to their historical and theological roots have provided Mennonites with a norm by which to judge their life and mission in the contemporary world.

The rediscovery of the Anabaptist vision, and the subsequent developments involving the revisioning of that vision, have resulted in the Mennonites no longer being able to carry on an undialectical relationship with culture.[33] They have been forced to consider their responsibility to the broader social order and to think in terms of entire historical processes. Moreover, they have also discovered within the tradition theological resources that challenge some of the basic assumptions that have prevailed both within the tradition and outside the tradition regarding peace and non-resistance.

As we noted earlier, this situation has been precipitated by a clear move from social withdrawal to social involvement to social responsibility to social justice. This metamorphosis of the Mennonite community has also contributed to an expanded understanding of the central concept of peace which was constitutive of these social ethical developments. For as Burkholder shows, peace in the Mennonite tradition was a basic attitude toward life rather than simply an attitude toward war.

Our analysis leads to several important observations: the developmental changes occurring in Mennonite social ethics; the internal critique which emerged and which has increasingly characterized the tradition; and the expanded historical and theological basis from which to engage in inter-confessional dialogue. Accordingly, the shape of contemporary Mennonite scholarship can more clearly be seen against the backdrop of historiographical developments internal to the tradition. History was the vehicle through which the Mennonite tradition was able to retrieve its theological roots and thereby reappropriate the central concept of peace for engagement with the modern world.

IV. Contemporary World as Text: Heuristical Considerations

The concept of peace in the Mennonite tradition relative to church-world relationships has been shaped internally by Mennonite ethnicity and externally by Niebuhrian ethics. These two interpretive frameworks have reinforced each other in defining Mennonite social reality as largely "separatist" in nature. Thus, Mennonite self-understanding and mainline Protestant typologizing have both contributed (mainly negatively) to rendering the Mennonite peace position as inherently "counter-culture."

So far we have demonstrated that major social and theological changes have taken place in the Mennonite tradition during the post-WWII period. Sociologically, there has been an important shift from a position of withdrawal to one of involvement in society. Theologically, as we have shown, there have been accompanying hermeneutical and historiographical developments in Mennonite social thought relative to this changing social reality.

Social Ethics after Niebuhr

What must also be noted in these developments is the emergence of the constructive critique of H. Richard Niebuhr, whose typologizing of the sectarian traditions, including the Mennonite tradition, became the standard for locating such traditions on the social-ethical map as "against culture."[34] The writings of John Howard Yoder have represented, both explicitly and implicitly, the most sustained and complete challenge to Niebuhr's definition of the "enduring problem" concerning the relationship of Christ and culture.[35] The Mennonite response to Niebuhr has been profoundly shaped by Yoder and remains an important baseline from which to carry on conversation with the Niebuhrian social ethical tradition and move beyond it.

However, it must also be noted that in recent years there have been other voices who have built on Yoder's critique and provide a basis for moving beyond the stage of antithesis in the Niebuhrian-Yoderian dialectic. One voice is that of Gayle Gerber Koontz, a writer within the Mennonite tradition.[36] She explores how confessional theology, committed to particularity, faces religious diversity within the Christian community—how a Protestant catholic vision and an ecumenical sectarian vision engage in dialogue and respond to diversity and division. In this context, she evaluates the relative strengths and weaknesses of Niebuhr's and Yoder's confessional postures in relation to inter-Christian and inter-religious dialogue. This study is a good illustration of seeking points of contact rather than merely divergences in inter-confessional dialogue. She seeks to show how their differences complement each other.

Gerber Koontz's description and evaluation of the differences and similarities between Niebuhr and Yoder is done in relationship to the goodness of the news, Christian conversion, permanent revolution, the conversion of culture, and theocentric versus christocentric ethics.[37] She shows how Yoder really belongs to the conversionist model, that is, to a tranformationist type.[38]

According to Gerber Koontz, Niebuhr sees ethics as a more descriptive and critical task. His is an ethic of response relevant to the social selves; yet he is more unclear in providing normative guidelines. His is an ethic of being, an act-oriented ethic. On the other hand, Yoder sees ethics as a critical and normative/constructive task. His is a community-based non-resistant ethic which is appealing but not always easy to locate in reality. His is an ethic of decision-making/action, a rule-oriented ethic.

In the end, Gerber Koontz argues that Yoder attempts to preserve the concreteness and specificity of the biblical story and of the Christian community in its expression of faith and ethics to a greater extent than Niebuhr does. This, she holds, has greater integrity than theological interpretations which attempt to move away from or transcend those concrete aspects and, indeed, enhances inter-religious exchange.

She maintains, however, that the particular type of non-resistant christocentrism modelled by Yoder, when it is corrected by the theocentric vision Niebuhr offers, has the potential to maximize both Christian integrity and fruitful intra- and inter-religious encounter.

A second voice is that of Charles Scriven.[39] Speaking as one who stands outside of the Mennonite tradition (although within the Free Church tradition), he draws conclusions which take us a step beyond Gerber Koontz's analysis. His thesis is that the true Niebuhrian way is the Anabaptist way. His proposal involves taking exception to the way in which Niebuhr has set up the enduring problem.[40]

For Scriven, it is the theological expressions of sixteenth-century Anabaptism and its reappropriation by the twentieth-century Mennonite tradition which reflects the true intention of the Niebuhrian "transformationist" ethic, properly understood. For Scriven, Christ transforms culture, as Niebuhr says, but the proper "mode" of that transformation is understood best by the Anabaptists. Christ is the transformer of culture, and Anabaptism knows best his way of doing so.[41]

Our analysis has served to illustrate several important points: the Yoderian influence on the changing shape of the agenda surrounding the classic Niebuhrian critique of the Mennonite tradition, especially as it relates to the concept of peace; the more positive interpretation of Niebuhr's original intentions regarding the "transformationist" strategy; the attempt to emphasize the points of convergence rather than contrast between Reformed and Mennonite positions; the inherent "transformationist" dynamic in the contemporary Anabaptist-Mennonite social ethic; and greater openness for inter-confessional dialogue.

The "against culture" typology characterizing Mennonites — as reinforced by sixteenth-century mainline Protestant historiography, traditional Mennonite self-understanding, and contemporary Niebuhrian church-world typology — is not only inadequate, but inaccurate in defining the fundamental dynamic of the Anabaptist-Mennonite peace tradition. The Anabaptist-Mennonite peace tradition is not intrinsically sectarian — even though historically at times it has been — but transformationist. The Anabaptist-Mennonite position does not reject culture, but discriminates and rejects certain expressions of culture while accepting others.[42]

A Transformationist Social Ethic

Our claim is that the Anabaptist-Mennonite peace tradition is inherently transformationist, not simply separatist, in character. We have made this claim largely on the basis of contemporary Mennonite theological self-understanding regarding Israel and the early Church, the Radical Reformation, and the contemporary Church-world issue. (See "Excursus on Mennonite Separatism," pp. 111-12.)

The contemporary Mennonite work which has done the most to provide a full-blown theological interpretation and application of the transformationist sensibilities of the Anabaptist-Mennonite tradition is that of Duane Friesen.[43] Central to his work is the extensive theological framework he brings to bear on understanding the relevance of peace theology for societal structures. He shows how the basic biblical themes of the biblical drama — the creation and fall, the redemptive process in history, and the new age to come — provide the basis for a Christian view of socio-political reality.

Under the biblical theme of creation, Friesen proceeds to develop a theological framework for the affirmation of institutional structure as "an aspect of God's created order." He shows how the Bible recognizes their positive (albeit provisional) role within God's purposes in history. The biblical basis for such institutional ordering of human life is the Genesis account of creation.[44]

Friesen clearly shows how "all human institutional life is affected to its core by human sinfulness," for "there is not always order and stability but also violence, oppression, and corruption of these 'sane' institutions." According to him "this rebellion has significant consequences for human social relationships." The fall is an interior breach between humans and God, a social breach between human beings themselves, and an exterior breach between humans and the earth.[45]

Since "the consequences of this sinfulness can never be separated from its expression in human, sociohistorical collectives," the "meaning of salvation therefore cannot be separated from the transformation of sociohistorical structures." For Friesen "it is not the existence of sociohistorical structures...but the absolutization of them that is sinful." For example, "war between nations is one form in which this absolutization expresses itself, in the protection of its interests."[46]

Friesen sees Jesus' life and teachings as "a continuation of the ethic of the prophetic tradition." Thus "Jesus chose the role of servant to inaugurate his kingdom, rather than exercise his messiahship through holy war in the Zealot tradition." In other words, Jesus rejects revolutionary violence. This "servant role and acceptance of the cross is the most fundamental and also widely held ethical model in all the various strands of the early church tradition."

According to him, "this servant Christ is Lord and is victorious over the powers and principalities, terminology which should be understood in sociopolitical terms." That is, in Christ human beings are set free from the institutionalized behaviour patterns of sexism, racism, classism, nationalism found in family, tribe, and nation. Now "the church is the institutional focus in history of the new ethical reality of the kingdom of God."[47]

Thus for Friesen "the NT eschatological vision does not completely destroy human cultural activity and institutional reality, but transforms it and gives it a new role in the eschatological future." However, the age to come is beyond history. For there is an already but not yet and one cannot finally resolve the tension in history. If we do, the result is either violent fanaticism or sentimentalism or escapism or an analysis of the human condition in terms of human possibilities. Yet for him "in Christ it is possible not to sin." This presupposes the possibilities of God's redemption here and now. But complete redemption remains an eschatological reality.[48]

V. Defining the Agenda Theologically
Peace as a Transformational Grammar

In this study we have attempted to engage in an intra-textual study of Scripture, history, and the contemporary world, with a view to writing a grammar for the language of peace in the Mennonite tradition, through which the meaning of the concept of peace is better able to be translated in inter-confessional dialogue. [49] Our attempt has been to forge the thesis that the Anabaptist-Mennonite peace tradition is not intrinsically separationist but transformationist. Throughout our intra-textual analysis we have tried to establish three crucial points.

The first is that the contemporary Mennonite tradition has been impacted by significant sociological, historiographical, and theological developments. By showing the shift and shape of contemporary developments in the Mennonite tradition, we have established important internal grounds for relativizing the Niebuhrian "anti-cultural" critique.

Secondly, we have tried to show that peace is a regulative concept. [50] Internally, it has functioned in that capacity for the Mennonite tradition. Externally, its associations have been with non-conformity and thus primarily separatism. By showing the way in which the concept of peace functions within the contemporary Mennonite tradition, we have tried to establish a regulative framework which can guide inter-confessional dialogue.

Thirdly, we have attempted to demonstrate that the Mennonite tradition is inherently transformationist in character. By showing the shape of theological developments and the way in which peace, as a regulative concept, functions in contemporary Mennonite theology, we have shown that the deepest theological instincts of the Mennonite tradition are not separatist, but transformationist.

It is this point which still needs further definition, especially in the context of inter-confessional dialogue. The concept of "transformation" has an established usage in Reformed social ethics in terms of the relationship of the Church to the world. For the Mennonite tradition to reappropriate that term for its confessional agenda needs some clarification. Therefore, what remains is the need to articulate the shape of a transformational grammar of peace in the Mennonite tradition with a view to providing a language that facilitates inter-confessional conversation.

For Mennonite social ethics, the biblical concept of *shalom* is the primary point of reference for giving definition to a transformationist theology of peace. As Perry Yoder has clearly shown, *shalom*, the biblical word for salvation, justice, and peace, lies at the heart of biblical faith and can be fully understood only through its linkage to a cluster of closely related key convictions—beliefs about God, the world, and humankind. [51] The concept of *shalom* consists of three interwoven strands of meaning which are constitutive of a transformationist theology of peace. They involve the physical/material, the social/communal, and the moral/spiritual dimensions of life.[52]

These three strands must be understood within the framework of the three corresponding theological themes which emerged from our hermeneutical considerations—the problem of God the warrior, the politics of Jesus the Messiah, and the powers that have been subjected by the Spirit of the risen Lord. The historical reality of the reign of God in the world as revealed in the message to Israel, the ministry of Jesus, and mission of the early church provides the theological grounding for a tranformational theology of peace.

Peace as an Embodied Virtue

A transformational theology of peace, first of all, involves concern for the physical and material well-being of persons and society. It addresses conditions of famine, disease, and war. It honours bodily existence and embraces the task of transforming human culture. The social ethic of a peace church witnessing to culture involves building upon the organic foundation the skills required for living, skills which are grounded in the practices and values commonly accepted in a particular tradition.

Peace as an embodied virtue is one of the great gifts of the Gospel. Its incarnation in bodily existence has significant implications for all basic human relationships and needs. Moreover, it is one of the profound forms of Christian witness, deeply rooted in the message to Israel, the ministry of Jesus, and the mission of the early church. In this incarnational role, the Church is an agent of conversion and transformation. It will necessarily function both as an alternative community with selective cultural involvement and as a tranformative example that functions as a lantern of righteousness, non-legalistically exhibiting the way of non-violence in a post-modern culture.

Thus, by "transformation" we do not simply mean cultural or political involvement but the incarnational dynamic of the reality of the Gospel of God culturally embodied in the world as light, salt, and witness to society. It involves an affirmation of a full-orbed cultural embodiment of the Gospel in its physical, material, and organic form. A transformationist theology of peace cannot, however, be accounted for in organic terms alone, where the definitional term is the "world."

Peace as a Powerful Practice

A tranformationist theology of peace also involves justice in the realm of social relationships. It entails the presence of positive and good relationships between persons, within a society, and between nations. The Church as an alternative community is to exemplify and foster *shalom* justice in all relationships. Moreover, the practice of peace within the Church as a social ethic involves nurturing co-operative human activities (such as friendship and marriage) through skills such as justice, courage, truthfulness, and integrity. These must be learned and maintained in a church community over a period of time and evaluated in light of the Gospel story of Jesus and the reign of God he proclaims through the Spirit in the Church and to the world.

A peace church must always, however, contend with the condition of a sinful world within and without. Contemporary theology has used the biblical concept of principalities and powers as an explanation of this condition.[53] Yet these "powers" (e.g., economic and civil) are not simply and always expressions of idolatrous forces at work. There must constantly be a discerning process regarding participation in or separation from these powers.

A transformationist theology of peace does not just acknowledge the presence of these powerful practices but responds to them transformatively. Such action requires that the individual and the community of faith stand in solidarity with Christ and practise the following virtues: social transformation in the context of non-conformity; trans-national identification in the context of cultural particularity; and responsible non-violent action in the context of violence.

A transformative theology of peace cannot, therefore, be abstracted from the narrative of the community.[54] It is not embarrassed about the particularity of confessional language. To celebrate confessionally that "light and truth have taken on the vulnerability of the particular" requires "a missionary ethic of incarnation."[55] In this way, peace functions as a powerful transformative practice, engaging the powers that be. Yet a transformationist peace theology cannot be defined solely in terms of the social strand where the definitional term is the "church."

Peace as a Spiritual Reality

The organic and social dimensions of a transformational peace theology must finally be grounded in the Resurrection. Here the definitional term is the "reign of God" in Christ. The Resurrection represents the authority of Christ in the context of an eschatological (Spirit), narrative (Jesus), and theocentric (God) vision. Through the Resurrection, God has inaugurated a new epoch between the times of the first and final advent of Christ. Its significance for social ethics lies in its new way of understanding and envisioning the world. It is a new reality on which you stake your life, a new world into which you enter through conversion and transformation.

It is by the envisioning power of this new reality that one is able to live the *shalom* ethic of straightforwardness, integrity, blamelessness, and non-violence. Only through baptism and communion, as the ongoing sacramental acts of the Church's faith, is one able to give birth to and nurture the embodied virtues anew; to say no to the powerful practices that continue to challenge God's people and would lead the Church into sin; and to say yes to the resurrection story of the one God in Jesus Christ who is Lord over history and creation.

A Christian social ethic therefore not only involves entering into the story of Jesus, remembering and expecting the Christ, or examining ourselves and entering into fellowship with God's people, but worshipping in word and deed the God above all who provides memory, unity, identity, and meaning to the story of our life.

Worship itself is a profound transforming, ethical act that says yes to the shared and lived story of God in Christ. Christian social ethics involves the discovery, understanding, and the creative transformation of a shared and lived story whose focus is Jesus and through which we are empowered and formed by the Resurrection Spirit of God.

Thus a transformationist theology of peace must be grounded in the power of the Resurrection. The way of peace must be shaped by a biblical paradigm in which there is a powerful Christological challenge to all previously formed cosmic visions. Here the definitional category is not world, culture, or civilization, but the rule of God. Embodying peace in the context of covenant loyalty to the rule of one Lord entails building concrete options based on the servant Lordship of God in Christ as manifested through the eschatological Spirit in culture and creation.

Peace as a Transformational Language

The language and life of *shalom* provides an inter-world transformational language to proclaim to our pluralist/relativist cultures that Jesus is Lord. It represents the embodiment of the peaceable presence of God's rule in the organic, communal, and spiritual spheres of life. This must be said in a variety of ways that add up to the proclamation of the Lordship of God in Christ through the Spirit. This language needs constantly to give shape to our response to the central biblical and theological question, "Whose are we?"

Critical to constructive, inter-confessional dialogue today is the recognition that conventional Western theism has collapsed and that an array of powers exists – the gods of humanity, nature, history, and religion – whose idolatrous threats against Christianity, culture and civilization should become the focal point to unite Christians so as to take them beyond obsolete debates and distinctions.[56]

It is anachronistic to continue to live as though the boundaries of conventional Western Christendom are still intact. We exist in an intellectual and cultural context where the Western theistic consensus no longer exists. A Christianized monotheistic culture has given way to a post-Christian polytheistic one. Yet most contemporary mainline and Mennonite Christians still act as though *corpus Christianum* and its modern extension in the "responsible society" is intact and that the Christian ethical options are still to be worked out within that reality.

The assumption of this study has been that we are no longer living under such conditions and that the articulation of a peace theology can no longer be carried on within the old lines of debate which assume such a self-understanding of the contemporary Western world. In short, we have attempted to write a grammar for the language of peace in the Mennonite tradition in order to make the concept of peace more translatable inter-confessionally in a post-modern world.

The language of peace must be linked to the paradigmatic way of Israel, Jesus, and the early Church in the world for a truly transformationist approach to culture to be found. Even though the reality of the fallen world does not yet offer us a lot of evidence that God's transforming rule is present, we do have enough to begin reconstructing a transformational grammar on this side of history and to promote the transformational language of peace as the way of proclaiming biblical faith to a post-modern culture.

Excursus on Peace as a Regulative Concept

Our purpose has not been to focus directly and narrowly on the concept of peace in the Mennonite tradition (it has not been an exercise in definition); nor to provide a definitive systematic treatment of peace in the Mennonite tradition (it has not been an exercise in making a comprehensive summary); nor to provide a descriptive historical overview of peace in the Mennonite tradition from its inception (it has not simply involved historical analysis); nor to provide an understanding of peace in the Mennonite tradition from a particular disciplinary perspective, be that biblical, historical, ethical, sociological, phenomenological, or theological (it does not represent the analysis of the expert in one field of study); nor to provide a standard comparison and contrast between Mennonite and Reformed views of peace (it is not simply drawing attention to possible points of convergence or divergence between two traditions).

Our approach does not clearly fall under any one of the descriptions above. Yet, in some sense, it encompasses all of them, for we have attempted to establish a conceptually broad and methodologically adequate framework in which peace, as a regulative concept in the Mennonite tradition, can be understood for the purposes of constructive inter-confessional dialogue.

Peace as a "regulative concept" refers to its function in second-order reflective discourse. "Concepts" attempt to orient motifs, metaphors, or symbols conceptually as instruments of thought in order to provide concrete subject matter. "Regulative" refers to an understanding of doctrinal "concepts" viewed, not as statements with unequivocal relationship to ultimate truth, nor as mere symbolic expressions of a prior and more important inner experience, but as the "regulative concepts" which determine how the persons and communities of faith actually live. "Doctrine" thus forms an individual's or a community's religious experience as well as expressing it. [See George Lindbeck, *The Nature of Doctrine* (Westminster, 1984) for an extensive definition of "regulative principles."]

Here we have adapted the term to describe the way in which the Mennonite concept of peace defines and influences a certain way of being Christian. The regulative concept of peace in the Mennonite tradition is not simply a perspective (a particular alternative theological method), a proposition (a dogmatic exposition with peace as the central locus), or a practice (a praxis involving ethical/social engagement). Rather, it is a first-level concept whose grammar must be understood intra-textually in conjunction with a series of other theological motifs: non-resistance, non-conformity, discipleship, service, servanthood, reign of God, the teachings of Jesus, and the ministry of the early Church. However, it is beyond the scope of this paper to explore the relationship of each of these motifs to the regulative concept of peace.

Excursus on Mennonite Historiography

Many theories concerning the origins and the essence of Anabaptism were promulgated in the years preceding and following the WWII period. The one that gained the widest currency among Mennonites was the view that Anabaptism is the culmination of the Reformation, the fulfillment of the original vision of Luther and Zwingli. It was a consistent evangelical Protestantism seeking to recreate without compromise the original New Testament church, the vision of Christ and the apostles. [See Donovan E. Smucker, "Anabaptist Historiography in the Scholarship of Today," *Mennonite Quarterly Review* 22 (1948): 116-27.

Harold S. Bender, the dean of Mennonite historians, articulated that vision in his classic work *The Anabaptist Vision* (Herald, 1944). He captured the Mennonite imagination by describing the "essence" of that vision in a threefold way: the essence of Christianity as discipleship, the Church as a voluntary community, and the ethic of love and non-resistance. The attendant theology of the Church as a visible fellowship of obedient disciples, exhibiting the way of suffering love, was one of the controlling features of Anabaptist theology. That theological paradigm has shaped the Mennonite ethos and ethic profoundly in the second half of the twentieth century.

Yet the Bender vision, which provided the impetus for the developments which moved Mennonite social ethics from a position of withdrawal to one of greater involvement, has itself come under criticism in the last two decades. The adequacy of its parameters for defining the Mennonite vision have been challenged. There are several reasons for this.

First, even though new understandings of social responsibility were brought about by this vision of discipleship, community and non-resistance, it still tended to interpret and implement this social vision within a strong sectarian (i.e., separatist) self-understanding. Moreover, themes such as separation of Church and state, individual freedom, and human ethical responsibility went in directions other than originally intended in the context of the spirit of the 1960s. Also, there was a growing realization of needing to affirm more the sinful nature of human beings and with that the impossibility of developing a pure church.

What has been critiqued is the tendency of the Bender vision and its advocates to idealize the edenic moment in history and not sufficiently recognize the need for perspective. Since the mid-1970s there has been a revisionist view proposed by a group of so-called "secular" historians. At the heart of their critique is the heavy employment of theology as a conceptual tool for the analysis of Anabaptism. Their alternative approach to Anabaptist-Mennonite history comes from the perspective of social, economic, and intellectual history rather than theology. Their first concern is to put together an historically reliable picture and then ask theological questions. [See Hans-Juergen Goertz, "History and Theology: A Major Problem of Anabaptist Research Today," *Mennonite Quarterly Review* 53 (1979): 177; and W.O. Packull and K. Deppermann, "From Monogenesis to Polygenesis: The Historical Discussion of Anabaptist Origins," *Mennonite Quarterly Review* 49 (1975): 83.

James Stayer's work, *Anabaptism and the Sword* (Coronado, 1972) is a good example of this kind of approach. He gives special attention to the interconnectedness of thought and social development. Moreover, he provides an extensive analysis of the Anabaptist view of the sword and argues that the rejection of the power of the sword was by no means as clear and general as held by the "normative vision" school. Employing a polygenetic rather than a monogenetic approach to the Radical Reformation (one which promulgates the multiple origins and diversity of the Anabaptist movement in various centres), he provides a thoroughgoing challenge to the traditional view of Anabaptism among Mennonites.

He limits the so-called essential or normative Anabaptism to one group and shows the futility of the search for mainstream Anabaptism as it is reflected in the monogenetic historiography. He disputes this group's right to primogeniture and attests the revolutionary character of early Anabaptism. Thus, he argues for a polygenesis of Anabaptism with sources in Switzerland, Central Germany, and the Netherlands.

Applying this analysis to the Anabaptist view of the sword, Stayer's thesis is that the essential qualities of the early Anabaptist teaching on the sword are apoliticism and radicalism. This was the most typical stance. According to Stayer, the mistake of those who say that all true Anabaptists are non-resistant (Mennonite tradition) is that they miss the movement's inherent illegitimacy and radicalism, which are in some cases compatible with violence. The mistake of those who would regard early Anabaptism as fundamentally violent (mainline tradition) is to miss the basic apoliticism of the movement. Stayer's view steers a course between a sixteenth-century mainline interpretation and a traditional doctrinaire Mennonite view.

In the past decade there has been a recognition, not only of the importance of sixteenth-century origins, but also of the subsequent confessional and theological developments within the tradition beyond its origins. [See, for example, the collection of essays edited by Willard M. Swartley, *Explorations of Systematic Theology from Mennonite Perspectives*, Occasional Papers, No. 7 (Institute of Mennonite Studies,

1984); or Howard John Loewen, *One Lord, One Faith, One Hope, and One God: Mennonite Confessions of Faith* (Institute of Mennonite Studies, 1985).]

Excursus on Mennonite Separatism

We have not in any sustained sense dealt with the long chapters of separatism in the Mennonite tradition. This study in no way denies the existence of those historical chapters, or that the Mennonite tradition, historically, fits to a large extent Troeltsch's sect type. Nor does it necessarily view those developments negatively. For the separation of the Church from the world does, in fact, need embodiment in some historical and cultural form. However, the Mennonite form of that separation is certainly not the only one and certainly was, and continues to be, less than ideal at points. Our concern in this study has not been to chronicle the history of Mennonite separatism and sectarianism but to engage in an intra-textual analysis of the regulative concept of peace in the contemporary Mennonite tradition.

Such an approach is necessary, especially in the context of inter-confessional conversation, because it has been the long stereotyped history of Mennonite separatism that has provided the primary frame of reference for both Mennonites and those who have become their interlocutors. That stereotyped frame of reference has been determinative in such conversations. Thus we have emphasized the modern recovery of the transformationist centre of the Anabaptist-Mennonite tradition in order to focus the theological heart of the tradition. This transformationist centre never really disappeared, but was at times overshadowed internally by the social reality of physical separation from culture and moral deterioration in the community, and externally by the theological definition given to this separatism by mainstream religion.

Yet the fact remains that confessionally and experientially the concept and reality of transformation remained at the heart of the Mennonite tradition, even in its socially separatist existence. At the heart of the Mennonite confessional tradition is a theological anthropology and soteriology in which regeneration and transformation of human character in its social context are central.

What often did not emerge in the past is an application of the transformationist ethos and ethic to the broader spheres of surrounding culture. However, what was certain is that the Mennonite tradition, even in its separatist mode, understood instinctively that transformation could be embodied in culture. The Gospel in Mennonite faith was something that could be truly incarnated in life. Thus the relationship between transformation and non-conformity in Mennonite experience is far more complex than the Niebuhrian typology makes it out to be. It presupposes a strong sense of the incarnational reality of the Gospel in culture. The problem that existed within the historical reality of a separatist existence, however, was the limitation of that insight to one circumscribed ethno-religious culture.

This historical fact does not, of course, invalidate the theological importance of separation from the world. We must still incorporate the concept of separation into the Church and theology, but it must be worked out in relationship to the central transformationist instincts of the Anabaptist-Mennonite tradition where the relationship of transformation and non-conformity involves all of what Paul meant in his challenge to the early Christians in Rome "not to be conformed to this world but to be transformed by the renewal of their minds" (Rom 12:2).

However, as we have shown in this study, major sociological, historiographical, and theological developments have occurred in the Mennonite tradition in the twentieth-century. Mennonites have moved from a position of social withdrawal to being full-fledged participants in twentieth-century culture. This renaissance which has occurred in the post-WWII period no longer makes it possible for Mennonites or their interlocutors to carry on conversations in an outdated language. Both are in need of learning a new language. The purpose of this study has been to develop a transformational language of peace that will assist Mennonites in inter-confessional and inter-world dialogue.

Notes

1. By calling Scripture, tradition, and the contemporary world "texts," we intend to make obvious the fact that our understanding of the grammar of peace must be derived and handled hermeneutically. That is, these "texts" do not straightforwardly evidence truth. Not only must they each be read interpretively, but they must also be interpreted intra-textually in order to render fully the meaning of peace in the Mennonite tradition and to ensure its translatability in inter-confessional conversation.

2. Following George A. Lindbeck [*The Nature of Doctrine* (Philadelphia: The Westminster Press, 1984), p. 114] we are using the term "intra-textual" to refer to a method which locates religious meaning within the text or symbolic system of a religious tradition rather than external to it. The notion of "intra-textuality" derives from a cultural-linguistic approach to religious understanding in which "meaning is constituted by the uses of a specific

language rather than distinguishable from it." It tries to see how texts operate within a religious community and thereby shape reality and experience "rather than by first establishing their propositional or experiential meaning and reinterpreting or reformulating their uses accordingly." It is in this sense that we are attempting to obtain an intra-textual understanding of peace in the Mennonite tradition relative to the texts of Scripture, history, and the contemporary world.

3. Historically, the Mennonite tradition has had a problem in entering into dialogue with most of the mainline traditions, not just because it refuses to go to war, but also because of the approach it brings to basic theological issues. Its central emphasis is on "living the faithful Christian life, rather than on holding correct theology." (J.R. Burkholder, *Mennonites in Ecumenical Dialogue on Peace and Justice*, Mennonite Central Committee, Occasional Papers, No. 7, 1988, p. 11). However, the parameters of most faith and order discussions are defined by creedal or confessional tradition. For traditions which claim the primacy of other norms — namely, Scripture, worship, ethics, and mission, not primarily creeds and confessions — to be decisive as tests of apostolicity and true faith, it becomes difficult for constructive dialogue to advance beyond a certain point. There is a sense in which this dilemma has made contemporary Mennonite scholarship much more self-conscious methodologically in how it proceeds in these kinds of discussions. There is a long memory of having its agenda shaped by its conversational partners. That point itself must become part of the dialogue, that is, clarifying the framework in which the conversational process begins, develops, and concludes and the language which is used to carry on the conversation between a minority and a mainline tradition.

4. That hermeneutical perspective affirms that the Old Testament (hereafter, OT) criticizes warfare and prepares for the New Testament (hereafter, NT) teaching of non-resistant love and pacifism. Since the OT prepares for the NT, it cannot be used for normative Christian ethics. Moreover, Jesus's life and teachings, as reflected in the apostolic writings, are clearly pacificist. The nature of God's reign and Jesus' messiahship supports the non-resistant position. Christ's atonement calls for a non-violent discipleship. Since peace is at the heart of the Gospel, the nature and mission of the church lead to the way of non-violence. Authority is linked to Christ and to the church community as the primary context in and through which the social ethic of peace is lived out.

5. In connection with the last view, there has been a more conscious reflection on the principles of pre-understanding which inform the reading of the biblical text. One of the important shifts has been that Mennonites are now making their case more from the Old Testament in the context of a diversity of views regarding the understanding of war in Israel.

6. There has been a shift in Mennonite scholarship away from a primary appeal to strong non-violent imperatives of Jesus in the NT — as strongly reflected, for example, in the Mennonite confessions of faith — to addressing more squarely

the theological problem of God as warrior as a central issue in biblical theology. The strong appeal to Jesus' words is seen in the predominant use of texts in Mennonite confessions from the Matthean discourses. Chapter 5 (Sermon on the Mount) is referred to the most extensively by far. Chapter 25 (on eschatology), Chapter 28 (the Great Commission) and Chapter 18 (church discipline) follow Matthew 5 in that order in frequency. Within Matthew 5, the section on love for one's enemies (vv. 43-48) receives the strongest emphasis by a margin of almost three to one. It is followed by the section on integrity and the oath. (See Howard John Loewen, *One Lord, One Church, One Hope, and One God: Mennonite Confessions of Faith* (Elkhart, Indiana: Institute of Mennonite Studies, 1985.)

7.   See Millard C. Lind, *Yahweh as a Warrior: The Theology of Warfare in Ancient Israel* (Scottdale, Pennsylvania: Herald Press 1980).

8.   According to Ben C. Ollenburger, what Lind has found is "that in the communities that produced those texts, God the Warrior did not function to legitimate or motivate warrior-like activity, but to correct or repudiate it." Therefore, "one cannot properly speak of the OT concept of God the Warrior apart from the larger symbolic construction of which it is a part." For "to speak of God the Warrior is also to speak of God the King and, hence, also of God the Creator." And "since the OT creation is almost always spoken of in terms of order, to speak of God is also necessarily to speak of justice and righteousness." To speak of God the warrior is to speak of God in a particular way that relates to God's universal dominion in justice and righteousness. "Peace Theology and the Concept of Warrior God," *Essays on Peace Theology and Witness*, Occasional Papers, No. 12, Willard M. Swartley, ed. (Elkhart, Indiana: Institute of Mennonite Studies 1988, pp. 112-34).

9.   See Willard M. Swartley, *Slavery, Sabbath, War, and Women: Case Issues in Biblical Interpretation* (Scottdale, Indiana: Herald Press, 1983), pp. 112-39.

10.   Swartley, *Slavery*, p. 146.

11.   For Mennonite peace theology, this has increasingly meant that a position of non-violence, defined by the privileged in the world as the passive avoidance of violence, of doing no overt violence, is really not a peace position at all but support for selective violence for it is "against violence by the oppressed but apparently comfortable with violence and injustice by the oppressors." See Perry B. Yoder, *Shalom: The Bible's Word for Salvation, Justice, and Peace* (Newton, Kansas: Faith and Life Press, 1987), p. 5.

12.   See John Howard Yoder, *The Politics of Jesus.* (Grand Rapids, MI: Wm. B. Eerdmans Publishing Co., 1972), p. 13.

13.   Yoder, *Politics*, p. 23.

14.   Yoder's analysis of Luke can be summarized in the following manner. For him the Annunciation story (1:46ff., 1:68ff.; cf. 3:7ff.) testifies to the political character of the good news. In the baptismal formula and the subsequent temptations, the economic, social, and political nature of Jesus' ministry is revealed (3:21-4:14). The calling of the twelve and the Lucan version of the Sermon on the Mount reaffirms Jesus' platform and marks the beginning of a

new social reality (6:12ff.). The feeding of the five thousand episode "marks the culmination of the popular Galilean ministry and the transition to a ministry centered on the disciples and moving toward Jerusalem." Jesus chooses "neither the way of quietism nor insurrection but increasingly the way of the cross as a true political alternative" (9:1-22, 51ff.). According to Yoder, there is "a continual shadow over the band of disciples moving to Jerusalem." The emphasis here is "that of calling a community of voluntary disciples, willing for the sake of its calling to take upon itself the hostility of the given society." This illustrates the social relevance of an inner group comprised of various people, including former Zealots and publicans (12:49-13:9; 14:25-36). The Lucan travel narrative reaches a culmination in Jesus' entry into Jerusalem. For Yoder, "every perilcope in the second 19:47-22:2 reflects in some way the confrontation of two social systems and Jesus' rejection of the status quo." For him "what is Caesar's and what is God's are in the same arena." Then "at the last moment Jesus again had to face the temptation of messianic violence." The trial in Gethsemane and the temptation in the desert are very similar. They reflect the real option of Zealot-like insurrection and kingship. But once more, as throughout his lifetime, Jesus rejects this option (22:24-53).

15. Yoder, *Politics*, pp. 62-63.

16. Yoder, *Politics*, p. 115.

17. See the proposed publication of John E. Toews, *Romans*, Believers Church Bible Commentary Series (Scottdale, PA: Herald Press). Also see Toews's article on "Paul's View of the State: What Romans 13 Says About Peace and Warfare," *Christian Leader* 41 (April 25, 1978):5.

18. For Mennonite theology, Romans 13 centres exegetically on two pivotal points: the exhortation (13:1a) and the recapitulation (13:5). With attention focused on the grammatical centre of 13:1a and 13:5 the concern remains predominantly with the life of the Christian, not the state. The primary emphasis does not fall on 13:1b-4, which is often used to fortify temporal authority. Verses 1b-4 represent an elaboration of the basic assertion in 1a, which is then recapitulated in verse 5b, namely, to be "ordered under" the governing authorities. The text does not provide warrants for a metaphysic of the state.

19. These powers can also be demonic. This concept of the "world" dominates all of Paul's writings (as can be seen in his many other texts on the "principalities and powers") and must also condition our interpretation of Romans 13. Thus the state does not possess absolute authority because the powers are subject to Christ and have been relativized.

20. What needs to be noted is the piling up of the Greek words for "order" (*taxis*); *hupotassestho* (being subject); *tetagmai* (has established); *antitassomenos* (resisting); *diatage* (have been established). It is significant that the word "order" has been chosen. In this context, "sub-ordering" by the Christian does not mean unconditional obedience but recognizing that one is placed below the authorities by God. Nor does "ordering" of the state mean that this text is

providing an ontology of the state, endorsing it as part of the structure of being comprehending heaven and earth. Rather it is a provisional order that functions as an extension of the powers (*exousiai*) which God, through Christ, brings into conformity with his purposes. The qualifying question is, In what sense is the state ordered by God? The consequent tension between Church and state is not an ontological one but a moral one. It is also important to observe that Paul avoids using the normal Greek words for obedience which denote a complete bending of one's will to the desires of another. The Christian is to be subordinate, to stand under, to recognize that they exist, and that the state is a provisional order which can serve God. It is an arrangement of God in which God through Christ as Lord reigns over human disobedience.

21.   In conjunction with the ministry of Jesus it is significant to note that Romans 13:1-7 is preceded by a periscope (12:14-21) whose subject matter has strong affinity with the words of Jesus. The specific content of these words in all likelihood come out of a Palestinian milieu (cf. Mt 5:39b, 44, 46). The unifying theme of the code in 12:14-21 which incorporates these sayings of Jesus is the proper attitude of the Christian toward the enemy: do not return evil for evil, live in peace with all persons, do not avenge yourselves. It is highly likely that in the Palestinian milieu in which Jesus taught, "to love your enemies" referred to a disavowal of a militant anti-Roman policy. Likewise it is probable that Paul's words are given in the context of Jewish nationalism manifesting itself throughout the Empire, including Rome. With an emerging Christianity caught up in the crisis of Jewish-Roman relations, a central question becomes, What is the right relationship toward Rome?

22.   See J. Richard Burkholder, *Mennonites in Ecumenical Dialogue on Peace and Justice* (Akron, PA: Mennonite Central Committee Occasional Papers, No. 7 (1988). According to Burkholder, "this theological development was especially enhanced through opportunities for dialogue with other Christian traditions" (p. 5). The "most important efforts in this area grew out of the presence of American Mennonites in Europe after World War II, in particular a core group of young men who had gone abroad in relief and reconstruction efforts and remained to study in European universities" (p. 8). In 1949, the renewed Historic Peace Churches developed a response to the 1948 WCC statement regarding war. Burkholder comments that "thus began an engagement with ecumenical circles that has continued up to the present" (p. 8). The most important chapter of this story is the conferences at Puidoux, Switzerland, held between 1955 and 1962 where, for example, the creative work of John Howard Yoder emerged, emphasizing the themes of the "Lordship of Christ" over all the powers of the cosmos and the recognition of acceptable non-violent action through such secular norms as equality and justice (pp. 5-6). This renewed theological perspective has in varying degrees become incarnated in Mennonite experience since the 1960s. According to Burkholder, "efforts at international dialogue have continued in other settings" (p. 8). Such efforts include the New Call to Peacemaking initiated by the Historic Peace Churches in 1976; the conference on "The Church and Peacemaking in the Nuclear Age"

in Pasadena in 1983; the 1983 WCC Sixth Assembly in Vancouver which emphasized justice, peace and the integrity of creation (pp. 5-13).

23.　See Harold S. Bender, *The Anabaptist Vision* (Scottdale, PA: Herald Press, 1944).

24.　J.R. Burkholder, *Mennonites*, p. 1.

25.　J.R. Burkholder, *Mennonites*, p. 2.

26.　J.R. Burkholder, *Mennonites*, p. 2.

27.　J.R. Burkholder, *Mennonites*, p. 4.

28.　J.R. Burkholder, *Mennonites*, p. 19.

29.　J.R. Burkholder, *Mennonites*, p. 5.

30.　See J. Lawrence Burkholder, *The Problem of Social Responsibility from the Perspective of the Mennonite Church* (Elkhart, IN: Institute of Mennonite Studies, 1989).

31.　J.L. Burkholder, *Social Responsibility*, p. 6.

32.　J.L. Burkholder, *Social Responsibility*, p. 213.

33.　J.L. Burkholder, *Social Responsibility*, p. 82.

34.　See H. Richard Niebuhr, *Christ and Culture* (New York: Harper and Row, Publishers, 1951), esp. chapter 2, "Christ Against Culture."

35.　See John Howard Yoder, "Christ and Culture: A Critique of H. Richard Niebuhr," unpublished manuscript, 1964.

36.　See Gayle Louise Gerber Koontz, *Confessional Theology in a Pluralistic Context: A Study of the Theological Ethics of H. Richard Niebuhr and John H. Yoder*, unpublished doctoral dissertation (Boston, MS: Boston University, 1985).

37.　Gerber Koontz, *Confessional Theology*, chapter 3, "Christian Confessionalism: Two Interpretations of the Gospel," pp. 67-136.

38.　Gerber Koontz, *Confessional Theology*, pp. 89f.

39.　See Charles Scriven, *The Transformation of Culture: Christian Social Ethics After H. Richard Niebuhr* (Scottdale, PA: Herald Press, 1988).

40.　Scriven maintains that in defining the "enduring problem" of the relationship of Christ and culture Niebuhr resorts to using the key operational term, "culture," inconsistently. In the separationist position, he uses culture positively to critique the position. In the transformationist position, he uses it negatively in order to legitimate the position. Thus the limitations of Niebuhr are that he fails to convey clearly the variety of ways in which culture expresses itself. According to Scriven, it is not useful to frame the problem in such a dichotomous way. Culture cannot mean the prevailing way of life in one context and everything that is human-made and human-intended in the next. Culture does have authority and shapes us all, but it makes no sense to oppose Christ's authority to that of culture since Christ is part of culture and his authority part of the authority of culture (see chapter 2, pp. 37-64).

41.　Scriven understands "solidarity with Christ" (trust, loyalty, likemindedness, union, and shared life) – including discipleship (with its emphasis on the self-giving, non-violent Jesus as a pattern to be emulated), new life, witness, community, apocalyptic consciousness – as the key to the various strands of Anabaptist dissent from the Magisterial Reformation. For Scriven, Niebuhr can be solicited to underwrite rather than dismiss the radical way (see pp. 20-26).

42. Here the legitimation of "the sword" is a central example. For the Anabaptist-Mennonites, the sword is not the essence of the civil order, nor the civil order the essence of the cultural mandate. Therefore an "against culture" response to the use of "the sword" does not *ipso facto* involve a negation of culture. The cultural mandate does not involve a monolithic response to culture, but involves a discriminating response to the various and multiple spheres of culture of which the civil order and its use of force are one aspect.

43. See Duane K. Friesen, *Christian Peacemaking and International Conflict: A Realist Pacifist Perspective* (Scottdale, PA: Herald Press, 1986).

44. Friesen understands the Bible "from the perspective of the drama of redemption culminating in the Christ event as normative for faith and life." For him, the Bible is most helpful in interpreting human experience when we look at the biblical story as a whole. He shows how the basic biblical themes – the creation, the fall, the redemptive process in history, and the new age to come – shape a Christian attitude to socio-political reality. He shows how different traditions have begun with one or the other of these perspectives. He contends, however, that they must all be held together. Any one by itself can distort. He describes Niebuhr's position as "a serious distortion of the Christian faith because it does not sufficiently emphasize the basic thrust of the whole biblical story.... Niebuhr is so preoccupied by the question of what human possibilities are that he underemphasizes the possibilities of God's redemption" (p. 99).

45. As social beings who have the capacity to create symbols and communicate, men and women are able to create culture with social institutions. In this they reflect the image of God as co-creators with God. This reflects a "fundamental goodness about human sociality." For Friesen "human sociality is expressed through and in the context of patterned institutional relationships." He maintains that "coercion is an aspect of being a social being. It means "being pressed together, shaped, structured into behavior that coordinates with others." Coercion in this sense is not entirely negative or sinful. For Friesen "some coercion is violent but some forms of coercion are not inherently evil or violent." He makes a distinction between coercion that is violent and "coercion which 'orders' human social behavior into patterns of cooperation that is not exploitive." The former is "essential to human social life." For the peacemaker, "the task of ordering life through institutions is important." For Friesen, this means we must create institutions which can solve human problems of conflict and injustice (pp. 55-61).

46. Thus the fall expresses itself in religion (spiritual), in history and humanity (social), and in nature (physical). This means institutions are infected by the fundamental breach of these human relationships – spiritual, social, physical: male over female, parents over children, master over slave, rulers over subjects.

47. For Friesen "salvation is not primarily the salvation of individuals but rather the salvation of people and their institutions — to make whole, to restore cultural and social reality to its intended purposes in the creative order of God." He points to the Old Testament concept of peace which is "a holistic spiritual-material condition in which well-being presupposes human spiritual-somatic unity." Therefore, "salvation is a transformation of the total person in his/her social environment." Personal and social peace are not separated (pp. 72-94).

48. Friesen states that "God created through Christ a new social reality which can transform human institutions." This "sets us free but also contributes to restructuring of the powers." Hence "the Christian position is neither total acceptance nor total rejection of the social structures." Rather, the Christian approaches these structures with a discriminating ethic (pp. 94-101).

49. Our procedure has been to explore three kinds of texts — the text of Scripture, the text of history, and the text of the contemporary world — and to understand how they interact concurrently, that is, how the language of peace functions intra-textually in a minority tradition in transition. We have tried to establish a grammar for ascertaining the meaning of the language of peace through its function in a variety of texts and contexts. We have attempted to demonstrate not only the obvious fact of its centrality in the Mennonite tradition, but also the shifts which have occurred and the shape it has taken in that regulative function as a central doctrinal concept. Ours is an attempt to establish a grammar for constructive inter-confessional conversation.

50. Peace as a "regulative concept" refers to its function in second-order reflective discourse. Here we have adapted the term to describe the way in which the Mennonite concept of peace defines and influences a certain way of being Christian. In that sense it is a first-level concept whose grammar must be understood intra-textually in conjunction with other theological motifs.

51. Perry B. Yoder's *Shalom: The Bible's Word for Salvation, Justice, and Peace* (Newton, KS: Faith and Life Press, 1987) is most helpful in giving definition to a transformationist theology of peace. He develops a biblical theology of peace under the rubric of *shalom*. He shows how the biblical concept of *shalom* has a threefold meaning. He demonstrates from the biblical narrative how the material, the relational, and the moral need to be present to have *shalom*, and how this tranformationist understanding of peace is constitutive of those clusters of convictions which constitute the redemptive story of Scripture. Materially, *shalom* is physical well-being and prosperity marked by absence of physical threats like war, disease, and famine; of right being and okayness. Relationally, *shalom* is justice in the realm of social relationships within a society and between nations, the presence of positive and good relations. Morally, *shalom* is straightforwardness in the arena of the moral or ethical; to be without deceit and without guilt; the presence of integrity and straightforwardness; the absence of fault, guilt, or blame.

52. I am relying on the analytical framework of James Wm. McClendon's *Ethics* (Nashville, TN: Abingdon Press, 1986) for the development of the threefold

emphasis on peace as a tranformational concept. McClendon's purpose is to show how ethics looks from the perspective of the believers' church (what he calls "baptistic") tradition and how ethics is the first, not last, step in the task of theological reflection. It consists of three inter-related strands: the organic, the communal, and the anastatic. I have analyzed McClendon's work in a recent article on "Rethinking Christian Ethics: From Moral Decisions to Character Formation," *Direction* 18 (1989):55. It is also noteworthy that Charles Scriven's threefold understanding of the radical vision parallels the threefold meaning of *shalom*. He contends that the radical vision (i.e., the concrete meaning of the cross) after Niebuhr involves the affirmation of the relationship of the Church to surrounding culture in a manner that manifests the following dimensions: that we honour our bodily existence and embrace the task of transforming human culture (organic); that the goal of the transformative process is a world whose form (people and structures) is Christ; and that the Church must be an agent of social conversion, an agent of the kingdom (Resurrection). In this role the Church functions both as an alternative society with selective cultural involvement and a transformative example that functions as a lantern of righteousness in a decaying culture where non-violence exhibited non-legalistically is a central feature of exemplary witness (see Scriven, chapter 6).

53.   These "powers" are the social and spiritual structures that can manifest themselves as replacements of God's powerful presence among the people (golden calves), as the political powers of nations (foreign gods), as the production processes among the people (false gods), and the powerful practices embedded in social and religious structures (principalities).

54.   Thus a transformationist theology of peace cannot simply be treated in terms of how a concept or idea functions within a tradition. It must be treated in terms of how the Church community actually works in its embodiment of its understanding of peace. This is not just a conceptual operation but a conversational process in a hermeneutical community where the Spirit, the gathering of the Church, and the Scriptures are indispensable elements of the process. Practical moral reason is essentially communal in a peace-oriented tradition. The particular narrative of the peaceable community is prior to the idea of peace or narrative. See John Howard Yoder, *The Priestly Kingdom: Social Ethics as Gospel* (South Bend, IN: University of Notre Dame Press, 1984), his most mature work, for a representation of such a narrative ethic, especially chapter 1, "The Hermeneutics of Peoplehood: A Protestant Perspective."

55.   Yoder, *Priestly Kingdom*, p. 44.

56.   This cultural transition can be characterized in a number of ways. There is the proliferation of old and new religions and pluralization of Christian and non-Christian theologies and traditions. This pluralization of faith commitments is accompanied by the fragmentation and individualism so rampant in North American culture and which has led to the erosion of the centres of life both at the personal and collective level. Moreover, the political

and economic decline of the Western world in general and North American hegemony in particular has begun to challenge the Constantinian mentality of the Western world. Linked to this is the growing awareness of the global economic disparity, inequity, and poverty which raises serious questions about the Church's relationship to our society and other societies. Then there is the ever-present shadow of the nuclear bomb, which has raised the spectre of apocalyptic despair. Together, these factors contribute to the need for the Church to continue to discern the nature of its relationship to society, culture, and state. See Howard John Loewen, "Biblical Faith and Citizenship: The Crisis and the Challenge" (Akron, PA: Mennonite Central Committee, U.S. Peace Section, 1983).

Chapter VI

CHURCH AND STATE IN THE CALVINIST
REFORMED TRADITION

Iain G. Nicol

While it is acknowledged that the Reformed traditions constitute a house in which a variety of views on ecclesiastical and secular polities live side by side, the focus of this paper will be to develop an historical and theological analysis of Calvin's understanding of the relationship between Church and state. He argued his position against three competing fronts, those of the Renaissance theorists, Lutheranism, and Anabaptism. In accordance with the theme of our dialogue, and in order to establish a yet sharper focus, particular attention will therefore be given to his consistently negative polemic against the Anabaptists.

The Reformed family of churches today lives in political and cultural circumstances quite radically different from Calvin's time and place in the *corpus Christianum*. Nevertheless, his theory of Church and state has been widely influential in effecting political and constitutional developments in the history of the West. It has also shaped the historic confessions and subordinate confessional standards of those churches which find their origin and *raison d'être* in sixteenth-century Geneva. However, if we are the beneficiaries of our respective traditions, we are also their victims. Calvin's legacy is no exception, for there can be no doubt that while his positive and constructive views on Church and state were on the whole reaffirmed in later confessional documents, his bitterly anti-Anabaptist sentiments tended to be formally endorsed as well. [1] It is only since the recent revival of interest and research into the "radical Reformation" that the corporate Reformed consciousness, confessionally so informed, has begun to be liberated. One of the consequences of this, among many others, is that one now hesitates to distinguish the so-called "magisterial" (authoritative?) Reformation from other related sixteenth-century reforming developments including those situated to the left of centre.

The broad scope of the given topic for this presentation is such that rather than giving equal attention to both Church and state in Calvin's thought, somewhat more space will be devoted to the latter. In order to establish the more general outlines of the confrontation between the Geneva reformer and the Anabaptists on the subject of Church and state, we shall first of all offer a brief analysis of his response to the statements on this topic expressed in the Schleitheim Confession of 1527. In a subsequent section we shall comment on his treatise on civil government in Book IV, Chapter 20 of the final 1559 edition of the *Institutes*, and in conclusion offer some questions about the Calvinian "model" for further reflection.

I.

Calvin's Response to the Schleitheim Confession[2]

Calvin's *Brief Instruction against the Anabaptists*[3] (*Briefve instruction pour armer tous bons fideles contre les erreurs de la secte commune des Anabaptistes*), was published in 1544, seventeen years after the publication of the Schleitheim Confession. Here Calvin's polemic against his opponents descends to the level of the virulent and vituperative. Even more emphatically than in the *Institute*, he characterizes the Anabaptists as unstable dreamers and questions even the sanity of those who commit themselves to unrealistic utopian fantasies. "They accept as revelation from heaven whatever fables they have heard from their grandmothers."[4] Or much worse, like vomiting drunkards "they spew out from a full throat the most exceedingly deformed blasphemies."[5] More specifically, in the context of his discussion of Article 6 of the Schleitheim Confession on Church and state, Calvin accuses its adherents of formulating pernicious conclusions on the basis of perverse assumptions about the nature and interpretation of Scripture. They are guilty of trampling underfoot what God has exalted. Consequently, they declare themselves at war both with God and the human race.[6] Would anyone, asks Calvin rhetorically, possessing even "une seule once de cervelle" ever conceivably be inclined to accept and promote such views as the Anabaptists do?[7]

Article 6 of the Confession on the subject of Church and state is closely related to Article 4 on separation from the world. Calvin notes some fairly minor areas of agreement between the Anabaptists and himself with regard to Articles 1: on Baptism, 2: on Excommunication, 3: on the Eucharist, and 5: on Pastors in the Church. It is on Articles 4, 6 and 7 (on the Oath) that there is clearly the most profound disagreement between him and his opponents.

Calvin's comments on Article 4 are relatively brief. He is by no means opposed to "separation from the abomination" if that means that the Anabaptists should distance themselves from "papal superstitions"[8] but he offers no further concessions. The "sting in the tail" of the Anabaptist argument, Calvin notes, is that any use of arms is "chose Diabolique." Of course, he agrees, our office is to suffer patiently even if violence is used against us. However, to condemn "the public sword" which God has ordained for our protection is an outright offence to God himself. Basing his rejection of the Anabaptist position on Romans 13:4, Calvin goes on to argue for the legitimate right of princes to wage wars of defence in the interest of the common good of their country. This is a last resort, only to be undertaken when all other means toward peace have been pursued and finally exhausted. With appeals to Luke 3:14 and to Acts 10:47ff., Calvin also comments that John the Baptist did not demand that the soldiers should lay down their arms; nor was Cornelius, a centurion, required to abandon his military vocation.[9]

Calvin then is in complete disagreement with the dualism which he perceives to be behind this Article: "For truly all creatures are in but two classes," according to the Confession: "good and bad, believing and unbelieving, darkness and light, the world and those who (have come) out of the world, God's temple and idols, Christ and Belial; and none can have part with the other."[10] Here, and even more explicitly in Calvin's extensive and more detailed commentary on Article 6, the Anabaptist logic of either-or and the Calvinian logic of both-and are shown, in the polemical nature of the case, to be necessarily and completely incompatible.

The sixth Article deals with the question of how Christians may conduct themselves in relation to the state.[11] This is the longest statement in the Confession and Calvin also responds to it at considerable length.[12] The following principal points may be briefly noted.

The article begins: "We are agreed as follows concerning the sword: The sword is ordained of God outside the perfection of Christ." In response to this, Calvin immediately notes that this affirmation of the sword as an ordinance of God to be used by the worldly magistrate represents a "quiet retraction"[13] of the statement in Article 4 where approval of *any* "devilish weapons of force" is expressly forbidden. Perplexing as this inconsistency may be, confusion is somewhat further compounded when the perspective is suddenly shifted from world to Church with the statement that "in the perfection of Christ...only the ban is used...without putting the flesh to death."[14] This is a confusion which Calvin is again quick to seize upon. However, it is difficult for any reader of the document, let alone Calvin, not to feel a sense of disquiet as the ambiguities proceed to multiply, for the essential problem which it poses at this point, namely, how to deal with the wicked person who is not a member of the believing community, is one which is by no means decisively faced, let alone resolved. The Church is in no position to excommunicate a non-member.

By way of illustration, Article 6 then goes on to cite the gospel account of "the woman taken in adultery." Calvin spares no effort in demonstrating that this move constitutes a disastrous exegetical mistake.[15] The Confession deploys the passage as an example of how in the Christian community the public sword has been replaced by the practice of excommunication, and of how a Christian may not take up the sword against the wicked for the protection of the good. The difficulty with this is the fact that the woman is not excommunicated. Nor can she conceivably be viewed as a symbol of that evil against which the good must be defended. Calvin, then, has no difficulty in pointing out the inappropriateness of this use of the passage. Unfortunately, his unrestrained polemic leads him to the further conclusion that his Anabaptist opponents simply follow the example of "les prêtres Papistiques." The blind have led the blind to the conviction that they, too, may commit adultery with impunity.

Article 6 concludes with two further points: Christians may not act as judges in worldly disputes; nor may they serve as magistrates in any political order for "the government magistracy is according to the flesh, but christians' is according to the Spirit."[16] In his response to these sentiments, Calvin charges the "malheureux phantastiques" with sedition and as committed to a course which will inevitably create civil and political chaos. Between Anabaptists he makes no distinctions[17] and seems to classify all of them as committed to the subversion of the state-church order. It is also important to note that in defending the legitimacy of politics as a Christian vocation, Calvin makes substantial use of the Old Testament to support his position. Unlike the Anabaptists, who viewed the government of the people of Israel as a "prefiguration" of the spiritual rule of Christ, Calvin insists that it was "un gouvernement politique."[18] The Church is therefore in no position to withdraw from the order of civil and political justice. The kings, princes, and judges of the Old Testament were "nourriciers" of the Christian Church.[19] In a fitting sense they may therefore be properly designated in a proleptic way as "protectors" of the Christian Church. Such exegesis is, of course, typically Calvinian.[20] Both covenants and both written testaments are equally valid, and the perfection of the law in the Old Testament is not displaced by the teaching of Christ.

In summing up to this point, it can already be seen that the differences and disagreements between Calvin and the Anabaptists on the nature of Church and state and the relations between them were profound. Many of his criticisms of the Anabaptist position can be traced to what may have been perceived to be the form of eschatological dualism[21] which pervaded it. The either-ors of flesh or spirit, world or heaven, darkness or light, Caesar or God, were alien to Calvin's way of thinking.

By contrast, Calvin was a both-and reformer and *pace* the strong polemics of his critique of Anabaptism (which was as much a pervasive component of the general sixteenth-century theological *zeitgeist* as it was of Calvin's writings in particular); this made him a master in the art of equivocation. Nowhere is this more apparent than in his constant insistence that like soul and body, both Church and state should be subject to the one Word of God. Christians are citizens both of the *civitas Dei* and the *civitas terrena*. In Calvin's view, as we shall see, the state should protect and promote the Church's public proclamation of the Gospel. Conversely, in its prophetic role, the Church must also bring the state into obedience to the same Word of God which governs both, for it is only in the light of this Word that government can properly understand its function as an ordinance and gift of God. Church and state must therefore exercise their distinct mandates in response to the one Word of God to which they are both subject.

We shall also see that Calvin advocates the middle way of ecclesiastical and political reform, a way distinguishable both from passive withdrawal and from revolutionary impatience. Such a course is not wholly incompatible with obedience to political rulers, or for that matter, even to tyrants. Yet Christians must discriminate between good and wicked political administrations. Conflict with civil and political government is always a possibility, but in such situations as in all, argues Calvin, Christians must obey God rather than men.

II.

The Origin and Purpose of the State

Calvin would not have taken exception to the view that life in sixteenth-century Europe was "nasty, brutish and short." As a matter of empirical observation and of biblical truth, human nature presented the bleakest of barren landscapes, a scene constantly exposed to threats of disaster and chaos.   Calvin was deeply concerned about what he frequently termed the "disorder" in social, ecclesiastical and political institutions.   Just as the mind had lost control of the lesser human faculties, desires and passions, so the ecclesiastical and political structures established in the interest of ordering human life had suffered a similar fate. A humanity so fallen and disordered lacks the capacity to re-order itself.   Only God, King of Kings and supreme legislator, can bring the world to order.

Disaster is always close at hand. "Innumerable are the evils that beset human life; innumerable too the deaths that threaten it."[22] However, for some at least, God has established a spiritual order, and for all, God has ordained the political order.   The first is the order of deliverance and incorruptible blessedness; the second offers no final release from the uncertainties and anxieties of this mortal and fleeting life but ensures at least the establishment and promotion of "general peace and tranquillity."[23] This is the "twofold government," the spiritual and the civil, under which human beings exist.   The one "resides in the soul or inner man and pertains to eternal life...(the other) pertains only to the establishment of civil justice and outward morality."[24] As distinct from each other but not at variance, both orders, Calvin insists, are ordained by God. Christians therefore possess a dual citizenship.

In its visible form in the world, the Church is never completely restored. It remains a captive to disorder and imperfection. Yet without its presence on earth, albeit imperfect, civil and political structures would collapse into complete disorder and anarchy. However, to ensure civil and political stability, the presence of the Church in history is not enough. Therefore, in his providence God has established political orders, not only to defend the earthly church, but also to protect society as a whole against those forces inherent in it which continually threaten its peace and order.

The constant threat of disorder and of the disintegration of the natural order of creation is rooted in sin. Its power is such, according to Calvin, that apart from common grace, creation would be annihilated and human beings reduced to a level subordinate to the beasts. However, God's act of grace ensures that human beings retain that measure of reason, a sense of right and wrong, by which they are distinguishable from the animals.[25] Further, in spite of the corrupting and alienating effects of sin, Calvin emphatically insists that human beings also retain their social instinct. By virtue of common grace this is an endowment common to believer and unbeliever alike:

> Since man is by nature a social animal, he tends through natural instinct to foster and preserve society. Consequently, we observe that there exist in all men's minds universal impressions of a certain civic fair dealing and order. Hence no man is to be found who does not understand that every sort of human organization must be regulated by laws, and who does not comprehend the principles of those laws. Hence arises that unvarying consent of all nations and of individual mortals with regard to laws. For their seeds have, without teacher or lawgiver, been implanted in all men.[26]

Calvin also holds the view that if human beings had remained in their original state of integrity, the political order would not have been necessary. For Calvin, then, unlike a later Lutheranism, the state is not an ordinance of creation. It is not organically related to creation and to human nature, but is rather a *post facto* expedient established as a remedy for disorder and for a corrupted human nature. Following Romans 13, he views the political order as a provision for the safety of human beings designed to ensure the protection and security of the good and to restrain the wicked. The state is therefore a transitory and temporary order provisionally established in human society to conserve it in the expectation of the end of time when the Kingdom of God will be realized.

This is the position which he defends against his "insane and barbarous" Anabaptist opponents "who furiously strive to overturn the divinely established order."[27] And Calvin adds:

> [if] God's kingdom, since as it is now among us, wipes out the present life, [then] all of this I admit to be superfluous. But if it is God's will that we go as pilgrims upon the earth while we aspire to the true fatherland, and if the pilgrimage requires such helps, those who take these from man deprive him of his very humanity.[28]

III.

In the following section, we will examine: a) the mission of the state in general; b) its mission in relation to the Church in particular; and c) the Church's mission in relation to the state.

The Mission of the State in General

a) In his *The Theology of Calvin*, Wilhelm Niesel mistakenly argues that Calvin was concerned about the state solely in its relation to the Church. He is "not concerned about the state as such, not even about the Christian State."[29] On the contrary, it is quite clear that Calvin's concern is to emphasize the fact that the political order exists to guard and promote the safety and well-being of all, and that it also exists to impress an outward morality on all its citizens. This corresponds to Calvin's (as to Luther's) understanding of the second use of the law.[30]

Unlike the more positive third use of the law which "finds its place among believers in whose hearts the Spirit of God already lives and reigns," its second use is "by fear of punishment to restrain certain men who are untouched by any care for what is just and right unless compelled by hearing the dire threats of the law...this constrained and forced righteousness is necessary for the public community of men." The law is like a bridle or halter which checks the actions of those inclined to lawlessness. In its second use, then, the function of the law is not excessively repressive or punitive, notes Calvin, for by bearing this "yoke of righteousness," human beings can be "partially broken in" and so tutored in the positive virtues of godly discipline.[31]

The political order is not a necessary evil. It exists not only as a bridle or as a remedy for the fall and for the universal disorder caused by sin. The political order finds its origin and justification in the will of God. The *rationale* for its existence is not located in the fact that it represents a concession to a corrupt and depraved humanity but in the fact that it is a divine and holy institution. Like the family, society, and the sphere of economic life, and corresponding to all the legitimate and divine callings which belong to these different spheres of human activity,[32] the function of the political order is not exhausted in its mission to resist evil. It also exists to promote good and thereby seek the further glory of God. As Ernst Troeltsch, for example, has noted:

> (Calvin) lays all the emphasis on that which is practical, possible and suitable. The result of this attitude, however, is that the institution of the state and of law both can and must be adopted to the two following ends: 1) the religious purpose of the maintenance of true religion; and 2) the social and utilitarian end of the promotion of peace, order and prosperity.[33]

Against his Anabaptist opponents Calvin is therefore arguing that all human beings are subject to political authority, and that Christians in particular are subject, not only to evangelical authority, as the Anabaptists suppose, but also to the authority of the state. So subject, however, it is also the duty of the state as divinely instituted to seek the welfare of its people and to promote a peaceful and harmonious life for all its citizens without exception. With its ethic based on the Decalogue, "the supreme rule of political life,"[34] the appointed end of civil government is therefore "to adjust our life to the society of men, to form our social behaviour to civil righteousness, to reconcile us with one another, and to promote general peace and tranquillity.[35]

These sentiments express at least two basic characteristics of Calvin's thought. The first can be stated in the briefest possible terms to the effect that, for Christians, it is impossible to ignore the world, let alone withdraw from it. Secondly, however, such a view as Calvin's, it may also be argued that the political order is not to be understood only as a *work* or ordinance of God but rather perhaps as a *gift* of God. Its source and cause is the divine *benevolentia* and it is ordained for the good of human beings. As a gift, and not as a necessary evil or "thing polluted," it should be *used* (not enjoyed), in the interest of the humanizing end to which it has been appointed by God.

b) *The mission of the state in relation to the Church in particular, or, the state as Defensor Fidei.*

According to Calvin, the state bears a primary responsibility toward the church in that the mission of the political order is also "to cherish and protect the outward worship of God, to defend sound doctrine of piety and the position of the church."[36] Similar sentiments are also clearly expressed in Calvin's *Commentary* on I Tim. 2:2, where it is noted that the mission of the state *vis à vis* the Church is to maintain true religion, to guarantee the liberty of the Gospel, and to ensure the orderly and reverent administration of the Church's ceremonies.[37] Specific warrant for this function of the political order is to be found also in the Decalogue, to which political rulers are subject, and in the example of "holy kings [in Scriptures]...who restored the worship of God when it was corrupted or destroyed, or took care of religion that under them it might flourish pure and unblemished...." God appoints rulers, therefore, not only to arbitrate in civil and political matters but also "that [God] himself should be purely worshipped according to the prescription of the law."[38]

These statements raise issues related to the question of "establishment." We may simply note that here Calvin affirms the right and duty of the state not only to defend the true Church but also to undertake its reformation and restoration in the event that it should succumb to idolatry and superstition. This is a principle which in turn is reaffirmed in most of the Reformed confessions directly or indirectly influenced by Calvin. It is clearly a dangerous one, not least in the sense that it may be invoked by an authoritarian magistracy intent upon depriving the Church of its independent spiritual jurisdiction and reforming it according to its own political image.

Reflecting on the principle that the state has the right to reform the Church, Karl Barth, in his Gifford Lectures of 1937-38, sounded a prophetic note. His comments on Article 24 of the Scots Confession of 1560[39] are as valid today as they were then:

> To maintain this is to go too far and indeed to do so in a way that is dangerous. Spiritual perversity must be overcome with spiritual force and not with political. If the church fails to recognize that, who is going to guarantee what reformation may one day be demanded of her by means of political force by some Josiah or other? If this view were true, Hitler would be right in his attempt to reform the church. But fortunately it is not the task of the state to reform the church. But it is correct to say that the significance of the political order as service of God becomes clear where the state provides and preserves *freedom* for the church.[40]

As we would expect, Calvin again sought the middle way. The Church and the political order are not in competition. Separate in theory, Church and state nevertheless relate, interact, and co-operate in practice. Derived from, and responsible to, one source in the divine goodwill, yet distinct, the one should not attempt to dominate the other but rather should reciprocally require, the one of the other, the fulfillment of their respective obligations to mutual and complementary collaboration. "As the magistrate ought by punishment and physical restraint to cleanse the church of offences, so the minister of the Word in turn ought to help the magistrate in order that not so many may sin. Their functions ought to be so joined that each serves to help, not hinder, the other."[41]

c) *The Church's mission in relation to the state.*[42]

In this respect, the Church's role may briefly be defined as essentially threefold. For one thing, the Church should pray for all those who exercise political authority.[43] Prayers should be offered even for those in authority who are hostile to Christians. However difficult this may be, Calvin urges, it is the enemies of the Church who are most in need of prayers of intercession. It is also the duty of believers to pray even for those who persecute them. For Calvin, the "order" even of tyranny is to be preferred above the chaos and disorder of anarchy.[44]

The Church, secondly, must also call political authorities to obedience under God. It must constantly remind rulers that they are invested with a divinely delegated power and mission. They must therefore exercise vigilance and earnestness in the service and pursuit of justice and take every precaution against any abuse of their power. If the Church should fail to fulfill this prophetic aspect of its mission, then it, too, becomes a willing accomplice in any injustice or neglect of duty committed by the state. In its prophetic role, then, the Church has every right actively and rigorously to exert strong critical pressure and influence on the state should its political policies be judged unjust or inequitable.

Finally, as A. Biéler has so ably shown,[45] the Church's prophetic role in relation to the state also includes the duty to recall the state to its commitment to defend and promote the interests of the poor and the weak against exploitation by the rich and powerful. Calvin repeatedly expresses the conviction that the validity and integrity of any political regime is to be judged according to the strength of its commitment to social justice and its defence and maintenance of the poor and afflicted in particular.

Thus to briefly summarize Calvin's theology of Church and state to this point: for this reformer the state poses no insurmountable obstacle to the authenticity and integrity of Christian life in the world. The political order exists as much for the good of Christians as for all who are subject to its authority. The state, therefore, has a positive role to play in the process of the redemption of the common life. Consequently, in these respects Calvin's position is clearly of a different order from that assumed by the Anabaptists against whom, on issues of Church and state among others, he was so vehemently opposed. Far from concluding that Christ's rule is exercised exclusively in the sphere of the spirit, Calvin affirms it as an active presence permeating every aspect of life. Thus, in terms of H. Richard Niebuhr's typologies of "Christ and culture," Calvin may, with reasonable safety, be classified as a "transformationist," as a reformer firmly committed to the view "that what the gospel promises and makes possible, as divine (not human) possibility, is the transformation of mankind in all its nature and culture into a Kingdom of God in which the laws of the kingdom have been written upon the inward parts."[46]

IV.

The Scope and Limits of Political Power

Civil government, according to Calvin, consists in three "parts": "the magistrate, who is protector and guardian of the laws; the laws, according to which he governs; the people, who are governed by the laws and obey the magistrate."[47]

a) The exercise of political authority is a divine calling.[48] This corresponds to Calvin's more general understanding of secular vocations as service to God, the Church, and the community. In contrast to the position of the Anabaptists, rulers exercise a divine vocation in accordance with the nature of the state as divinely instituted. Those who occupy this office are therefore to be respected and obeyed, for in the exercise of political authority the magistrate is God's "lieutenant," God's representative on earth: "they have a mandate from God, have been invested with divine authority, and are wholly God's representatives, in a manner acting as his viceregents." Commenting on John 10:35, Calvin writes: "they are gods...," adding: "this is no subtlety of mine." He then concludes this passage with the resounding affirmation that:

> The Lord has declared his approval of their offices. Accordingly no one ought to doubt that civil authority is a calling, not only holy and lawful before God, but also the most sacred and by far the most honourable of all callings in the whole life of mortal men.[49]

Today we are not so sanguine. However, it is clear that these statements are directed against two competing fronts: against Anabaptism for one, and against the contemporary and pre-Reformation politicised ethic of precepts and counsels of perfection which rendered the political office subordinate to the sacerdotal.

In response to the former, and to the objection that since all human beings are equal in the freedom of Christ before God and that Christians therefore have no business with the requirement of civil government that the few rule and the majority obey, Calvin argues that rulers in themselves are not to be treated with servile obsequiousness. As he notes elsewhere: "princes are but puffs of smoke, poor earthworms; nevertheless it is true that they are to be honoured to the extent that God has put his mark on them; but in themselves, they are nothing."[50] The importance of the magistracy, therefore, is the office itself, the function which the magistrate is called to fulfill. Rulers themselves are not expected to be perfect. Nevertheless, Calvin does insist that it is by virtue of their divine office that they are to be respected and obeyed, for to disobey rulers is to disobey God.

b) In what respects, if any, are the powers of rulers ordered and limited? Realist that he was, Calvin observed that rulers are very likely to magnify their offices. They are by no means immune to *hauteur* or to the temptation to abuse their power. From their position of authority, human rulers will frequently be disposed to pursue the satisfaction of their own ambitions, and even to abuse and distort religion in the interest of state policy. Deploring such an attitude, Calvin roundly condemns those "clever men who have devised many things in religion by which to inspire the common folk with reverence and to strike them with terror."[51]

Calvin's response to such abuses is to invoke the principle of the *double regime* of state and Church subject to the one word of God. Rulers are limited in the exercise of power in at least the following respects: their rule of life and vocation is the Decalogue. To this divine law they must be subject. Further, God has entrusted the Church to the care of the magistrates so that it may be nourished and protected by them in their role as "foster fathers."[52] A sense of high calling and responsibility toward those over whom they have been placed in authority should also act as a check on the power with which they are invested, for "as vicars of God...they should represent in themselves to men some image of divine providence, protection, goodness, benevolence and justice."[53] Should they fail to fulfill the obligations of their office, the Church also exists to remind them that the mighty fall much further than those under their care, and should the crushing burden of such responsibilities prove to be insufficient inducement to exercise caution and restraint on the part of rulers, the Church also exists to warn them that they are also finally subject to the judgment of God.

c) As primarily accountable to God, rulers also nevertheless bear a moral responsibility to support and advance the common good. Under God they in turn are also servants of the people, appointed "to provide for the common peace and safety of all."[54] Such obligations of rulers toward their subjects are not based upon some mutual contract or covenant between ruler and ruled, but again, upon the divine law to which both rulers and people are subject, namely the Ten Commandments and the Golden Rule, subject to which rulers in particular will seek to fulfill the demands of their office as "father(s), shepherd(s), guardian(s) and protector(s)."[55]

In his recent biography of Calvin, William Bouwsma has drawn attention to Calvin's frequent preoccupation with the first of these metaphors and his application of the duties and feelings of fatherhood to the vocation of the magistrate. Reflecting on Calvin's references to the family as an *ecclesiola* and to the body politic as an extended family, Bouwsma cites this concern as another aspect of Calvin's understanding of the extent to which the powers of the state are limited, of his "deep attachment to the traditional paternalistic model of politics," and of his perception that "this paternal chain from heaven to earth means that no father is strictly secular, and thus that there can be no *ultimate* separation of realms" (emphasis mine).[56]

V.

The Duties and Rights of those under Authority

A high sense of calling and a commitment to cultivate those qualities essential to its proper exercise should therefore encourage rulers to self-discipline and restraint in the deployment of their delegated power. However, the question which must now be addressed, given that power and its exercise are invested in divinely appointed rulers, is whether Calvin is also prepared to recognize that power may also in some sense be invested in the ruled. He does not hesitate to affirm the explicit *duties* toward the political order that citizens are obliged to fulfill. The question is essentially whether rulers can be trusted. If not, then do citizens not also have *rights*?

Concerning the conduct of citizens toward rulers Calvin is quite adamant that their duties are to honour, reverence, and esteem their office as a jurisdiction ordained by God. As owed to God's representatives, Calvin adds, such duties should not be rendered grudgingly. Nor should they be motivated by fear. Rulers are rather to be held in reverence and esteem for the same reason that God is to be honoured, for after all it is God's power and authority with which they are invested.[57]

It is also essential that citizens not only honour and reverence those who rule but also that they obey them. According to Calvin, this is the clear rule of Scripture, which itself is the sole source of truth in such matters.[58] Such obedience to magistrates is demonstrated "by obeying their proclamations, or by paying taxes, or by undertaking public offices and burdens which pertain to the common defence."[59] Alternatively, it is the duty of the magistrate to punish a people or an individual who chooses to withhold such obedience to the ruling office. Again, it may be noted that the duty of political obedience is not motivated by mutual agreement, contract, or covenant either between rulers and ruled or between God and the ruled. If "the mouth of God" says that we must be subject to the governing authorities (Romans 13:1),[60] then "the will of the Lord is enough. For if it has seemed good to him to set kings over kingdoms, senates or municipal officers over free cities, it is our duty to show ourselves compliant and obedient to whomever he sets over the places where we live."[61] Thus to the extent that good and just rulers are so honoured and obeyed, and to the extent that rulers in turn fulfill their obligation to safeguard and promote the good of the community, political, social, and economic expression is given to the command to love one's neighbour as oneself.[62]

Clearly, however, such mutual duties are predicated on the obvious condition that rulers be just and benevolent and committed to the development and codification of just and humane laws in the light of the Decalogue and the command to love.

But not all rulers are just, and Calvin is acutely aware that many are unjust and malevolent and that some prove to be cruel and oppressive tyrants.[63] But whatever their qualities, good or bad, Calvin firmly insists that they must be obeyed. His already noted intransigence is nowhere more apparent. He knows well that submission to just rulers is difficult enough for human beings more naturally inclined to the opposite. How, then, can he counsel obedience even to tyrants? Must the ruled simply accept as divine that God ordains rulers, along with the historical reality that some are just, some unjust, some indifferently slothful, and some cruelly tyrannical? Not untypically for Calvin, his answer is: yes and no. His response can be briefly summarized under five heads:

1) In his discussion of obedience to unjust and tyrannical rulers in the *Institute*,[64] Calvin classifies Nebuchadnezzar as "an abominable and cruel tyrant" (Jer. 27:5-8), a classic example of the kind of ruler for whom we naturally have an "inborn feeling to hate and curse." However, Calvin adds, no good can come of such feelings of outrage at injustice, cruelty, or wickedness. Judgment must therefore be left to God "in whose hands are the hearts of kings and the inclinations of kingdoms." Our duty is therefore to suffer patiently and obey.

2) It is God's prerogative to avenge "unbridled despotism."[65] God executes judgment upon arrogant kings and intolerable governments by raising up avengers to punish their lawlessness.[66] Sooner or later, God's judgment will meet up with them.

These are not counsels of resignation, but rather represent a call to suffer in eschatological patience and restraint. "They also serve who only stand and wait."[67]

3) Certain forms of passive resistance may be situationally permissible. For example, Calvin defends Daniel's disobedience of the King. He was justified in taking the course he did because the King "in lifting up his horns against God, had himself abrogated his power."[68] In another example, Calvin observes that it would have demonstrated "an inexcusable contempt for God" if the Hebrew midwives had obeyed Pharaoh's order to kill the male infants of the Hebrew mothers.[69] Passive resisters must nevertheless calculate carefully and be prepared to accept the consequences of their actions, for it is common knowledge,

according to Calvin, that "kings bear defiance with the greatest displeasure."[70]

4) Some situations may also demand active resistance. Again, in his Commentary on Dan. 6:22, Calvin urges that when princes rob God of his rights and thereby dishonour him, our duty is not to obey, but to "spit on their heads."[71] In a sermon on the same passage, having emphasized that one must normally submit to the authorities, he adds a qualification: "But if they rise up against God they must be put down, and held of no more account than worn-out shoes." [72]

5) The question of *how* wicked and unjust rulers should be put down is one which Calvin addresses only in the closing paragraphs of the *Institute*.[73] Here he outlines a strategy for resistance to political oppressors through the power invested in the "lesser magistrates" who, by virtue of their divine office, have the right actively to oppose princes who defy God. To cite also his *Instruction in Faith*: "it is fit to endure those who tyrannically abuse their power, until, *through legitimate order*, we be freed from their yoke"[74] (emphasis mine). In failing to resist tyranny, the lesser magistrates would "betray the freedom of the people, of which they know that they have been appointed protectors by God's ordinance."[75]

Firmly committed to law and order, Calvin refused to sanction any theory of popular resistance or revolution. To do so would have been to advocate anarchy. Later followers would pursue Calvin's logic further and conclude that active resistance to tyranny could involve armed rebellion as a religious duty. This development gave rise, for example, to the establishment of the Reformed Churches in Scotland and England, and to the Congregational Church of the Puritan Commonwealth. Calvin's carefully formulated reservations had not been forgotten. They were nevertheless set aside by saints less patient and less skilled in his capacity for fine distinctions.

VI.

In the interest of further reflection on the Calvinian paradigm which today to varying degrees still continues to inform Reformed responses to Church-state relations and issues, the following concluding points are offered for consideration.

Like so many other aspects of his theology, Calvin's understanding of Church-state relations has tended to be interpreted in the light of the scholastic seventeenth-century confessional statements on the subject rather than according to a more objective and detailed exegesis of

Calvin's own writings. On such a reading, one is inevitably bound to conclude that the notably dominant *motif* in his Church-state theology is the intransigent insistence on obedience to political authority. What is more remarkable, however, if less frequently noted, is that to the political order in partnership with the Church is also committed the more dynamic mandate of implementing a comprehensive vocation to establish a just social order, of turning to face the world in the struggle to reform society as a whole and institute the holy commonwealth on earth. Judgment will begin with a plague on both houses if this divine commission is refused or neglected. Emphasizing the nature of the state as *agency* rather than as order, Calvin's insistence is on constant reform.[76] This includes the reform of government, particularly if the machinery of the state is unequal to the task of implementing the social vision. It is on the basis of this particular understanding of the function of the state that Calvin enters his reservations on the duty of political obedience.

In his arguments against the Anabaptists, Calvin could not envision this commonwealth as a separate society. Among the historical reasons for this is that his thought was still deeply rooted in Constantinianism. He assumed that there was virtually no discontinuity between being a member of the Church and a member of society. If there was, then perhaps it was simply a matter of "changing hats." The visible Church was viewed as a *corpus mixtum*. No matter how strongly affirmed, Calvin's doctrine of election provided no appropriate objective criteria for distinguishing between those who were elect and those who were not. The Church was understood to be a society in which one "learned Christ," an institution in which the Christian life might be developed, rather than a "believers' church" or a community of already sanctified persons abstracted from and independent of the world's structures as a separate divine commonwealth.

These are some of the convictions which still exert a powerful influence on the doctrines and practice of the Reformed family of churches. The both-and logic so integral to Calvin's state-Church theology still survives. Nevertheless, in our post-Christian era, there is by no means any clear family consensus on Church-state theology. It is impossible to venture a safe opinion as to what the precise nature of the relation between Church and state should be, or rather between churches and states each with their own histories and developing traditions.

In some state-Church contexts the logic of both-and operates effectively enough even though the particular political and legal arrangements derived from it may not necessarily preclude the possibility that serious difficulties may yet arise between civil and ecclesiastical powers. In other contexts where, for example, state and Church may represent two solitudes, the logic of either-or is much more pervasive. Between and beyond these positions there is a variety of finely nuanced options.

In our contemporary, pluralistic complexity little is to be gained by attempting to attach the historic labels of Erastianism, *cuius regio*, two kingdoms, co-ordinate jurisdiction with mutual subordination, to cite but a few, to present day Church-state relations. Apart from the fact that today different models such as these may be found within one church, no theory has been or will be sufficient finally to resolve the kinds of difficulties that are likely to arise between churches and states as long as conscience perceives that we do not do justice, nor love kindness, nor walk humbly with God.

Perhaps one thing is clear. If the traditional *theories* of Church-state relations are now presently viewed as transcripts of formerly activated theological/political consciences and therefore as historically relative, the forms of Church *praxis vis à vis* the state formulated by Calvin and his successors remain the same: active identification with the agency of the state and its projects; critical and constructive solidarity and co-operation; prophetic protest, perhaps involving passive or active resistance; and then the option which Calvin himself refused to advocate but which was endorsed by some of his successors who defended the right and even the obligation of citizens to violate the law and take up arms against tyrannical and godless rulers.

Whether or not this last course of action involving violence as a component in resistance to the state is ever morally permissible is clearly the most difficult issue that certain churches face today in their struggle against injustice and life-diminishing deprivation.

Notes

1. This is carefully documented in "The Attitude of the Reformed Churches Today to the Condemnations of the Baptists in the Reformed Confessional Documents." Various editors, *Mennonites and Reformed in Dialogue* (Geneva: World Alliance of Reformed Churches, 1986), pp. 42-56.

2. For some helpful detailed historical background to this see, e.g., Willem Balke's *Calvin and the Anabaptist Radicals* (Grand Rapids: Eerdmans, 1981), pp. 169-95.

3. *Corpus Reformatorum*, Calvini Opera, Vol. 7, pp. 49-142, Brunsvigae, 1868 (hereinafter referred to as *Opera*, VII, followed by Column No.). An English

translation of Calvin's *Brief Instruction* was published in London in 1549 under the title *A Short Instruction for to arm all Good Christian People against the Pestiferous Errors of the Common Sect of Anabaptists*.

4. *Opera*, VII: 95.
5. *Opera*, VII: 90.
6. *Opera*, VII: 92.
7. *Opera*, VII: 84.
8. *Opera*, VII: 77.
9. *Opera*, VII: 79.
10. John H. Leith, ed. *Creeds of the Churches* (Atlanta: John Knox Press), 1973, pp. 286-87.
11. Leith, *Creeds of the Churches*, pp. 287-89.
12. *Opera*, VII: 80-92.
13. *Opera*, VII: 80.
14. Leith, *Creeds of the Churches*, pp. 287-88.
15. Leith, *Creeds of the Churches*, p. 289.
16. Leith, *Creeds of the Churches*, p. 289.
17. In his *The Origins of Sectarian Protestantism* (New York: Macmillan, 1964), Franklin H. Littell comments: "(Calvin) made no distinction between the spiritualising and biblicist wings of the movement — if, indeed, he was aware of the distinction" (p. 147).
18. *Opera*, VII: 81-82.
19. See especially Calvin's *Commentaries*, e.g., on Ps. 72:11; Is. 49:23. See also *Opera*, VII: 82.
20. This topic should be given priority in further Reformed-Mennonite discussions.
21. See, e.g., Willem Balke, *Anabaptist Radicals*, p. 267.
22. *Inst.* I., xvii, 10.
23. *Inst.* IV, xx, 2.
24. *Inst.* IV, xx, 1.
25. *Inst.* II, ii, 12.
26. *Inst.*, II, ii, 13. It may also be noted that this is an aspect of Calvin's thought to which Michael Walzer has paid scant attention. See his *The Revolution of the Saints: A Study in the Origins of Radical Politics* (Cambridge: Harvard University Press, 1965) where, in chapter two he argues that in Calvin's understanding the state is exclusively an order of repression. Walzer argues that according to Calvin, the fall "had created a second nature and an *a*-social man" (p. 31, emphasis mine).
27. *Inst.* IV, xx,1.
28. *Inst.* IV, xx,2. We may note here that in his *Calvins Lehre vom Staat und Kirche* (Breslau: Markus, 1937), p. 171, Josef Bohatec concisely sums up the three causes to which the existence of the political order may be attributed: a) the disorder effected by sin is the provocative cause; b) God's grace is the efficient cause; c) the preservation of the race is the final or teleological cause. In addition to "preservation" one might also suggest: "and humanisation."

29. Wilhelm Niesel, *The Theology of Calvin* (London: Lutterworth Press, 1956), p. 230.

30. *Inst.* II, vii, 10-11.

31. *Inst.* II, vii, 10.

32. In this connection see especially André Biéler's *La Pensée économique et sociale de Calvin* (Geneva: Georg et Cie., 1961).

33. *The Social Teaching of the Christian Churches*, vol.II, p. 615 (London: Allen & Unwin, 1931).

34. M.-E. Chenevière, *La Pensée politique de Calvin* (Geneva: Editions Labor, 1937), p. 141.

35. *Inst.* IV, xx, 2.

36. *Inst.* IV, xx, 2.

37. Eds., D.W. and T.F. Torrance (Grand Rapids: Eerdmans, 1964), pp. 205-207. "I urge that supplications prayers, intercessions, and thanksgivings be made for all men, for kings and all who are in high positions, that we may lead a quiet and peaceable life, godly and respectful in every way" (R.S.V.).

38. *Inst.*, IV, xx, 9.

39. The passage which Barth addresses here runs as follows: "Kings, Princes, Rulers and Magistrates...not only are appointed for Civill policie, but also for maintenance of trew Religioun, and for suppressing of Idolatrie and Superstition whatsoever: As in David, Josaphat, Ezekias, Josiah, and Utheris highlie commended for their zeale in that caise."

40. *The Knowledge of God and the Service of God* (London: Hodder and Stoughton, 1938), pp. 225-26.

41. *Inst.* IV, xi, 3.

42. Here I am dependent mainly on A. Biéler's *La Pensée économique*, pp. 292-300.

43. Calvin articulates this aspect of the Church's ministry in relation to the state most clearly in his *Commentary* on I Tim. 2:2. See n. 39 above.

44. "It is indeed bad to live under a prince with whom nothing is permitted; but much more worse under one by whom everything is allowed" (*Inst.* IV, xx, 10).

45. Biéler, *La pensée économique*, pp. 306-45.

46. *Christ and Culture* (New York: Harper and Brothers, 1951), pp. 217-18.

47. *Inst.* IV, xx, 3.

48. *Inst.* IV, xx, 4.

49. *Inst.* IV, xx, 4.

50. Quoted by M.-E. Chenevière, *La pensée politique*, p. 153.

51. *Inst.* I, iii, 2.

52. *Inst.* IV, xx, 9.

53. *Inst.* IV, xx, 5.

54. *Inst.* IV, xx, 6.

55. *Inst.* IV, xx, 24. Michael Walzer takes no account of these metaphors in defending the thesis that Calvin's state is an order of repression, see n. 28 above.

56. *John Calvin* (New York and London: Oxford University Press, 1988), pp. 211-13. Bouwsma also makes the interesting observation that implicit in Calvin's understanding in this connection is "the ancient association, at once classical and Germanic, of fatherhood and priesthood."

57. *Inst.* IV, xx,22.

58. According to M.-E. Chenevière it is this appeal to the biblical tradition which explains Calvin's "intransigeance" on this point (*La pensée politique*) p. 303.

59. *Inst.* IV, xx, 3.

60. In his *Commentary* on this text Calvin again takes the opportunity to accuse the Anabaptists of "despising the providence of him who is the author of political power" because of their disrespect for the divine ordinance of the state and the corresponding obedience which this involves. (*Commentary* on Romans 13.1).

61. *Inst.* IV, xx,8 (on the Diversity of Forms of Government).

62. See, e.g., John T. McNeill, *Calvin: On God and Political Duty* (New York: Bobbs, Merrill Co., 1950) "Preface," p. xviii.

63. It is frequently noted by commentators on Calvin that nowhere does he show any interest in how rulers acquire their power. One notes that he regarded such enquiry as a "frivolous curiosity": cf. W.A. Mueller, *Church and State in Luther and Calvin* (Nashville: Broadman Press, 1954), p. 133.

64. *Inst.* IV, xx, 24-29.

65. *Inst.* IV, xx, 31.

66. *Inst.* IV, xx, 30.

67. John Milton, "On his Blindness," 1652.

68. *Inst.* IV, xx, 32.

69. Cited by W. Bouwsma, *John Calvin*, p. 209.

70. *Inst.* IV, xx, 32.

71. *Comm.* Daniel, *Calvin's Commentaries*, trans. T. Myers, vol. XII (Grand Rapids: Eerdmans, 1979), p. 382.

72. *Opera*, XIX, 415f: "il faut qu'ils sont mis en bas, qu'on ne tienne plus compte d'eux, non plus que de savattes."

73. *Inst.* IV, xx, 31-32.

74. Edited and translated by P.J. Fuhrmann (Philadelphia: Westminster Press, 1959), p. 77.

75. *Inst.*, IV, xx, 31.

76. The feeling of guilt arising from inactivity is the other essential component in the Calvinist *psyche*!

Chapter VII

CHURCH AND STATE IN THE

ANABAPTIST-MENNONITE TRADITION:

CHRIST *VERSUS* CAESAR?

Harry Loewen

In his paper "The Anabaptist Vision,"[1] Harold S. Bender argued some forty-five years ago that the Swiss Brethren who emerged from the Zwingli circle in Zurich, and those who believed and practised their faith as they did, were the genuine Anabaptists of the sixteenth century. Stressing discipleship, brotherhood, non-resistance, and separation of Church and state, these early radical reformers, according to Bender, "arrived to bring into full...realization" what Luther and Zwingli had originally intended to accomplish but failed.[2] And the two reformers failed, according to Bender, because they "decided that it was better to include the masses within the fold of the church than to form a fellowship of true Christians only." "May it not be said," Bender asks, "that the decision of Luther and Zwingli to surrender their original vision was the tragic turning point of the Reformation?"[3]

This emphasis in interpretation has not only led to a one-sided understanding of the nature of sixteenth-century Anabaptism, but also to deep-seated differences between the Anabaptists and the Reformers with regard to key issues, including the relationship between Church and state. Because the Swiss Brethren were seen by Bender as the "original" Anabaptists, it was believed that their understanding of the "two kingdoms" with its stress on withdrawal from the world and worldly institutions was both "normative" for evangelical Anabaptists and direction-setting for later Mennonites.[4] The "Brotherly Union" of Schleitheim (1527) was regarded as a Confession of Faith of the true Anabaptists, and its seven articles were considered the heart of what they believed and sought to practise. Any deviation from this Confession was seen as a deviation from genuine Anabaptism, and individuals and groups of Anabaptists who did not follow Schleitheim were seen as "marginal" Anabaptists at best.[5]

Today this earlier view of Anabaptism has become problematical, and some issues of the early Anabaptist movement appear to be more complex. As has been shown by more recent scholarship, the Swiss Brethren and Schleitheim represented but one form of Anabaptism among a variety of other forms.[6] While Swiss Anabaptism exerted a considerable influence on the more peaceful groups within the movement, there were several individuals and groups who understood important Reformation issues differently from the Swiss Brethren, and whose practice varied accordingly. Particularly with regard to Church and state issues there soon appeared and developed at least two traditions: the one which generally followed Schleitheim stressed withdrawal and non-involvement in matters of secular society and the state; the other, while most sympathetic to the Swiss position, stressed what might be called selective participation and involvement in matters of government.[7]

In my attempt to show the development of these two traditions, I shall first deal with the Anabaptist legacy with regard to church-state relations; secondly, examine representative Confessions of Faith on the subject; and thirdly, summarize Mennonite beliefs and practices relative to their involvement in government. My conclusion will suggest that in matters of Church-state relations there is definitely an histori-cal-theological basis for dialogue between Mennonite and Reformed to take place.

I.

It has been shown that initially the radical reformers in Switzerland and south-west Germany sought to affect a large-scale reformation of society similar to what reformers like Luther and Zwingli were doing.[8] Radicals like Grebel, Mantz, and Blaurock in Zurich, and Balthasar Hübmaier in Waldshut and later in Moravia provide convincing examples of this original intent. However, when these Anabaptist leaders experienced opposition from the magisterial reformers, society, and governments, they began to withdraw from the hostile world and instead sought to establish free and independent sectlike congregations.[9] These separated communities were to model Christ's intent and ideals for society and thus advance the kingdom of God in the world. However, such things as discipleship, brotherhood, non-violence, and generally a Christian lifestyle were not to be prescriptive for society at large, for society would not acknowledge the rule of Christ as binding for itself.[10]

This changed view of early Anabaptism was reflected in what became, in effect, the first Confession of Faith of peaceful Anabaptism. Michael Sattler, a former monk and sympathizer of the peasants in 1525, together with other Swiss and south-German Anabaptists, drafted in 1527 the "Brotherly Union" articles which then were accepted by the Swiss Brethren and some south-German radicals. [11] Other important Anabaptist leaders like Hans Denck, Hans Hut, and Hübmaier were not part of this "union,"[12] and some of these "outsiders" even seemed to oppose the seven articles of Schleitheim, particularly those which dealt with the sword and the state.

According to the "Brotherly Union" of Schleitheim, the temporal state exists as a valid institution established by God himself. At the same time the articles state clearly that followers of Christ are to withdraw from governmental involvement and to have nothing to do with the sword, the symbol of power, punishment, and violence. The sword and all that it represents is "outside the perfection of Christ" and hence to be shunned.[13] This dualism of Schleitheim is absolute. In the kingdom of God (i.e., the Church) the Spirit of God and the power of love rule. The only means of settling internal disputes and correcting serious moral issues is the ban. And even the ban or excommunication is practised in love and for the correction and salvation of the members. In the kingdom of this world, however, law and order are upheld by means of governmental authority and the use of the sword, means which are contrary to Christian faith and life. Hence disciples of Christ are not only free in Christ, but also free and separated from temporal institutions like the state and its functions.[14]

The dualism of the "Brotherly Union" was similar to Luther's dividing all of life into two separate realms.[15] However, Schleitheim differed from the German reformer in that it did not allow Christians to function differently in the two realms but insisted that they live consistently as Christians in the Church and in society. Thus, while Luther was most critical of rulers and their governments, he taught that Christians were not only subject to them but that they must also serve as magistrates and in other governmental capacities.[16] According to Schleitheim, on the other hand, a Christian had nothing to do with temporal government. Thus, if there was a conflict between the two claims, a Christian, according to the Schleitheim Confession, was obliged to "obey God rather than men."[17]

Schleitheim also differed from Zwingli's less negative view of society and governmental institutions[18] in that it rejected, at least by implication, the *corpus Christianum* idea and instead stressed the sectlike Christian community as a redeemed society. Zwingli believed that since the state was part of a more or less Christian society, it should be involved in the spiritual work of the church. The Swiss radicals, on the other hand, insisted that the Church must be free and separate from the state to do its work. Similarly, Calvin, in his criticism of the Schleitheim articles in 1544, underlined the difference between himself and the Swiss Brethren with regard to their understanding of the Church's role in society.[19] In opposition to Schleitheim's complete separation of Church and state, Calvin not only assigned important Christian roles to magistrates but he also sought to work closely together with the state to bring about the transformation of society according to Christian ideals, goals, and standards. To despise these "servants of god," as Calvin called rulers and governments, was tantamount to despising God and would lead to chaos in society.[20]

This is not to say that Luther, Zwingli and Calvin were uncritical of rulers, governments, and states. Luther and Calvin in particular added their prophetic voices to the Church's witness to secular and ungodly governments.[21] However, withdrawal from government and separation of Church and state as Schleitheim demanded it were foreign to the magisterial reformers.[22]

Long before Calvin wrote his response to the articles of Schleitheim, Balthasar Hübmaier, some four months after the "Brotherly Union" was drafted, wrote what appears to be a reply to Schleitheim, particularly with regard to the articles dealing with government and the sword.[23] It might be noted in passing that it would be instructive to compare Hübmaier's *On the Sword* (1527) with Calvin's pamphlet *Treatises Against the Anabaptists* (1544). The parallels between the two arguments are striking indeed.

Before focusing on Hübmaier's argument against Schleitheim's view of the Christian and the state, we need to sketch in Hübmaier's political involvement and work as a magisterial reformer. In an attempt to bring about a reformation on a larger societal scale, Hübmaier managed, with the help of the rebellious peasants and the magistrates of Waldshut, to convert the town to Anabaptism.[24] Political and military complications, however, and pressures from the Hapsburgs and the Roman Catholic church caused Hübmaier to leave Waldshut, and thus this early political, social, and religious Anabaptist experiment came to naught. Shortly thereafter Hübmaier fled to Nickolsburg, Moravia, where the Liechtenstein nobles favoured Anabaptism and provided a haven of refuge for these persecuted radicals. In Nickolsburg, Hübmaier, faced with an Anabaptist government, sought to work out a Christian view of the state and a Christian's responsibility to it. The problem Hubmaier had to solve was: How can Christian rulers and subjects combine their faith, including belief in non-violence and love, with the need to uphold law and order and to defend their territory against outside attack? The booklet *On the Sword* was Hübmaier's answer to this question.

Like Calvin in 1544, Hübmaier uses harsh language against what he considers simple-minded Christians who are out of touch with reality. "Even a blind man can see," Hübmaier states, "that Christians may with a good conscience be a judge and council member to judge and decide in temporal matters."[25] And if a Christian must judge in spiritual matters, Hübmaier reasons, how much more may he "also be a protector with the hand of justice and a punisher of the unrighteous."[26] Hübmaier sees a contradiction in the view that the state is divinely instituted, yet Christians cannot participate in its temporal functions. "What good is a shoe if one dare not wear it?" he asks.[27] "Observe, dear brothers, that councils, courts and laws are not unjust...a Christian may — according to the order of God — bear the sword in God's stead against the evildoer and punish him."[28]

Like Luther, Hübmaier believes that in discharging his duty as a magistrate a Christian can and must act in love and for the good of his fellowmen. As Hübmaier puts it: "a Christian magistrate should never hate or envy anyone, but love everybody. Thus a Christian magistrate has no enemy, for he hates and envies no one. What he does with the sword, he does not out of grudging or hate, but at the command of God."[29] Both God and the Christian, according to Hübmaier, must restrain and punish evil, not from hate or envy, "but from justice."[30]

Hübmaier, however, like Luther and Calvin, was not absolute in his call for obedience to the government and he was certainly most critical of unjust rulers. As Calvin would argue later, Hübmaier believed that only just governments deserved obedience. Christians were thus advised to test "the spirit of rulers" and if they found that the magistrates were not equipped to govern, then "that government may justifiably be put away and another chosen.... If, however, such putting away cannot be done legally and peacefully without great harm and insurrection, one must be patient."[31] While Hübmaier foreshadows Calvin in this, Hübmaier does not say — as Calvin does — how a wicked government is to be replaced.[32]

Hübmaier further argues that not only kings and princes are responsible to God and ought to rule justly, but also magistrates on all levels of government must act in the place of God and thus be ultimately responsible to God himself.[33] This means that a magistrate cannot hide behind his superior's orders. If a magistrate is ordered by his superior to act unjustly, then the magistrate ought to "obey God rather than men." For Hübmaier, just causes and obedience are closely linked. Even a "just war" was not excluded from Hübmaier's thinking. In his "Justification" (1528),[34] Hübmaier argues that Christians are responsible to defend just rulers and causes—which no doubt was written with the nobles sympathetic to Anabaptism in mind—but he rejected the idea of a holy war for the Gospel. As Walter Klaassen comments: with regard to holy wars "the magisterial Anabaptist Hubmaier differed basically from his Protestant and Catholic contemporaries, most of whom accepted the necessity of the war for the gospel."[35]

Having summarized the two extreme Anabaptist positions with regard to Church-state relations, we now turn to a few Anabaptist leaders who held views somewhere in between these opposites.

Writing in his *Concerning True Love* (1527), the south-German Hans Denck, who had not been part of the Schleitheim consensus, expresses a somewhat ambivalent position with regard to a Christian's involvement in power politics. "It is not that power in itself is wrong, seen from the perspective of the evil world," he writes, "but rather that love teaches her children a better way, namely to serve the graciousness of God."[36] According to Denck, if a government were to act in love, justice, and toward the betterment of society, "it could well be Christian in its office."[37] However, since the world will not tolerate such Christian behaviour, "a friend of God should not be in the government...that is if he desires to keep Christ as a Lord and master."[38]

Denck's thinking reveals the basic dilemma Anabaptists and later Mennonites experienced with regard to their relationship to the temporal state. On the one hand they accepted government as an "ordering of God" and sought to be submissive to it. On the other hand, their negative and often painful experiences of government and the means governments used to accomplish their ends caused Anabaptists to withdraw from them.

Similarly, Pilgram Marpeck, a mining magistrate in Austria prior to his becoming an Anabaptist and later a city engineer in Strasbourg and Augsburg, believed in total separation of Church and state, but admitted in his *Confession* of 1532 that earthly rulers were servants of God in earthly matters.[39] Moreover, worldly rulers, according to Marpeck, have received special gifts and wisdom for their important service. However, these gifts and wisdom have nothing to do with Christian faith, nor will a Christian necessarily be a better ruler just because he is a Christian. This means that the natural wisdom God gives man is sufficient for his function in the magisterial realm where the Spirit of Christ cannot function. This appears to be the only place in Anabaptism where one encounters a specific application of a natural theology.[40]

On the specific question of whether a Christian may enter governmental service, Marpeck states in his *Defense* that Christians may not "administer cities and protect countries" because the kingdom of Christ is not of this world and because as a magistrate a Christian would have to use force in his office.[41] "It is difficult for a Christian to be a worldly ruler," Marpeck concludes. Even if a Christian in power were to act properly and in love, Marpeck asks, "how long would his conscience allow him to be a magistrate...since no one can serve two masters."[42]

Menno Simons, after whom the Anabaptists were later called Mennonites, went through several stages in his views on government.[43] In reading his writings on this subject, however, there appears generally a vacillation between withdrawal from temporal government and acknowledgement that rulers are Christians and answerable to God for their actions. In addressing the rulers of his day who persecuted his fellow Anabaptists, Menno appeals to them as brothers who ought to take their Christian profession seriously.[44] If rulers claim to be Christian, Menno argues, then they are enjoined not only to rule justly but also to promote the kingdom of God in society.[45] Menno went so far as to say that, in addition to upholding law and order, governments were to protect Christians and to punish or restrain manifest heretics and destroyers of the Christian faith, provided that such punishment is carried out "without tyranny and bloodshed."[46] Thus, while recognizing the Christian nature of governmental institutions, Menno limits their coercive powers and in doing so even questions the moral validity of capital punishment.

Menno Simons does not state explicitly whether a Christian may enter politics, but in addressing rulers as fellow Christians and admonishing them to govern justly and in love, he at least implies that a Christian might serve as a magistrate.[47] Menno certainly would not have agreed with Peter Riedemann, a Hutterite leader and contemporary of Menno, that true believers must withdraw from the world and have nothing to do with the state.[48] But neither did he concur with the

Melchiorite Anabaptists who rebelled against the governments of their time and established an earthly kingdom of their own.[49] It was precisely this caricature of Anabaptism which Menno opposed and which became the occasion for his decision to leave the old church and join the radical movement in the hope that he might help to bring these "erring children" back to the ways of peace and Christian discipleship.[50]

Menno Simons and Pilgram Marpeck, the two so-called second-generation Anabaptists, the one from the north and the other from the south, in a sense bridge the gap between those early Anabaptists who withdrew from the world and lived in sectlike communities, and those later Mennonites who entered society and gradually began to enter state functions on many levels. While they experienced the tension between withdrawal and participation, they at least opened the way for Mennonites to serve God in "high places of power" as well.

Given Menno Simons's sympathetic view of rulers and government, a view generally shared by the northern Anabaptists, it is not surprising that the Dutch Mennonites as early as the second half of the sixteenth century were favourably disposed toward the state, especially after they were granted religious toleration under William of Orange. The Dutch were among the first Anabaptists to enter politics and to serve in government departments. There is some truth to the criticism that this openness to the world among the Dutch was a reflection of their "worldliness" and their forsaking of the earlier Anabaptist ways, especially if the Dutch Mennonites are measured with the yardstick of Schleitheim.[51] As we have seen, however, the less negative position with respect to the state existed among Anabaptists from the very beginning, and the Dutch Mennonites and their descendants developed along the continuum of this particular tradition.[52] Some of the southern Anabaptist groups continued much longer along the tradition of Schleitheim.

II.

Having dealt with the Church-state legacy of Anabaptism, we shall now look at representative Mennonite Confessions of Faith from the seventeenth century through to the present time. It is in the Confessions of Faith that Christian communities express what they believe and wish to practise and the tensions which they experience in the world.

The Dordrecht Confession of 1632 was no doubt the most important Mennonite faith statement since the Schleitheim Confession of

1527. The Dordrecht Confession was adopted, not only by the more conservative Mennonites of the Netherlands and North Germany, but also by the Alsatian and Palatinate Mennonites in 1660 and the Amish who originated in 1694.[53] The Confession's English version was introduced to the Pennsylvania Mennonites as early as 1727.[54]

The Dordrecht Confession acknowledges that "God has instituted civil government for the punishment of the wicked and the protection of the pious...wherefore we are not permitted to despise, blaspheme, or resist the same; but are to acknowledge it as a minister of God and be subject and obedient to it in all things that do not militate against the law, will and commandments of God."[55] The article on government concludes with an admonition to Christians to pray "that the Lord would recompense [the rulers], here and in eternity, for all the benefits, liberties, and favours which we enjoy under their laudable administration."[56] The Confession does not say whether Christians may serve in politics.

In 1747 Cornelis Ris, a minister of a church in Hoorn, north Holland, formulated a Confession which was intended to satisfy the more liberal Waterlander Mennonites and churches of the more orthodox Frisian Mennonite persuasion.[57] Article 28, dealing with the office of "Temporal Government," acknowledges the necessity of government and its institution of God "for the observance of right and good order in social life" and for "the punishment of the evil and the protection of the good."[58]

With regard to a Christian's involvement in government, Ris is ambivalent. "Should, however, such an office be conferred upon us," the Confession states, "we would hesitate and would not dare to accept it, not knowing the will of Christ as to how such office should be administered."[59] The article concludes with an expression of gratitude to "the benign government" for exempting Mennonites "from participation in government, from taking oaths, and from military service."[60]

While Ris's Confession was not widely accepted in the Netherlands — presumably because it was not sufficiently liberal — it came into common use among the German Mennonite churches; in 1902 it became an acceptable statement of faith for the General Conference Mennonite Church of North America.[61]

The Penner-Richert Confession was generally followed by the churches in Russia, West-Prussia, and in parts of North America.[62] In a footnote to Article 13, which deals with the "Office of Government," the Confession states: "To what extent the individual Christian may become an official of state, must be decided by himself according to his calling and inclination and his personal religious position. We do not consider the acceptance of a government position as being wrong nor sinful, since according to the clearest pronouncements of holy scriptures such an office is not only permitted by God but also established and instituted by him."[63]

This was generally the view of the great majority of Russian Mennonites prior to World War I. The Russian Mennonite historian P.M. Friesen devotes some fifty pages to the attitude and actions of the Mennonites with regard to the Russian state.[64] Friesen goes to great length documenting that while Mennonites were peace-loving people whose principle of non-resistance was sacred to them, they nevertheless had proven their love for the tsars and the Russian people and contributed generously their money, goods, and services to the support of Russia's wars against Napoleon, the Turks, the enemies of Russia during the Crimean War, and the Japanese war in 1905.[65] This nationalism and patriotism among the Russian Mennonites found eloquent expression in letters, poems, and songs written by Mennonite leaders as early as the mid-nineteenth century. Even such teachers, preachers, and evangelists as Heinrich Heese and Bernhard Harder sang the praises of the Russian tsars and their military valour and exploits.[66]

Back in North America, a shortened version of a Mennonite Confession established in Beatrice, Nebraska, in 1918, expresses both tension and ambivalence with regard to the state.[67] While it follows other European and North American traditions, it adds to the article on government a significant modification: "To accept a government position we feel only then duty-bound when the office does not conflict with our duties toward God. We desire only to live like the humble ones in the land."[68] Thus, while the Confession advocates the more traditional non-involvement stance, it does not altogether forbid members to take part in some forms of government.

I shall conclude this section with references to the Confessions of two large North American Mennonite denominations, the Mennonite General Conference (MGC) and the Mennonite Brethren Conference (MBC). The MGC Confession, adopted in 1963, sees itself as being in the tradition of the Dordrecht Confession of 1632 and "other statements adopted by our church."[69] In Article 19, "the Christian and the State," the Confession acknowledges the validity of the state under God and states that Christians should "witness to the authorities of God's redeeming love in Christ and of his sovereignty over all men."[70] The article then adds: "In law enforcement the state does not and cannot operate on the nonresistant principle of Christ's kingdom. Therefore, nonresistant Christians cannot undertake any service in a state or in society which violates the principle of love and holiness as taught by Christ and His inspired apostles."[71]

As shown in this Confession, questions of state and members' involvement in it are always tied to the Mennonite tradition of pacifism. At the same time the Confession leaves the door at least partly open to Christians' involvement in politics, provided that such involvement does not violate the principle of pacifism. Also, this Confession includes an important statement about witnessing to the authorities in government, although it does not specify how such witnessing can or should be done.

The MBC Confession, adopted in 1975, states in its Preface that the Mennonite Brethren are historically rooted in "evangelical Mennonite-Anabaptism" of the sixteenth century in general and Menno Simons in particular.[72] With regard to the state (Article XIV), the Confession makes no provision for those who might wish to enter politics. However, in stating that "the chief concern and primary allegiance of all Christians should be to Christ's kingdom,"[73] the Confession is sufficiently ambiguous to allow for service in the political arena if members can retain their allegiance to Christ and his kingdom. It is thus not coincidental that Mennonite Brethren church members are entering politics on all levels in increasing numbers, while at the same time remaining church members in good standing.

III.

From the ideals of the Confessions, however ambivalently expressed, we now turn to the actual practices of Mennonites in the "real world." By the middle of the sixteenth century, as we have indicated, many Dutch Mennonites permitted their members to hold at least local political offices not involving capital punishment. The so-called "Swiss" Mennonites, however, continued to observe as much as possible the Schleitheim tradition of withdrawal and political non-involvement. When this position became increasingly difficult to maintain, many Mennonites left for North America. The early settlers in Pennsylvania and other parts of America continued to adhere to their strict confession, shunning political involvement and participation in the military. In the twentieth century the writings of Guy F. Hershberger, for example, not only reflect this withdrawal position among the (Old) Mennonites but also advocate that non-involvement continue to be the norm for non-resistant Christians.[74]

While the principle of avoiding politics persisted as an ideal among the Swiss Mennonites in America, "the reality hardly reflected the theory," as John H. Redekop has pointed out.[75] Mennonite leaders in Pennsylvania, Ohio, and Ontario became political activists as early as the eighteenth century, petitioning the governments for military exemption and other issues pertaining to Mennonite life. Such "Swiss" Mennonites as Abraham Erb and Moses Springer of Waterloo, Ontario, were political leaders in municipal affairs, and Springer was eventually elected to the provincial legislature.[76]

According to Theron Schlabach's recent history of the American Mennonites, three things made the "Swiss" Mennonites more politically conscious and open to political activism in the nineteenth century: the coming of the "Russian" Mennonites to America; progressivism; the politics of prohibition.[77] However, despite the new progressive voices among the American Mennonites, most groups of Swiss descent, including the Amish, "still put little faith in government to perform God's positive work."[78] "Most Mennonites and Amish," Schlabach concludes, "had not shifted their confidence away from faith and congregation and toward politics and governments.... In the final years of the [nineteenth] century, the classic two-realm outlook still prevailed."[79]

In northern Europe, among the so-called "Dutch-Prussian" Mennonites, the picture was different in the late eighteenth and nineteenth centuries. In Poland and Prussia they soon followed the early example of their Dutch forebears. They negotiated terms with the governments concerning exemption from military service and other "privileges" such as religious toleration, educational and language matters, and issues relating to land, settlement, and taxes. At times they even used the courts to uphold their traditional practices.[80] During the time of Chancellor Bismarck, however, Mennonites were fighting a losing battle with the government. While they still lobbied government officials in Berlin, hoping that their time-honoured traditions, especially pacifism, would be recognized, after 1868 the German Mennonites became increasingly integrated in society, losing their traditional distinctives and entering all areas of life including services in government and the military.[81]

Beginning around 1800, the Russian Mennonites were well on their way to establishing what has been called a "commonwealth," that is, a virtual church-state on the South-Russian steppes.[82] Already, before the Mennonites settled in Russia, they had negotiated settlement terms with the Russian authorities. Historian D.H. Epp shows how intelligently and skilfully Bartsch and Höppner, the Prussian Mennonite deputies to Russia in 1786, had worked out good deals with the Russian officials.[83] Living in separate colonies, the Russian Mennonite settlers administered their own affairs, including local government, agriculture, education, industry, and, of course, church life. Beginning in 1870, when the imperial government announced drastic changes for the colonies, including an end to military exemption and the loss of autonomy, Mennonite loyalty to Russia was put severely to the test. Nevertheless, through protracted negotiations, trips to St. Petersburg, and threats of emigration, Russian Mennonites worked out terms with the government with which the majority could live.[84] The relationship between the Mennonite church-state and St. Petersburg remained fairly close until the end of World War I. By the turn of the century, Mennonites had their first representative, Hermann Bergmann, in the Imperial Duma (parliament). With the abdication and death of the Tsar in 1917, the political experiment of the Mennonite commonwealth in Russia came to an end, only to be resurrected in the late 1920s in Paraguay, where it still exists today.

With regard to the present situation in North America, I have time just to sketch the most salient points of Mennonite participation or involvement in the political arena. Among Mennonites in the United States and Canada, the two traditions — that is, non-involvement and selective participation — are still alive, and one might say at war with one another. Nevertheless, while the tension between the two positions remains — as it no doubt does in other Christian communities as well — the post-World War II period has seen increasing Mennonite participation on all three levels of government. Even the (Old) Mennonites in the United States now vote, approach their senators and congressmen on behalf of themselves and various causes, and maintain an observer office with the assistance of Mennonite Central Committee (MCC) in Washington.[85] Delton Franz and his staff have developed this office into a significant national political voice, addressing issues of justice, arms buildup, U.S. intervention in Central America, and peace-war concerns. In a recent issue of their organ, *Washington Memo*, they write: "On the problematic side, many current Mennonite adherents to 'two-kingdom' theology, interpret it to mean that the church should not be engaged in efforts to influence the direction of government. But even in the sixteenth century, the radical dualism of

Michael Sattler and those who adhered to the Schleitheim Confession was seen as an outlook that was too passive and too separatist by Anabaptists like Pilgrim Marpeck, Hans Denck, Menno Simons and others.... We cannot, therefore, look to the sixteenth-century Schleitheim Confession for ready guidance as to whether, or for what purpose, we might speak to our government in 1989."[86]

Similarly, Canadian Mennonites are close to the corridors of power in Ottawa. The influence and mediation of William Janzen's office are well respected by both Canadian Mennonites and members of Parliament; the good that this office has been able to achieve is considerable. Considering Janzen's political involvement, it is no doubt ironic that he had an uncle who was excommunicated by a Mennonite church for voting![87]

Canadian Mennonite involvement on the municipal, provincial, and federal levels of government has apparently burst all restraints. In several western provinces, Mennonites hold important positions in the legislatures, and there are prominent lawyers and judges who are practising Mennonites. On the national level, there has been no shortage of Mennonite candidates since the 1950s. In the 1974 election, the total number of candidates reached 16, in the 1980 election, 11.[88] According to John Redekop's tabulation, a total of 17 Mennonites were candidates for the House of Commons in the 1988 election. Of these, four were elected, three for the Progressive Conservative party and one for the New Democratic Party.[89] Jake Epp, Member of Parliament for the Provencher riding of Manitoba, is well known as a senior cabinet member in the Brian Mulroney government. Even though Mr. Epp has formally withdrawn from the Mennonite Brethren Church in Steinbach, Manitoba, and joined an evangelical congregation, he is nationally known as a Mennonite and closely connected to the Mennonite community.

How the majority of Canadian Mennonites — particularly those of Russian Mennonite background — feel about politics and involvement in government is perhaps best expressed by John Redekop. In a pamphlet, *Making Political Decisions*, Redekop states: "here and there we find citizens who are convinced that God wants them to enter politics. I see some problems in such cases, particularly where party ideology is specific and party discipline strict. But let us not become judgmental.... I am convinced that God directs some Christians to serve their fellowmen in political service."[90] And in his conclusion to this pamphlet Redekop writes: "Although...I do not see political involvement as a top priority of the church, the corporate nature of the body of believers leads one to conclude that even in the realm of political activity the group has an important place."[91] What that place or role of the Church might be has been repeatedly articulated by John Howard Yoder, Mennonite theologian at Notre Dame University. Like the early Anabaptists who, through their suffering and pleas for religious toleration, exposed the states' injustice, cruelty, and resistance to God's ways, so Christians today must witness to the state concerning justice, peace, and humanity, and insist that governments live up to their profession and declaration of human rights.[92] If a Christian is led to serve God and society through government, Yoder agrees that he do so "as long as he can," implying that a principled Christian might not last long in the corridors of political power.[93]

Conclusion

Anabaptists and Mennonites have experienced the temporal state as being "outside the perfection of Christ." Because they suffered persecution at the hands of the state, the Anabaptists saw more clearly than other Christians in sixteenth-century society that the state operated primarily according to laws which for them were symbolized by the sword. If in the Church Christians were governed by the law of Christ, namely love and obedience to God, in the state society was held in check through power and violence. Because of these diametrically opposed realities, Mennonites throughout the ages experienced a tension between complete withdrawal from the state and the desire to effect wholesome changes in society through participation in government. Partly because of the changed nature of Western democratic states and the enormous problems which face society in modern times, Mennonites today have become more open to and positive about greater participation in government. They believe that they can thus better contribute to governments and society values which the world needs if it is to survive.

In light of these changed views and practices of Mennonites with regard to their responsibility to the state and society, it is now possible for Mennonites and Reformed to engage in meaningful dialogue about what it means to be a follower of Christ in a world which is basically alienated from God. While Mennonites are no doubt much more skeptical about their ability to "transform the world" through political processes than the Reformed have been historically, they nevertheless realize that they can no longer be *die Stillen im Lande* (the quiet ones in the land) but must become involved with suffering humanity around them and bring about needful changes in society through the most effective means possible.

That the political process is a powerful means in this regard there is little doubt.

I suggest that in matters of Church-state relations the dialogue between Mennonites and Reformed deal with two related questions: 1) What are the differences and similarities in our understanding of what it means to be *in* the world and yet not be *of* the world? 2) How can Mennonites and Reformed become effective witnesses *to* and *within* governments? Such prophetic witness to and within the powers that be would no doubt address issues and questions related to justice, human rights, immigration, the environment, third-world development, poverty at home and abroad, war and peace, and many other social, economic, and political ills which plague our world.[94]

It seems to me that Mennonite and Reformed churches have much to contribute to making our governments more responsible toward what can and must be done for their citizens and the international communities.   Mennonites, with their historic peace position and traditional skepticism of the nature and ways of temporal governments, and the Reformed, with their centuries of experience in matters of government and political involvement, can unite in planning strategies and providing powerful voices on behalf of the Kingdom of God and humanity on the highest decision-making levels of our time. That our governments need to and can benefit from such united witness there is no doubt. How such witnessing to the state is to be accomplished requires much thought and dialogue with one another. It may be that our united Christian action will not only prevent the world from destroying itself but make it a little better place for all people.   And that is no mean achievement.

Notes

1.   Harold S. Bender's "The Anabaptist Vision" was first presented at the American Society of Church History, December 1943, and then appeared in *Church History* 13 (March 1944):3 and *Mennonite Quarterly Review* 18 (April 1944):67. I am following the article as reprinted in Guy F. Hershberger, ed., *The Recovery of The Anabaptist Vision*: A Sixtieth Anniversary Tribute to Harold S. Bender (Scottdale, PA: Herald Press, 1957), pp. 29-54.

2.   Hershberger, ed., *The Recovery*, p. 37.

3.   Ibid., p. 41.

4.   This emphasis on withdrawal and normative Anabaptism in earlier Anabaptist historiography is more implied than stated explicitly. See the following works on this: Harold S. Bender, *Conrad Grebel c. 1498-1526: The Founder of the Swiss Brethren Sometimes Called Anabaptists* (Scottdale, PA: Herald Press,

1950), pp. xiii, 213-14; Robert Friedmann, *The Theology of Anabaptism: An Interpretation* (Scottdale, PA/Kitchener, Ont.: Herald Press, 1973), pp. 36-48. For the "Brotherly Union" articles, which stress withdrawal as an Anabaptist way of life, see *The Schleitheim Confession*, trans. and ed. by John H. Yoder (Scottdale, PA/Kitchener, Ont.: 1973).

5.   Hans Denck, Balthasar Hübmaier, Hans Hut, Ludwig Haetzer, and others were seen as "marginal" Anabaptists because their theology and practice were not in accord with the Swiss Brethren and the Schleitheim articles. See Yoder's notes in *The Schleitheim Confession*, pp. 22-24. See also the articles on Hans Denck and Balthasar Hübmaier in *The Mennonite Encyclopedia*, vol. II, pp. 32-35; 826-34.

6.   See especially Klaus Deppermann, Werner O. Packull, and James M. Stayer, "From Monogenesis to Polygenesis: The Historical Discussion of Anabaptist Origins," *MQR*, XLIX (1975).

7.   I am borrowing "selective" participation or involvement from John H. Redekop, *Making Political Decisions: A Christian Perspective*, Focal Pamphlet No. 23 (Scottdale, PA: Herald Press, 1972).

8.   On this see James M. Stayer, *Anabaptists and the Sword* (Lawrence, Kansas: Coronado Press, 1976), and C. Arnold Snyder, *The Life and Thought of Michael Sattler* (Scottdale, PA/Kitchener, Ont.: Herald Press, 1984) among others.

9.   See, for example, Michael Sattler who at first seemed to sympathize with the peasants and their concerns and then in 1527 drafted the Schleitheim Confession which stressed separation from the world and apoliticism.

10.   The Anabaptists understood well the basic difference between the Church and the state. While the church included believers who sought to be obedient to the claims and ethical standards of Christ, the state in its very nature was outside of Christ and his rule. See especially John H. Yoder, *Täfertum und Reformation im Gespräch. Dogmengeschichtliche Untersuchung der frühen Gespräche zwischen Schweizerischen Täufern und Reformatoren* (Zürich: EVZ-Verlag, 1968), pp. 117-205.

11.   I am following the English version of *The Schleitheim Confession*, trans. and ed. by John H. Yoder.

12.   See Yoder, ed., *The Schleitheim Confession*, pp. 22-23, for a discussion concerning this exclusion of "marginal" Anabaptists and Spiritualists.

13.   Ibid., pp. 14-15.

14.   Ibid., p. 15.

15.   On Martin Luther's view of the "two kingdoms," see his "Temporal Authority: To What Extent it Should be Obeyed," in *Luther's Works*, vol. 45 (Philadelphia: Muhlenberg Press, 1962), pp. 75-129.

16.   Ibid., pp. 95-104.

17.   While Anabaptists accepted responsibility for their moral actions, Luther tended to shift such responsibility, especially in matters of government, to rulers who were responsible for law and order and the defence of the realm. *Luther's Works*, vol. 46, pp. 130-31.

18.   On Zwingli's "Realpolitik," see Stayer, *Anabaptists and the Sword*, pp. 49-69.

19. See John Calvin, *Treatises Against the Anabaptists and Against the Libertines*, ed. and trans. by Benjamin Wirt Farley (Grand Rapids, MI: Baker Book House, 1982), pp. 13-91.

20. Ibid., p. 79. See also George L. Mosse, *Calvinism. Authoritarian or Democratic?* (New York/Chicago/San Francisco/Toronto/London: Holt, Rinehart and Winston, 1957), p. 5.

21. On Calvin's criticism of rulers, see Mosse, *Calvinism*, pp. 4, 9-10.

22. See especially Calvin, *Treatises Against the Anabaptists*, pp. 79-80: Since God assigns rulers "a place so honourable in the midst of His people as to grant them the honor, I say, of ordaining them 'protectors of His church,' what impudence is it to exclude them from it altogether?" (p. 79). For an excellent discussion of the differences between the Anabaptists and Calvin with regard to Church and state issues, see Willem Balke, *Calvin and the Anabaptist Radicals*, trans. by William J. Heynen (Grand Rapids, MI: Eerdmans, 1981), pp. 253-300.

23. There is good reason to believe that Balthasar Hübmaier wrote his *On the Sword* in direct response to the Schleitheim articles. See the Introduction to "On the Sword" in Balthasar Hübmaier, *Schriften* (Quellen und Forschungen zur Reformationsgeschichte Band XXIX, Quellen zur Geschichte der *Täufer* IX), herausgegeben von Gunnar Westin und Torsten Bergsten (*Gütersloh*: Verlagshaus Gerd Mohn, 1962), pp. 432-33.

24. Ibid., pp. 27-30.

25. Quoted in Walter Klaassen, ed., *Anabaptism in Outline: Selected Primary Sources* (Kitchener, Ont./Scottdale, PA: 1981), p. 248.

26. Ibid., p. 248.

27. Ibid.

28. Ibid.

29. Ibid., p. 249.

30. Ibid.

31. Ibid., p. 271.

32. Calvin believed that subordinate magistrates and lesser nobles are sometimes used by God to punish wicked rulers. Mosse, *Calvinism*, p. 5.

33. Klaassen, ed., *Anabaptism in Outline*, p. 271.

34. Ibid., p. 250.

35. Ibid., p. 246.

36. Ibid., p. 249.

37. Ibid., p. 250.

38. Ibid.

39. Ibid., p. 251.

40. Ibid., p. 262. I am indebted to Walter Klaassen for this point.

41. Ibid., p. 263.

42. Ibid.

43. See Stayer, *Anabaptists and the Sword*, pp. 309-28.

44. Menno Simons, *The Complete Writings*, trans. from the Dutch by Leonard Verduin and edited by John Christian Wenger, with a biography by Harold S. Bender (Scottdale: Herald Press, 1956), p. 193.

45. "In all love, without force, violence and blood, you may enlarge, help, and protect the kingdom of God with gracious consent and permission, with wise counsel and a pious, unblamable life." Ibid.

46. Ibid.

47. Cf. Cornelius Krahn, *Menno Simons (1496-1561): Ein Beitrag zur Geschichte und Theologie der Taufgesinnten* (Newton, KS: Faith and Life Press, 1982, reprint of 1936 edition), pp. 164-77.

48. Peter Riedemann, in his "Account" of 1542, insists that Christians cannot be part of temporal governments and that if rulers become Christian they must leave their office: "It is clear that not only governmental authorities but all who still cleave to created things, and forsake them not for Christ's sake, are not Christians." Klaassen, ed., *Anabaptism in Outline*, p. 262.

49. See Menno Simons's "The Blasphemy of John of Leiden" of 1535, *The Complete Writings*, pp. 33-50.

50. Ibid., pp. 670-71. It would have been useful to rehearse the genesis of Menno's view of government, stemming from Hoffman, whose view was Lutheran, through *Münster*, a proto-puritan experiment (i.e., reformed tradition).

51. For a criticism of the Dutch Mennonites, see John Horsch, *Mennonites in Europe* (Scottdale, PA/Kitchener, Ont.: Herald Press, 1942), pp. 233-58.

52. See Harry Loewen, "The Anabaptist View of the World: The Beginning of a Mennonite Continuum?" in *Mennonite Images: Historical, Cultural, and Literary Essays Dealing With Mennonite Issues*, ed. by Harry Loewen (Winnipeg: Hyperion Press, 1980), pp. 85-95.

53. C. Henry Smith, *The Story of the Mennonites* (Newton, KS: Mennonite Publication Office, 1950), p. 747.

54. Ibid.

55. Howard John Loewen, *One Lord, One Church, One Hope, and One God: Mennonite Confessions of Faith*, Text-Reader Series No. 2, Willard M. Swartley, ed. (Elkhart, IN: Institute of Mennonite Studies, 1985), p. 67.

56. Ibid., p. 68.

57. Smith, *The Story of the Mennonites*, p. 210.

58. Howard Loewen, *One Lord*, p. 97.

59. Ibid., p. 98.

60. Ibid.

61. Smith, *The Story of the Mennonites*, p. 211.

62. Howard Loewen, *One Lord*, p. 143. This Confession is not dated.

63. Ibid., p. 147. Translation mine.

64. Peter Martin Friesen, *The Mennonite Brotherhood in Russia (1789-1910)*, translated from the German (Fresno, CA: Board of Christian Literature General Conference of Mennonite Brethren Churches, 1978), pp. 575-625.

65. Ibid., pp. 575-86.

66. Ibid., pp. 702-705; Bernhard Harder, *Geistliche Lieder und Gelegenheits-Gedichte*. Gesammelt und herausgegeben von Heinrich Franz sen. (Hamburg: Verlagsanstalt und Druckerei A.-G. [vorm. J.F. Richter], 1988), pp. 580-83.

67. For the entire Confession, see Howard Loewen, *One Lord*, pp. 129-41.

68. Ibid., p. 139. Translation mine.

69. Ibid., p. 73.

70. Ibid., p. 77.

71. Ibid.

72. Ibid., p. 175.

73. Ibid., pp. 177-78.

74. See especially Guy Franklin Hershberger, *War, Peace, and Nonresistance* (Scottdale, PA/Kitchener, Ont.: Herald Press, 1944).

75. John H. Redekop, "Politics," in *The Mennonite Encyclopedia*, vol. V, forthcoming.

76. Ibid.

77. Theron F. Schlabach, *Peace, Faith, Nation: Mennonites and Amish in Nineteenth-Century America* (Scottdale, PA/Kitchener, Ont.: Herald Press, 1988), pp. 158-71.

78. Ibid., p. 166.

79. Ibid., p. 172.

80. See, for example, the legal wranglings with regard to David von Riesen who was expelled from membership in a West Prussian church for serving in the army in the War of Liberation in 1815. G.L. von Reiswitz and F. Wadzeck, *Beiträge zur Kenntnis der Mennoniten-Gemeinden in Europa und Amerika* (Berlin, 1821), pp. 233-315. See also the earlier affair of the "Potsdam guards" under Frederick William I (1713-1740) when Mennonites in Prussia protested to the King about infringing on their privilege of exemption from military service. *The Mennonite Encyclopedia*, vol. II, p. 386.

81. John Friesen, "The Relationship of Prussian Mennonites to German Nationalism," in *Mennonite Images*, Harry Loewen, ed. (Winnipeg: Hyperion Press, 1980), pp. 61-72.

82. For a good historical discussion of the Russian-Mennonite "state," see David Rempel, "The Mennonite Commonwealth in Russia: a Sketch of its Founding and Endurance, 1789-1919," *MQR* XLVII (1973):259; *MQR* XLVIII (1974):5. See also the monumental work of James Urry, "The Closed and the Open: Social and Religious Change Amongst the Mennonites in Russia (1789-1889)," dissertation, Oxford University, 1978.

83. D.H. Epp, *Die Chortitzer Mennoniten. Versuch einer Darstellung des Entwicklungsganges derselben* (Steinbach, Man: Die Mennonitische Post, 1984, reprint of the 1889 original), pp. 10-26.

84. See P.M. Friesen, *The Mennonite Brotherhood in Russia*, pp. 586-625. For a thorough discussion of introduction of military service in Russia and Mennonite emigration to Canada and the U.S.A., see James Urry, "The Closed and the Open," Part X.

85. Redekop, "Politics."
86. *Washington Memo*, vol. XXI (Jan.-Feb. 1989), 1:3.
87. Redekop, "Politics."
88. Ibid.
89. John H. Redekop, "Mennonite Politicians," *Mennonite Brethren Herald* (December 23, 1988), p. 8.
90. Redekop, *Making Political Decisions*, p. 36.
91. Ibid., p. 38.
92. See especially Yoder's *The Politics of Jesus*.
93. Yoder in a discussion in September 1979 concerning Christians and political involvement. See one of the papers he gave on that occasion, "Mennonite Political Conservatism: Paradox or Contradiction," in *Mennonite Images*, Harry Loewen, ed. (Winnipeg: Hyperion Press, 1980), pp. 7-16.
94. See Urbane Peachey, ed., *The Role of the Church in Society: An International Perspective* (Carol Stream, IL.: Mennonite World Conference, 1988), pp. 3-12.

PART TWO:
THE RESPONSES

Chapter VIII

CHURCH, STATE, AND THE REFORMED

TRADITION: A PHILOSOPHER'S RESPONSE

Hugo Meynell

I.

I always enjoy the story of the Anglican dignitary who was interrupted by a Catholic heckler while giving a speech. "Where was your church, Sir, before the Reformation?" The answer was: "Where was your face, Sir, before you washed it?" I am here as a representative, so to say, of the unwashed face of the Church. The old days of mutual vilification are, fortunately, largely over, at least so far as the scholarly community is concerned; and we are now far more capable than before of trying to share one another's wisdom on such difficult questions as the proper relations between Church and state, and the nature of the sacraments. Not that "blandness is all" ought by any means to be the watchword; against a general background of charity and the search for mutual understanding, and a willingness by each party to admit its shortcomings, there is still room for brotherly or sisterly correction. It sells all parties to the Reformation short if one implies that the issues which divided Western Christendom at that time were not really of any significance. At all events, it is a great honour to be asked, as an outsider, to contribute to the proceedings of a conference dealing with that Reformed tradition which has played such an outstanding part in the life of the universal Church since the sixteenth century. But perhaps "outsider" is not after all quite the *mot juste*; as Karl Barth remarked in a letter to Hans Küng, we are divided in faith, but divided in *the same* faith, so far as from our different viewpoints and in our different ways we acknowledge the same Lord.

No thinking Christian is able to avoid the question of what relation the Christian community ought to have with the established political order. At one extreme, one may see no positive relation at all; as when Christians feel committed to leaving the political order to perdition, or even actively to subverting it. Both of these options were taken up by some radical sects at the time of the Reformation. As we have been told in Dr. Loewen's paper, at first the radical reformers in Switzerland and south-west Germany aimed at a large-scale reconstruction of society; it was only when they met determined opposition that they began to withdraw from the world. Both attitudes are very understandable. If the life of the Christian is to be devoted to proclaiming the Kingdom of God in word and deed, what can she have to do with submission to, let alone control and administration of, the old order which is passing away? And if any stance at all is to be taken up to the powers of the human world which has fallen into sin, should it not be one of active resistance?

At the other extreme, there is close Christian involvement with the affairs of the state. There are obvious *prima facie* tensions between administration of human affairs as they are, and the proclamation of the Kingdom of God and implementation of its demands. When these tensions arise, as they must sooner rather than later, there are two obvious, simple ways of resolving them. They are both based on the premise that when push comes to shove, either the state must submit to the Church or the Church must submit to the state. The former solution is what is usually and misleadingly known as "theocracy"; if this were actually the reign of God it would be all very well, but in fact it is almost invariably the rule of those who blasphemously sanctify their own group interest by identifying it with God's will. Hume's Philo was possibly exaggerating when he caustically remarked that there was no group to whom it was more dangerous to give power than the clergy;[1] but history, ancient and modern at least, indicates that the exaggeration was a pardonable one. As to the opposite state of affairs, when the Church submits to the state, no desertion of an appointed task could be more contemptible than that of a church which abandons her prophetic office. We have it on the highest authority that, when the salt loses its savour, it is good for nothing but to be trampled underfoot.[2]

It has been said, in my view wisely, that the Christian faith comes into the world as the supernatural solution to the problem of evil; but that human beings being as they are, some are apt to treat it as all supernatural, and others as all solution. The former party tends to seek a life with God which is totally detached from the concerns of the world, while the latter devotes itself to politics and social action.[3] But much experience goes to show that politics and social action, if they are to be effective at all, necessarily have their vicious side. Constantine would not be baptized until the very end of his life, since the coercion and shedding of blood necessary for the efficient running of an empire seemed plainly incompatible with Christian principles. When the Emperor Vladimir of Russia became converted to Christianity at the end of the tenth century, he wished to abolish capital punishment throughout his dominions and was only with difficulty dissuaded by his bishops, who understandably maintained that the step would be quite impractical.

It was the great merit of the fathers of the Reformation that they insisted on looking at the practical problems of the Christian life with fresh eyes; however, the problems remained the same. We have been informed by Dr. Loewen how the "Brotherly Union" of Schleitheim had admitted that the temporal state was established by God but insisted all the same that the followers of Christ were to have nothing to do with it. Balthasar Hübmaier rightly saw a contradiction in the view that while the state is a divine institution, Christians cannot be involved in the running of it. His solution to the problem leans heavily on appeal to motive; while the Christian magistrate must use the sword at God's command, he is always obliged to love everyone. For all that it is obviously liable to abuse, I believe that Hübmaier's suggestion about motive is a helpful one. It is one thing to exercise coercion, or even occasionally to have people killed, because it is necessary for the preservation of a social order, the loss of which would lead to a substantial increase of unhappiness and injustice; it is quite another to do such things out of spite, fear, or the desire for gain. Christians may well use such a criterion as a basis either for informed criticism of the political order or for conditional participation within it.

But if to participate in the running of the state necessarily involves connivance at such intrinsically un-Christian practices, is it after all permissible for the Christian? From this perspective, what has been called the "vacillation" of Menno Simons is at least readily intelligible. The sole business of a Christian, it might well be insisted, is to accept the supernatural gift of God and radically to apply it to the whole conduct of her life. At this rate any political involvement would be liable to seem merely a distraction and a delusion. Yet it seems a rather central part of the Christian vocation to be concerned with the good of all people; and how can one be so concerned without striving to ameliorate so far as possible the actual circumstances in which they live? Particularly if the rulers claim to be Christians, can they not be exhorted, as they were by Simons, to perform their task in a manner which is so far as possible compatible with their Christian vocation? That involvement in politics has, as we learn from Dr. H. J. Loewen's paper, been a question of conscience for Mennonites right up to our own times serves as a remarkable witness to Christendom at large and perhaps as an indictment of its complacency; Mennonite hesitation between "non-involvement and selective participation" does at least take the measure of the difficulty of the problem.

I have already touched on two very simple ways of resolving the tensions between Church and state. A rather less simple solution to the problem is that associated with Luther. Though Luther never recommended the overthrow of the state, some of his more inflammatory early pronouncements were easily misunderstood in this sense; it has often been pointed out that experience of the results of this misunderstanding in the chaos and carnage of the Peasant's War of 1525 influenced his mature teaching on the matter. According to Luther, Christians in respect of their inner being in Christ are lords over creation; but in respect of their outer being they are subject to obedience, and above all to the political authorities of their country.[4] The splendour of this conception, and the profoundly Christian insight which it conveys, has of course to be acknowledged; surely the freedom which the Christian has in Christ is a freedom not to domineer over or be indifferent to but to serve others, to renounce her selfish ends for work for the good of her neighbour. But most would now agree that the political consequences which Luther drew from this insight have been rather unfortunate. When Martin Niemoller with exemplary courage arraigned Hitler for his policies, Hitler was able to reply that, as a good Lutheran, Niemoller should attend to the needs of people's souls and leave the conduct of material and terrestrial affairs to Hitler himself. One can hardly wonder at Dietrich Bonhoeffer's suggestion that, had Luther lived in Germany in the late 1930s, his political teachings would have been exactly the opposite of what in fact they were.

It is one of the special glories of Reformed Christianity that it confronts the problem of Church-state relations directly and thinks them through consistently and thoroughly. The position of Calvin on the matter has been set out for us with great clarity and power by Dr. Nicol; I will summarize it as briefly as is consistent with the purposes of my paper. While the state ought to protect and promote the proclamation of the Gospel, which is the primary office of the Church, the Church on her part should guide the state into obedience to the Word of God, which governs Church and state alike. In his estimate of human affairs, Calvin was impressed by what he saw as an unremitting tendency to disorder which was liable to bring about disaster at any moment short of stringent measures. In order to meet this peril, and to promote peace and tran-

quillity, God has established a political order for all human beings as well
as a spiritual order for the elect; consequently Christians have a dual
citizenship. If human beings had remained in a state of integrity, there
would have been no need for the political order; the latter is
consequently not an order of creation, as Luther thought, but essentially
transient and temporary.

Now we come to the more controversial side of Calvin's teaching.
Even a tyrannical order, as he sees it, is to be preferred to the chaos of
anarchy. Whether rulers are good or bad, Calvin firmly insists that they
must be obeyed; the punishment of unbridled despotism is the
prerogative of God alone. Calvin does take pains to protect his views
from possible misunderstanding. He points out that princes are to be
honoured only for the office that they hold and that in themselves they
are nothing. The Christian must disobey the civil authority when it
requires her to flout the law of God, thus in effect abrogating its own
powers. Lesser magistrates, in accordance with their own divinely
bestowed commission, may oppose unjust princes; indeed, if they fail to
do so, they betray the freedom of the people whom they have been
appointed to protect. However, Calvin gave no sanction to popular
resistance or revolution on the grounds of justice, the effect of which, in
his view, would merely have been to release anarchy.

If we disagree with Calvin, as I think we are entitled to do, in his
view that revolution against a tyrannical state is never justified, at least
we should take the measure of the arguments which he uses to support it.
Dr. Nicol reminds us that Calvin did admit (in the manner of Aristotle
and Aquinas rather than of Augustine, whose authority he was most
inclined to follow) that human beings are by nature social and possessed
of a certain natural instinct to foster and preserve society; we may
properly wonder whether his refusal in any circumstances to countenance
revolution in the cause of justice took this admission sufficiently into
account. (It is perhaps more true of Calvin than of any other Christian
theologian that one should not lightly make against him the charge of
inconsistency.) A revolutionary Calvinist may cite as precedent his
followers in England and Scotland who clearly acted against his teaching
on this particular matter. However, the Christian who contemplates
revolution, in the light of Calvin's warnings about the chaos which
threatens human affairs, ought at the least to ask herself a number of
questions. Do I take sufficient account of the good which is done by the
present regime as well as of the devils of which it is guilty? Do I have
reason to suppose that the regime with which I intend to replace the

present one is likely on balance to be better? Am I morally certain that the violence by means of which I and my party intend to achieve our end is the only means by which that end can be achieved and that the end is worth the means employed in attaining it?

II.

The review of the relation between the Christian community and the state which may be said to be classical for Western Christianity is that of St. Augustine. Love of an object, Augustine says, unites all those who share it into a society.[5] If we call each such society a "city," then it may be inferred that every human being will belong to at least one of two cities, that united by love of temporal goods and that united by love of God.[6] Now every society wants peace; even wars are only waged ultimately for the sake of peace.[7] But the condition without which peace is at best temporary and unstable is order. Just as the parts of an organism have all to be in their right place for the organism to function as it should, so must the diverse wills which constitute a society if that society is to have peace.[8] Peace is in fact the tranquillity which is derived from order.[9] While the order of the earthly city is the merest mockery in comparison with the true order of the city of God, it is good as far as it goes.[10] The city of God brings together human beings of widely differing languages and customs, destroying nothing useful and striving to preserve whatever each has to contribute to worldly peace, provided of course that there is nothing in conflict with the true peace of God.[11]

The eternal city is accordingly the only true city.[12] Still, given the *de facto* existence of the two cities, how are they to settle down together at all?[13] Christians, like others, need the material goods for which the earthly city has been organized; they benefit from its advantages and share its burdens.[14] Yet the two cities never really mix thoroughly with one another; even where the same action is done by a member of the one as is done by a member of the other, it is done in quite a different spirit. For members of the earthly city, temporal goods are to be *enjoyed* for their own sake; to those of the heavenly city, they are merely for *use*, means to the achievement of beatitude.[15] In theory one might say that material things belong by right only to those who know how to use them, that is, with a view to God. However, redistribution on this basis would involve a social upheaval which is neither possible nor desirable; where would we find the just human beings to whom to allot the goods which are now possessed by the unjust in a wrongful way? Civil laws at least restrain those who use their goods badly from using them badly in order to inflict undue harm on one another.[16] It must be concluded that here below, unless the peace of society is harmed thereby, it is legitimate possession of things, and not good use of them, that forms the basis for the right of ownership.[17]

It must be remembered that while order is in the interest of both cities, the relative order of the earthly city by no means coincides with the true order of the eternal city and is in many ways opposed to it. This must be so, since while temporal law is for social peace here below, eternal law demands that what is temporal be subjected to what is eternal.[18] Thus some conflict is inevitable; the problem is to determine the proper stand of a Christian when such conflict arises. "Will he have to reform everything, or put up with everything?"[19] The earthly city has nothing to fear from the city of God; on the contrary, Christian principles demand more effectively what the laws of the earthly city are aimed to achieve. Civil law, for example, forbids revenge, which amounts to the return of evil for evil. Christian morality goes further than this by exhorting us to return good for evil and so helps to establish that dominion of good over evil which is the surest foundation for civil order. No conflict can arise so long as the earthly city conforms to the principles of justice; a state which had all of its citizens, especially its magistrates and soldiers, living according to Christian principles could ask for nothing better.[20] It is when the earthly city flouts its own laws that the difference between the two cities appears most clearly in relief; the Christian goes on observing the law when the earthly city cannot or will not any longer enforce it, precisely because she has a higher end in view in complying with it at all. At this stage, Christians will have a lot to put up with; they will set right whatever they can set right without flouting their own principles (of love of their persecutors, non-violence and so on), and what they cannot thus set right they will endure.[21]

What follows on this view for particular conflicts between the Christian and the state? When the state claims what is due to it, the Christian is to meet its demands (here we have direct divine warrant[22]), but out of love of God, not of state itself. When an unjust authority demands what is not its due, the Christian should remember that such an authority has its power from God, for reasons which we do not know, but must exist all the same since nothing within the scope of divine providence happens only by chance. The Christian will prefer submission to injustice over resort to violence and the undergoing of undeserved punishment rather than abandonment of the divine law of love.[23] Of course when the state exceeds its prerogatives so far as to demand what is due only to God, the Christian must refuse, not, however, out of hatred of the state, but out of love for God.[24] What about collaboration between Church and state? Augustine's *practice* in this matter changed a great deal in the course of his life as a Christian. For many years he detested the idea of any collaboration between civil and ecclesiastical authorities; gradually, however, he came to accept it more and more, growing meanwhile ever less scrupulous about use of the powers of the state against schismatics and heretics.[25] He was impressed that his own town had been converted more or less *en masse* to Catholic Christianity owing to fear of the laws of the empire.[26]

In considering the merits and the defects in Augustine's position, it is important to bear in mind that he does not, strictly speaking, identify the heavenly city with the empirical Church, or the earthly city (consisting of those leading sensual and selfish lives, and so bound for damnation) with the secular state. But he does sometimes tend to blur the differences, and it seems to me that, when one considers how his teaching ought to be applied and modified, the necessary distinctions should be made sharply and kept carefully in mind. There are many outside the empirical Church who at least strongly suggest, by their zeal for truth or justice, that they belong to the eternal city without knowing it;[27] whereas it is notorious that individuals claiming to be Christians, and sometimes even the empirical Church at large, can present exactly the opposite appearance. It should be a painful reflection to Christians in general, as it was to Vladimir Soloviev, how many advances towards the ideal of justice in society have not only been made by unbelievers but have been actively opposed by members of the Church. It seems to be not untypical of the official representatives of the Church that, as Veronica Keon remarked[28] of the Irish Catholic clergy among whom she was brought up, they purvey spiritual treasures of whose nature they themselves apparently have very little notion.

Only the *de facto* identification of the empirical Church with the eternal city and of those outside her with the "earthly city" consisting of those bound for damnation, could begin to justify the use of state power against heretics *as heretics*. It was quite proper, I believe, for Augustine to appeal for state protection against those Donatists who tried to ambush him on his episcopal rounds. However, it is of crucial importance that, in the name of the justice which is the essence of the eternal city, the Donatists should have had just the same right to protection against coercion or violence at the hands of the orthodox. The Church exists, of course, to proclaim the coming of the kingdom of God and to bring about its ideals in society so far as possible by word, action, and example; so identification of the empirical Church with the kingdom of God is quite a natural one, for all the deplorable discrepancy between the ideal that the Church represents and her empirical reality, which was probably less obvious from Augustine's historical perspective than it is from ours.

In connection with Karl Marx, I have suggested elsewhere[28] that it is useful to distinguish between state A and state B , where state A is nothing more than a device by which some sections of society may exploit others (the essence of the state as such in Marx's view) and state B, a means of control which is actually exercized in the public interest. (Marx thinks that such a state is impossible in the present and will be unnecessary in the future, but I shall argue below that there are substantial reasons for disagreeing with him.) Augustine often clearly admits the limited good realized by actual secular states; yet in other contexts he runs together the idea of the secular state with that of the "earthly city" bound for perdition. So one can properly say that the distinction I have drawn between aspects of actual states is latent in his thought. State A has plenty to fear from the kingdom of God or the eternal city and consequently ought to fear the Church; it is state B which, as Augustine says, has nothing to fear from them.

That Christianity (in common with other religions) provides a special and uniquely compelling motive for submission to state B is an important insight of Augustine; hope for the coming kingdom of God should hearten the Christian to submit to the public interest when this conflicts with her own immediate interest or that of her class or group. On the other hand, the distinction between state A and state B provides the rationale for possible Christian sponsorship of revolution to an extent that would by no means have been countenanced by Augustine himself, or indeed by Calvin, his close disciple in this as in so many other respects. There is a very great difference between struggle against injustice as such, which may be undertaken by a person whether she is a victim or not, and mere retaliation for actual or imagined injury received. Augustine is clearly right that the latter sort of behaviour is always wrong for the Christians, but his arguments do not touch the former. One may conclude that, so far as an actual state partakes of the nature of state A rather than state B, the Church ought to provide support for efforts to change it, perhaps in extreme cases even giving her reluctant and conditional sanction to violence.

III.

They say that one who sups with the devil had better use a long spoon. The crucial question about the proper relation of Church and state, it may be said, is how long a spoon the Church needs to use when it sups with the state. Too close a proximity leads to one set of abuses; too great a remoteness to another. The Church has to proclaim the kingdom of God in word and deed and must resist any encroachment of the state which prevents her from doing so—hence the necessity for independence. However, one aspect at least of her proclamation is to remind the state how far its policies and enactments fail to conform to the ideal of the just and happy society, which is one aspect of the kingdom of God; hence, the necessity for close involvement in the state.

What have Christians to contribute to knowledge of this political ideal of the just and happy society? My impression—perhaps this is a hard saying—is that they have no special *knowledge* of what such a just and happy society would amount to in detail, or of the means by which it might be realized. What they do have to contribute is a special *motive*. As Luther brought out with incomparable force, since the life of Christians is hid with Christ in God, they have the heart as well as the obligation to devote their lives to the good of their neighbour, and the good of one's neighbour consists very largely of the implementation of the social and political ideal of which I have spoken. How are we to go about finding the nature of this ideal and the means by which it might be achieved? The answer to this question is at once rather obvious and rather obscure. It is obvious, in that everyone has some sense of what it is to be fulfilled and happy, as opposed to frustrated and miserable, and also of what is fair and just, as opposed to unfair and unjust. A good state is nothing other than a state which promotes happiness and fairness so far as possible. The business of ethical theory is to clarify and mutually adjust our intuitions about what is good and right and so about happiness and fairness; the business of political theory, to apply its results to society and the state and to the good and evil to which they are prone. The obscurity of our problem is due partly to the real difficulty of reconciling the different elements of the social and political good and partly to the ingrained human tendency to prefer the indulgence of moral outrage to the facing of intractable problems. It is much more satisfying, and gratifying to one's self-esteem, to blame on the folly and knavery of others the persistent failure of utopia to arrive than to attend to the actual circumstances which prevent it from doing so.

On the question of what actual or possible states are good, political philosophers are the experts. The results of looking at recent work on the subject are not, however, wholly encouraging. While "emotivism" and "prescriptivism" reigned in ethics[30] — to call something good or bad was essentially not to describe it but to evince a positive or negative emotion towards it and to get people to act in a certain way in relation to it — there was not much reason to expect enlightenment from political philosophers about what kinds of states or societies were really better or worse than others. In that "heyday of Weldonism,"[31] the business of the political philosopher was thought to be nothing more (or less) than to analyze the vocabulary of politics, to set out precisely the way in which political terms and expressions are in fact used. While this might be useful as far as it went — as a "first word" if not a "last word" on the treatment of political problems — it can hardly by itself provide a solution to the crucial problem which concerns us of what kinds of states and political policies are good or bad and why they are so.

Where a rational political theory, with specific conclusions and recommendations derived from first principles, is lacking, there is a natural tendency for the perplexed to grab whatever offers itself. What has most conspicuously offered itself in recent times is Marxism. Marxism very properly appeals to a sense of justice which is almost universal, to the effect that it is obviously wrong that the few should enjoy the good things of life while the many have to work long hours in unpleasant conditions in order to produce them. It has, in its theory of ideology, an interesting and quite largely sound account of the manner in which the economic status of human individuals and groups may dominate the manner in which they think about the natural and social world and their place within it. It gives shape to life and a direction for moral effort, while not, at first sight at least, demanding a faith which goes beyond or even opposes reason. It affirms an optimism about human nature which can seem refreshing and liberating against the background of more austere religious views and has a plausible account of the sources of the human selfishness and perversity with which religions have been preoccupied. What is much more morally questionable, it effectively discharges human impulses to self-righteousness and aggression towards others of their kind; the enemy (the capitalist) is clearly identified and the member of the righteous (communist) group need not be unduly afflicted by self-doubt. It is perhaps no wonder that, stung by the Marxist gibe that they are essentially sponsors of oppression and reaction, some Christian groups have been tempted to take over lock, stock, and barrel the Marxist account of community and society. After all, it is difficult not to agree with Berdyaev's judgment that the notion that pure capitalism, with its rampant and crying exploitation and injustice, is more Christian than Marxism with its championship of the poor and oppressed is so absurd as not to be worth a moment's serious consideration.

However important its contributions may prove to be to that knowledge and implementation of the social and political ideal which we may hope to achieve in the future, it is by no means obvious that Marxism is without its defects even as a socio-political doctrine when one abstracts from its consequences for religion. It is not entirely clear at the present time that the "dictatorship of the proletariat," in countries which have had their revolution, has brought significantly nearer the "withering-away of the state" prophesied by Engels, or the classless society supposed to ensue from this. Indeed, there seems to have been a clear tendency recently for leading Marxist states to adulterate the purity of their doctrine with concessions to capitalist notions of private enterprise and the beneficent operation of market forces. The devout Marxist is liable to protest that one country after another has betrayed the revolution; however, when there have been more than a certain number of failures in a doctor's treatment one may not unreasonably wonder whether it was perhaps the treatment rather than the patients which was at fault.[32]

Faced with ethical subjectivism and relativism on the one hand and the inadequacies of Marxist dogmatism on the other, one might well despair of secular assessments of the social and political good. I think, however, that such despair would be premature. The notions of happiness and fairness which, as I have argued, are at the base of our political ideals, are nicely caught respectively by the utilitarianism of Jeremy Bentham and J. S. Mill and by the universalizability criterion sponsored by Immanuel Kant.[33] Where each party falls short, I think, is in failing properly to take into account the aspect of the matter which is emphasized by the other. Mill thought that the principle of justice could be inferred from that of the greatest happiness of the greatest number; Kant held that if justice, as formulated in the principle of universalizability, was the basic criterion, the matter of happiness could be left to look after itself. The arguments against the obvious thesis, that a political system is good so far as it promotes human happiness while not impugning fairness, though they have enjoyed considerable vogue in philosophy during the last few decades, will not stand up to examination.[34]   A virtually necessary component of human happiness is a certain freedom of maneuver, to work out what is best to do and to decide to do it, both in particular situations and in the overall course of one's life.   The really serious problem in politics, both practical and theoretical, it seems to me, is not with articulation of the basic ideals. Everyone agrees, implicitly if not explicitly, that the happiness which includes freedom is intrinsically desirable and that fairness is so as well. The problem is how the realization of the one ideal is to be reconciled with that of the other.   The tendency of the political left is to assume that if fairness is assured, the problem of freedom can be left to look after itself; the right is apt to stress the freedom, at least of some few people, to such a degree that fairness drops out of sight.   It appears to me that the beginning of wisdom in political thought, and so in Christian assessments of the state, is to realize how far the reconciliation of these two ideals constitutes a perennial problem.

Many examples could be mentioned of the difficulty, of which I will take two more or less at random. Almost everyone agrees that it is deplorable that some people should beat and starve the children under their care.   But how can they be prevented from doing so without an intolerable degree of interference with family life by police and social workers and without an excessive proportion of the resources of the state being devoted to the salaries of these officials? Again, most people agree that parents should have some freedom of choice as to how their children are educated, which would seem to entail that they should have the option of sending them to private schools rather than those run by the state.   Is this now, however, bound soon to lead to inequitable class divisions within society, the children of rich and thrifty parents being unfairly advantaged over those of the poor or feckless?

The Marxist solution to this problem is that it is an inevitable feature of some political and economic systems but will disappear when these are replaced, as they certainly will be in the long run, by another more satisfactory one. Under the capitalist state, affairs are conducted exclusively for the benefit of the bourgeois few, and the proletarian many are oppressed. Under the socialist state, in the immediate aftermath of revolution, they are conducted for the benefit of the proletarian majority, and the bourgeois oppressors are in their turn oppressed.   When communism finally arrives, there will be no more state, since coercion of one individual or group by another will no longer even seem to be to anyone's advantage when each is spontaneously acting for the good of all, and all for the good of each.   It appears to me that this account of the matter greatly underestimates the stability of human predispositions over changes in economy and society.[35]   But at least Christians should sympathize with Marxists to the extent of looking forward to and striving for a political system in which the uncharitable and anti-social predispositions of the old Adam are minimized rather than exacerbated by the environment, as they seem to be in a situation of unrestrained capitalism.

Among recent authors who have reflected on our problem, two deserve special mention. It seems to me that Robert Nozick, with his advocacy of a "minimal state," confined to protecting its subjects against force, theft, and fraud and to the enforcement of contracts, definitely upsets the balance of fairness and freedom in favour of freedom against fairness. If the relief of the needy and unfortunate is to be managed entirely by voluntary charity, and is not to be the province of the state with its powers of coercion, it will be managed at best very inadequately; few inductive arguments based on the course of human history can surely be more soundly based than that. Yet we have to attend very carefully to Nozick's powerful arguments to the effect that a state which has a more extensive mandate will necessarily come to violate basic rights of individuals.[36]

In contrast to Nozick, John Rawls is particularly impressive in his facing of the problem of how individual and collective interests are to be balanced against one another and in his proposed solution to it. There is, he points out, a certain identity of interest which prevails within communities, since co-operation makes possible a better life for each individual than she could achieve if left entirely to her own resources. However, there is a conflict, too, since persons will hardly be indifferent to whether they get a greater or lesser share of the benefits produced by collaboration.[37] One cannot expect a rational person to accept loss for herself just in order to bring about a greater overall degree of satisfaction in society.[38] (It is failure to take this point into account which is, as Rawls sees it, the central defect of classical utilitarianism.)

To determine the principles of justice in these conditions, Rawls proposes that they should be conceived as chosen by rational persons behind a "veil of ignorance," which would ensure that the natural chance or social circumstances which affect each individual in different ways would not influence her choice.[39] A rich person, for example, would find it to her advantage not to live in a society which imposed taxation to pay for social welfare, whereas a poor person would find just the opposite; so from behind a veil of ignorance, one does not know if one is to be rich or poor.[40] Rawls maintains that rational persons behind a veil of ignorance would choose two principles, one assigning equality in basic rights and duties, the other affirming social and economic inequalities to be just only if they issue in compensatory benefits to all, particularly the least advantaged.[41] "All social values — liberty and opportunity, income and wealth, and the bases of self-respect — are to be distributed equally unless an unequal distribution of any, or all, of these values is to everyone's advantage. Injustice, then, is simply inequalities that are not to the benefit of all."[42] If a society which was just in a Rawlsian sense, the greater expectations permitted to entrepreneurs would encourage them to take risks which, if they came off, would raise the long-term prospects of persons in the labouring class.[43]

The trouble with many social and political programmes is that they set their sights so high as inevitably to break down sooner or later under the pressure of human nature; those whose hearts are larger than their heads may press for policies without working out their probably long-term consequences. Rawls's ideals impress by their sobriety and by the fact that they seem at once to meet our basic intuitions and to confront fundamental political and social dilemmas. Is it not proper, for example, that a brain surgeon, with her enormously difficult and laboriously acquired skill, which is furthermore of the greatest use to the community, should have social and financial rewards greater than those of a crossing-sweeper? Yet it is equally proper, indeed more so, that the crossing-sweeper should earn enough to feed and clothe herself and her children, and also, perhaps, that her children should have equal opportunities for good health and education as compared with those of the brain surgeon.

The resolution of such problems and dilemmas is at once difficult and urgent; there are aspects of the game of politics which are not only intellectually and morally degrading in themselves, but very dangerous as tending to divert the mind from them. A few weeks ago, there was dropped into my mailbox a pamphlet on behalf of one of our political parties which described a leading politician of an opposing party as though he were criminally insane. Now this politician may have his defects as a public or private person, as some of the rest of us do; criminally insane he certainly is not and it does no good whatever to speak of him as if he were so. We too easily accept such speech as part of the game of politics, and I suggest that the Church, which has a mandate to keep in mind the long-term public good, has a special duty at the present time to combat this almost universally accepted evil.

As has been pointed out by Peregrine Worsthorne, there are many contemporary social and political problems which urgently need solution, but the solution to which is known by nobody; all of them are rendered the more difficult of solution by the comfortable expedient of blaming their existence on the folly or knavery of our political opponents. How is the bulk of industrial work to be made sufficiently interesting to fire the workers' enthusiasm? How is inflation to be controlled without the bringing about of even worse social evils than are brought about by failure to control it? How are we to hit off the balance between industrial growth and the preservation of nature? How is one to cope with the exacerbation of age-old inter-racial human antipathies by the possibilities of worldwide travel? And so on and so on. "Because the human imagination is so clouded with agitational ideologies, which prevent a clear perception of the intractability of these questions, and no seer or prophet has yet found the clarity of vision capable of dispelling them, there they remain, preventing the light of reason from ever breaking through."[44]

It is sometimes felt that the complexity of contemporary political and social problems is such that they can only be left to experts, and that the Church consequently has no useful say in these matters. At this rate, the Church must be reduced either to silence, or to the propounding of ineffective moral *clichés* about the most urgent questions that confront humanity. But the fact is that people are inclined to forget the most elementary moral principles when preoccupied with details of economic or political policy. Whatever political party one belongs to, one should not countenance the poor taking more than their share of the tax burden, and it was salutary for the Canadian bishops a few years ago to draw attention to evidence that they were doing so. Again, to be prepared to blow millions of one's fellow human beings to smithereens, and irrevocably to pollute vast tracts of the planet while one is about it, is hardly a morally tolerable position; it did no harm for the American Catholic hierarchy to remind us recently of this.

IV.

Christians have been told to "hunger and thirst for righteousness' sake";[45] one important aspect of this should be acknowledging and facing frankly the balance of virtual incompatibles which is justice in the political order. It has been said, I believe rightly, that "it is not propaganda and it is not argument but religious faith that will deliver human reasonableness from its ideological prisons."[46] The point of this remark, which would seem almost insanely paradoxical in some quarters (do not some people *know* that religion is of the very essence of the ideological?), is simply that the believer, relying on the hope that she has in God will be the more likely to gain the courage to try to envisage what is true and to implement what is good at all hazards in spite of the enormous pressure exerted by worldly desires and fears and by the prejudices due to her upbringing, her class position, and so on. I have said that the ideal society maximizes happiness without sacrificing fairness and that an essential element in happiness is a degree of freedom. The ideology of the right is apt to emphasize freedom at the expense of fairness and pillories the left for its tendency to neglect freedom, whereas the ideology of the left has exactly the opposite characteristic. The arduous labour of clearly and distinctly conceiving, and them of implementing, the conditions of a just and happy society, is not helped, indeed it is greatly impeded, by the mutually opposed demonologies of the extremists. Each is determined not to take into account the viewpoint of the other and is too apt to blame the delay of utopia on its folly and knavery.

I believe it is one special vocation of the Church to ensure that both sides be listened to and that the real difficulties of articulating in detail, let alone of achieving, the political ideal of the just and happy society be taken into account. This requires a nice combination of detachment and commitment, perhaps anticipated by what may seem to be the inconsistent attitudes of Menno Simons. Unless the Marxists and anarchists are right in this matter, and I see no reason to believe that they are, a political authority will always have to have some resort to coercion, if not actually to bloodshed. The Christian has to try to ensure, whether by criticism from without or by action from within the political apparatus, that such resort is minimal and that it is always for the public good rather than in the private interest of powerful individuals or groups. Here we have to learn from Hübmaier's drawing of attention to the special motives which should influence the Christian politician or legislator. A political arrangement which is at once beneficient and clear-sighted must take into account human nature as it is, fallen in Adam yet redeemed in Christ, without uncritical deference either to the determined pessimism characteristic of some ideologies or the excessive optimism of others. If we are now too apt to assume that human beings when left to themselves are invariably or even usually altruistic and co-operative, Calvin's austere vision can help to provide us with the necessary corrective.

Appendix

As a Catholic contributing to such a conference as this, I can hardly sign off without saying a word on baptism as a sacrament. My initial prejudice on the matter is to the effect that either baptism and the eucharist are to be taken seriously as rites through which God confers grace, which is essentially the Catholic view, or they degenerate into pious habit or venerable folklore. I was glad that Dr. West recognized the essentially Catholic character of at least one standard Protestant view.

A word seems in place on the much-misunderstood Catholic doctrine that the sacraments function *ex opere operato*. This doctrine preserves rather than impugns the sovereignty of God, amounting as it does to the claim that God will infallibly confer grace through the rite when it is performed under the specified conditions, regardless of the worthiness of the minister. As Augustine rightly declared against the Donatists who denied the validity of sacraments received at the hands of those who had renounced their faith in face of persecution, the actual giver of grace through the sacraments is Christ himself and the human being who administers them is merely his more or less unworthy instrument.

Karl Rahner has made the profound suggestion that a great deal of harm is done by assuming that infant baptism is a paradigm rather than a limiting case of a sacrament. In infant baptism, obviously, something is *done to* the recipient without her doing anything on her own account. It appears to me — I have much sympathy with the position of Karl Barth and the Anabaptist tradition on the matter — that this practice is tolerable only when confirmation is bestowed strictly on the adult who demands it for herself. Of course, the view condemned by Rahner has prevailed in the churches in such a way as to encourage early confirmation (here Catholics seem in general worse offenders than Protestants). The underlying assumption is that it is better to get both baptism and confirmation *done to* a person before she is in a position to think and act for herself when she might decline the privilege. (I am delighted to find myself in agreement with Dr. Stackhouse on this matter.)

In paradigm cases of sacraments (adult baptism, adult reception the eucharist), the attitude of the recipient is of the essence. As the Thomists (in this matter opposed by the Scotists) say of the sacrament of penance, the penitence of the one who receives it, her real desire to amend her life, constitutes the *matter* of this sacrament; in other words, it is an essential part rather than a mere desirable concomitant of it. (This is obviously a specifically Catholic example but it seems to have application to rites which Protestants would regard as genuine sacraments.)

I believe that the point of Karl Barth's famous or notorious attitude to sacraments is to emphasize that it is the gracious action of Jesus Christ alone which is at issue in baptism and the eucharist; so soon as they appear to gain some significance independently of him, they are just blasphemous travesties. It is this, I suggest, that we have primarily to learn from the attitude to this matter of the original Reformers. I do not think that, when Barth refused to speak the sacraments in the way traditional among Lutheran and Reformed, let alone among Catholic, Christians, the great theologian chose the best way of making his point.

Notes

1. "Is there any maxim in politics more certain and infallible, than that both the number and authority of priests should be confined within very narrow limits, and that the civil magistrate ought, forever, to keep his *fasces* and *axes* from such dangerous hands?" David Hume, *Dialogues Concerning Natural Religion*, XII; *Hume Selections*, Charles W. Hendel, Jr., ed. (New York: Charles Scribner's Sons, 1955), p. 395.
2. Matthew 5:13.
3. Perhaps the clearest and most telling exposition of this view is to be found in Luther's *On the Liberty of the Christian*. Of course, the writing of this pamphlet antedated the Peasants' War by several years.
4. See E. Gilson, *The Christian Philosophy of Saint Augustine* (London: Gollancz, 1961), p. 172. I am heavily indebted to this work for this paragraph and the following three.
5. Augustine, *Enarr. in Ps.* 64.2; *The City of God* (CG in subsequent notes) XIV, 28.
6. CG XIX, 12.1.
7. Gilson, *The Christian Philosophy*, p. 173.
8. CG XIX,13.2.
9. CG XIX,12.2. Gilson, *The Christian Philosophy*, p. 174.
10. CG XIX,17; Gilson, *The Christian Philosophy*, p. 182.
11. CG XIX,23.5. Gilson, *The Christian Philosophy*, p. 174.
12. Gilson, *The Christian Philosophy*, p. 175.
13. CG XIX,26.
14. CG XIX,17; Gilson, *The Christian Philosophy*, p. 176. This distinction between use and enjoyment is fundamental to Augustine's ethics. Most Christian authorities have conceded that we are not only entitled to enjoy material things in moderation, but that we ought to do so. Even Calvin, who is no hedonist, remarks that God, in creating the world, has provided not only what is

necessary to our life, but also for our comfort and delight (*Institute* III,X.2). And Thomas Aquinas declares roundly that "a man cannot lead a reasonable life if he avoids all pleasure," and is apt in these circumstances to be "boorish and ungracious." (*Summa Theologica* IIa IIae 142.1).

15. *De bono conj.*, 14, 16; *The Christian Philosophy*, p. 177.
16. Gilson, *The Christian Philosophy*, pp. 330-31.
17. *De lib. arb.* I,15.
18. Gilson, *The Christian Philosophy*, p. 178.
19. *Epist.* 138.2.12-15. Gilson, *The Christian Philosophy*.
20. One may compare the case of Russian dissidents in recent times, who have upbraided the Soviet government for failing to abide by the principles of its own constitution.
21. Mark 12:17 and parallels.
22. CG XIX,4.5; 26.
23. *Epist.* 185.2.8; Gilson, *The Christian Philosophy*, p. 179.
24. Cf. *Epist.* 93. 1,2; 2.8; 5.16; 5.17.
25. Gilson, *The Christian Philosophy*, p. 180.
26. Gilson, *The Christian Philosophy*, p. 182.
27. Cf. Matthew 25:37-38.
28. In conversation.
29. See Hugo Meynell, *Freud, Marx and Morals* (New York: Barnes and Noble, 1981), p. 91.
30. For emotivism, cf. A. J. Ayer, *Language, Truth and Logic* (New York: Dover Publications, n.d.), chapter 6; for prescriptivism, R. M. Hare, *The Language of Morals* (New York: Oxford University Press, 1964).
31. The central contention of T. D. Weldon's *Vocabulary of Politics* (Harmondsworth: Penguin Books, 1953) has been summarized by Anthony Quinton as follows: "There really is no such subject as political philosophy apart from the negative business of revealing the conceptual errors and methodological misunderstandings of those who have addressed themselves in a very general way to political issues." *Political Philosophy*, ed. A. Quinton (London: Oxford University Press, 1967), p. 2.
32. On the merits and defects of Marxism, and what can be salvaged from it, see Meynell, *Freud*, chapters 4 and 7.
33. The classical expositions are: J. S. Mill, *Utilitarianism* (New York: Dutton, 1964); and I. Kant, *Groundwork of the Metaphysics of Morals*, translated under the title *The Moral Law* by H. J. Paton (New York: Harper Torchbooks, 1964).
34. What underlies this claim is the contention that to call anything good is not a matter of describing it, but rather of commending it or evincing a positive attitude towards it. For a refutation of this view, cf. Meynell, *Freud*, chapter 6.
35. See Meynell, *Freud*, pp. 80, 101-102, 178-79.
36. Robert Nozick, *Anarchy, State and Utopia* (New York: Basic Books, 1974).
37. John Rawls, *A Theory of Justice* (Cambridge, Mass.: Harvard University Press, 1971), p. 4.
38. Rawls, *Theory*, p. 14.

39.   Rawls, *Theory*, p. 12.
40.   Rawls, *Theory*, pp. 18-19.
41.   Rawls, *Theory*, pp. 14-15.
42.   Rawls, *Theory*, p. 73.
43.   Rawls, *Theory*, p. 78.
44.   In the London *Sunday Telegraph*, quoted in *Encounter*, April 1979, pp. 12-13.
45.   Matthew 5:6.
46.   B. Lonergan, *Method in Theology* (London: Darton, Longman and Todd, 1972), p. 117.

Chapter IX

THE STATE AND PEACE:
A SOCIOLOGIST'S RESPONSE

Harry H. Hiller

As a sociologist, my comments are restricted to the matter of Church and state, and the issue of war and peace, since it is clear that the societal implications of theological positions on these particular items are especially significant.

I. Church and State

The notion of inter-church dialogue suggests that there is some common ground which the groups engaging in dialogue possess. The danger in searching for this common ground is that we can ignore some basic sociological principles.

As a careful exegesis of the writings of John Calvin, the paper by Professor Nicol points out the disagreements Calvin had with Anabaptist reformers. We learn about the ideals and thinking of one man who was clearly influential. What we do not learn is what impact these ideas had on people in terms of actual Church-state relations either in Switzerland or elsewhere, or how his ideas were adapted by people in the press of daily living. Sociologists are always skeptical about accepting theological ideals as expressing reality in practice. Furthermore, ever since Max Weber's classic study, we are alerted to the totally different meaning which ideals and teachings may have in everyday life. Weber pointed out that an unexpected consequence of Calvin's teaching of the doctrine of predestination was the production of insecurity and anxiety in the life of the believers about their election, to which pastoral advice was to encourage parishioners to prove they were one of the elect through intense and dedicated worldly activity. What is critical, then, is not just to examine the teachings, but to determine how people responded to them and interpreted them at the grass roots.

The first principle in dialogue, then, is not just to study the teachings, official doctrines, or confessional statements, but to examine how these teachings are operationalized in local churches and how they are interpreted by local believers. While I would argue that the official position of a church body has always been at some variance with ideas held and practices carried out at the grass roots, those issues are even more timely in the contemporary era, when individual opinions vary widely within church communions. Witness the official Catholic position on birth control and the actual practice of Catholics. How much more is this a critical issue in churches with more congregational forms of government as opposed to a hierarchical system. So my first point is that even when it comes to Church-state relations, we must distinguish between the official model and grass roots thinking.

My second point is that we often assume a homogeneity within a church tradition that is seldom there. Ever since Ernst Troeltsch proposed his Church-sect typology, we have been aware that there exists within the Gospel an inherent tension between a churchly style embracing the world and a sectarian style of withdrawing from or being different from the world. Troeltsch argued that this tension was inherent in Christianity. Sociologists have discovered that how one resolves this tension may be related to social class, ethnicity, the possession of power or alienation from power, worldview and personal taste, and finally, personal conviction. This means that rather than view church traditions and doctrines as a monolithic entity possessing relative uniformity, we can expect considerable difference in theological worldview from local church to local church, dependent on the makeup of the local congregation and the worldview of its pastor. Churches in an inner city community and consisting of mostly lower class persons frequently see the state much differently from churches in middle-class suburbs — even in the same denomination.

Differences, then, *within* church families may be almost as great as differences *between* them. What I read in these papers is a tendency to overlook these internal differences, for the sake of dialogue between the two groups, and to neglect the internal diversity which is clearly an important characteristic of religion in the modern world. In other words, it is not so much the seminal differences *between* Reformed and Mennonites which need to be considered but differences *within* these two groups. Historic positions may even be relatively unimportant as local congregations deal with contemporary realities in their own way. Dr. Howard Loewen provides some evidence on this point with regard to Mennonites, but much more needs to be made into a continuum whereby we discover differences between local congregations and individuals within them on these points, *within* both religious traditions, rather than assume the differences are only *between* the two groups.

The third point that a sociologist should make is that there is a need to do cross-cultural research comparing practices and conditions pertaining to Church and state within both religious communities. The objective should be to try to understand what national/cultural circumstances contribute to differences in theological worldview. Attitudes towards Church and state vary greatly from country to country in many denominations. We have only to begin with Canada and the United States to note that the separation of Church and state is a hallowed theme staunchly reiterated by many Protestant groups in the United States, but seldom heard in Canada, to know that cultural context does make a difference. Furthermore, it is not just political and cultural context that may vary but the nature of political regimes and the religious affiliations of the population that may make a difference. A church operating in a predominantly Muslim country may see the state much differently (perhaps preferring passive withdrawal) than one operating in North America, where the group has an established presence and lobbying agencies in Washington and Ottawa. Or, churches operating in South Africa, Nicaragua, Poland, Great Britain, or Mozambique must each deal with very different political systems, which are likely to affect their views on Church and state. Again, the evidence is that we ought to be careful not to assume too much homogeneity within each of these two groups when differences from one cultural and national context to another are enormous.

Fourth, it is incumbent on a sociologist to point out that positions about Church and state are essentially positions expressing different views about power. I say this because the emphasis in the papers was that of description rather than explanation. We learn about differences that exist between Church and state, but an attempt also needs to be made to explain why these differences may exist. I prefer an explanatory model that points out where a group stands in relation to the locus of economic and political power. To a peasant group standing on the margins of society, it is difficult to talk about confronting or reforming the state—in fact, withdrawal seems the most viable course. To a group being persecuted by the state, it is difficult to obey political authority. To a group large enough to wield influence, it is much more possible to view the state as a protector or promoter of church interests. To a religious group closely linked to the state, it is much easier to view the state as an acceptable instrument to deal with theological deviants or heretics. In all of these instances, a theological position about Church and state is arrived at from the social context in which a group finds itself.

Thus it is not surprising to find that theologies of Church and state undergo modifications over time in response to changes in their advocates' position in the social structure. Nowhere is this more visible to us in Canada than to see the transformation of the Mennonite community from a rural-based community to an urban community of upwardly mobile well-educated members. In sum, a group's views about Church and state vary with the amount of power a religious group may feel within that society, as well as the level of individual power its members possess.

One final point needs to be made about the contemporary period where, particularly in the Western world, religious pluralism makes it difficult for any group to feel closely tied to the state. In fact, in a pluralist situation which insists on a secular state, all religious groups may find themselves more and more in opposition to the actions and policies of the state. Furthermore, congregations are increasingly divided over appropriate responses to actions of the state. When these factors are combined with the decline of what Peter Berger calls "product loyalty", leading to the phenomenon of "switching" between denominations as well as out of them, and increasing religious intermarriage, it becomes clear that while churches may have a doctrinal heritage about Church and state which is part of their historical tradition, ideas about Church and state are much less monolithic, more individually idiosyncratic, and changing with the issue at hand.

I am suggesting, then, that where congregational forms of government prevail, inter-church dialogue needs to be aware of the realities of the modern world, namely that there is enormous diversity beginning at the level of the individual, moving to the local church, and from nation to nation and culture to culture. All of these factors constrain the dialogue on which you have embarked.

II. War and Peace

Among the central characteristics of sectarianism are the emphases on fellowship and in-group solidarity, resistance to compromise, and rejection of dominant societal values and structures. Whatever institutions represent the dominant values of society, whether they be church, state, or even education and the economy, sectarians view with suspicion, distrust, and even disdain. Because the state is the instrument to uphold this structure, it is not surprising that the refusal to bear arms in the name of the state is sometimes resisted by closely knit, intensely committed sectarians. From this perspective, the refusal to bear arms is not primarily a commitment to the principle of the sanctity of life but a statement of rejection of the authority of the state and all that the state stands for. Why put one's own life at risk or take the life of another when one rejects the cause, the values, and the structures which are to be preserved by the battle? Pacificism, then, I am arguing, originated as a consequence of the act of rejection of society's values and structures. In contrast, the idea of a just or holy war is urged by those who feel that society's values and structures are worth defending. Putting one's own life or the lives of others on the line only makes sense if the current shape of society is viewed as inherently good or even superior to another.

This rather simplistic overview suggests why some religious groups were more likely to ally themselves with the state, and viewed the state as at least partially an instrument to support their own interests and objectives, while other groups at the margins of society, frequently rejected by society as well as themselves rejecting society, were totally unwilling to defend the state upholding that society. Thus, historically, one can easily see how differences between Reformed and Mennonites developed regarding war.

However, in the contemporary era, two significant changes have altered these two classic positions. In the first place, the position of Mennonites in society has been drastically altered. No longer rural peasants, but increasingly urban and well educated, Mennonites no longer exist on the margins of society as a powerless, persecuted minority. Howard Loewen's paper points out that it is primarily since the Second World War that the meaning of peace has been conceptually broadened to include an attitude toward life and not just towards war.

I would hypothesize that it is not coincidental that this change occurred when it did for Mennonites. As an increasingly urban people, Mennonites found themselves participating in the general societal changes experienced by all rural-urban migrants of the post-war period in North America, as post-secondary educational institutions boomed, professional and entrepreneurial skills developed, and both rural and urban prosperity abounded. Some have even argued that the "achievement orientation" of this new generation of Mennonites, in combination with a persistent clannishness, produced a group distinctiveness almost equivalent to another group with a history of persecution and high achievement orientation, namely, the Jews. The point is that social change, upward mobility, greater intellectual sophistication, and increasing prosperity have moved Mennonites away from the margins of society to active participation in society. As this shift has occurred, the classic sectarian position slowly eroded and the state was less likely to be viewed with hostility and more as a defender of their own interests. Thus, Loewen's important conclusion that Mennonites became more transformationist rather than separatist can be viewed as a product of their changing position in society.

I propose that the broadened concept of peace that emerged among Mennonites came to mean intense involvement in those activities that would make war unnecessary rather than just opposition to war itself. Feeding the hungry, reducing disparities in the Third World, and mediating conflict, even promoting strong families, all became concerted efforts not primarily of a social Gospel but a way of maintaining peace. Thus pacifism, as a way of rebelling against authority that sustained a society with which they could not identify, was transformed into peace activity that would preserve the best of the status quo (in which they had interests) and minimize conflict that could produce war at both the macro (international) level and micro (personal) level (but primarily the former). Nowhere is this changed view of the world clearer than in the work of the Mennonite Central Committee. The global work of this organization (which I highly respect), in my view, has not received sufficient attention in these papers, for it truly represents the changed socio-economic position of North American Mennonites and their changed attitude towards society.

The second change that has affected the two classic positions noted earlier is the growth of religious pluralism, not only in North America, but increasingly elsewhere as well. Even in countries with a state-supported church, there has been increasing toleration of religious diversity, individual choice, and even disaffiliation. The end result is that the state becomes more and more secular, putting all religious groups into a minority situation. These different religious groups may not be equal because of variations in size and influence, but, at the very least, the religious hegemony which had prompted alliances between church and state has disappeared. Many religious groups, then, including those that formerly possessed preferential status, find themselves at odds with state policies, and only one among many interest groups pressuring the state for policies which it favours. Thus, as Professor Stackhouse has pointed out, it is not unusual to find "forms of disengagement or opposition to society" within Reformed churches to policies of the state. Instead of the old, holy alliance of Church and state playing together in the same bed, now it is the new unholy alliance between economy and state in the same bed to which the Christian Gospel brings its challenge.

What I am arguing is that a pluralistic secular society reduces all churches to almost equal status, almost approaching a counterculture, where Christian values oppose materialist values when invoked to do so, where no religious group has more power than the other, and all attempt to influence the state as one of many pressure groups.

If this assessment is correct, Mennonites and Reformed have much reason to dialogue because they are increasingly both operating from a similar position. Since Mennonites have transformed peace from a position of anti-war to one of minimizing conflict in all its dimensions, and have become active participants in society; and in view of the fact that Reformed churches have in large measure been relieved of the obsession to control the state, preferring instead to challenge it from the outside to overthrow evil and defend the innocent, both groups have more in common than ever before. If the situation has changed for both groups, perhaps sufficient cynicism about the possibility of a just war exists in both groups, and a common commitment to the social, political, and psychological dimensions of peace is jointly shared. In that sense, it may now be appropriate to call both sides pacifist, using the broadened definition which has been outlined here.

Chapter X

A SYSTEMATIC THEOLOGIAN'S RESPONSE

Andrew D. MacRae

I. Church and State

In presenting his theological statement on Church and state, Professor Iain Nicol concentrates almost exclusively on the work of John Calvin. His comments on Calvin's antipathy to the Anabaptists gives the paper special point in the context of discussion with Mennonites. The intentional limitation of the paper to the work of John Calvin may give the impression of a unified body of Reformed thinking on the subject. That impression is neither intended nor real, however, since Reformed thought manifests significant deviations from the Calvinian position. Indeed, Professor Nicol draws attention to Karl Barth's divergence from the Scots Confession of 1560, which was firmly based on Calvin's views of the state's right to reform and restore the Church if it should fall to idolatry. On page 140 he cites Barth's insistence that "spiritual perversity must be overcome with spiritual force and not with political." Many other instances of Reformed divergence from Calvin's position might be noted, but my purpose is simply to take note of the limitations of the treatment of the subject matter, as the author clearly intends.

While Calvin's arguments on this subject are based on a biblical hermeneutic, the conclusions at which he arrives are more theologically dogmatic than biblically coherent. His tendency, perhaps excusable in a young man, to indulge in bitter polemic against his Anabaptist enemies, tends to be a sign of the weakness of his case, rather than the strength of his argument. To accuse his opponents of believing fables received from their grandmothers is no more than a cheap shot, even in Calvin's day, which casts more doubt on his own integrity than on theirs.

It is, perhaps, characteristic of some Reformed theologians to follow Calvin in extrapolating from certain biblical tenets conclusions which go beyond the legitimate implications of Scripture. Calvin's extension of the notion of civil authorities taking action against wrongdoers to an argument in favour of waging wars in defence of one's own country is simply not responsible exegetically, but is the insertion of nationalist sentiment into a passage designed simply to uphold, on theological grounds, the responsible rule of law.

Also, to illustrate the weakness of Calvin's biblical exegesis in the polemical areas of his theology, it is worth noticing, as the author reminds us, that he actually argues against a pacifist position on the grounds that John the Baptist did not demand that soldiers should lay down their arms. One might as well argue that the New Testament could not have been opposed to slavery or the letter to the Ephesians would never have urged slaves to be obedient to their masters.

Of course, we should note the validity of some of his protests against the Schleitheim Confession, in particular his legitimate complaint about the poor exegesis of the story of the woman taken in adultery. He took strong exception to the Anabaptists' opposition to Christians holding civil office, and argued against that particular kind of "separation of church and state."

However, it is clearly demonstrated that, when Calvin is arguing *for* the responsible roles of Church and state, civil and ecclesiastical authorities, he assumes a situation where the state recognizes, as clearly as the Church, that it operates its mandate under the Word of God to which it, like the Church, is subject. He sees the state, and civil authorities, as Divinely ordained, and therefore to be obeyed. While sin threatens to corrupt, Calvin argues for a common grace which produces in the human mind a sense of civic fairness and order. While he sees the state as a temporary expedient to sustain justice in a sinful world, under God, he opposes the Anabaptists as being, effectively, anarchist in their attitude to the state, and insists that Christians, far from withdrawing from the world and its civil governments, should use the civil order as a Divine gift to be used as part of our stewardship of life. In contrast to the Anabaptist view he attacks, he sees the state as responsible to defend, and even reform, the Church! Such a view would have been a totally unwarranted interference in the life of the Church for the Anabaptists.

Likewise, his view that the Church must call political authorities to obedience under God, in contrast to the alleged Anabaptist view of two separate kingdoms, one of God and the other of Satan, has clearly been foundational to some contemporary expressions of the Reformed movement, as in the case of modern Presbyterianism in the Church of Scotland, which insists, while taking the national name, that it is not a state church, but rather the conscience of the nation, calling it to account in matters spiritual, and on issues like human liberty and social justice, which, let it be said, it frequently does effectively, through pronouncements of its General Assembly. Calvin clearly saw the Christian role as transformationist in the life of society.

Accordingly, Calvin's insistence on the accountability of civil powers to God is expressed in his assertion that civil authority is the most sacred and honourable of all callings. This led him to attack the civil anarchy he saw in the Anabaptists, while also opposing with bitterness the spiritual authoritarianism he saw in the Papacy, usurping the God-appointed rule of civil authorities.

His arguments in favour of total obedience to the civil "powers that be" are fraught with difficulty, ranging from the insistence on patient endurance under bad government, to the possibility of passive, and even active, resistance in situations where God's name is not held in honour. He comes close to undermining his own premise about the sanctity of civil office by his attempt to adopt a middle-of-the-road position.

Calvin seems to struggle with the assumption that civil rulers recognize, as much as we, the rule of God, and the obligation to uphold his honour. His Anabaptist opponents, in their attempts to protect the honour of God, tended to withdraw from state involvement, and he despised them for it.

The reading of the paper by Dr. Harry Loewen is a salutary reminder of the inadequacy of Calvin's treatment of the Anabaptists. His tendency is to caricature them on the basis of the Schleitheim position of 1527. Loewen makes it very clear that there was a variety of views which is simply not reflected adequately in Calvin's tunnel-vision attack.

It is undoubtedly true that the Anabaptists largely withdrew from a hostile world into sectlike congregations, separated communities, which expressed the concept of the believers' Church in contrast to the much more inclusive church of the Calvinian position. Loewen goes so far as to write of Church-state relations as frequently rendering Christian participation in government impossible, since, although the state is established by God, its way of righting wrong, by the sword, is quite unacceptable to those who belong to the Prince of Peace. The most violent action the separatist Anabaptist position would allow in the Church was "the ban," or excommunication in the case of serious moral deviations.

Yet it should be noted that a wide variety of Anabaptist views on the relation of Church and state exists. The "Brotherly Union" statements of Schleitheim do not reflect anything like the universal Anabaptist position as a review of the positions of Hübmaier, Menno Simons, and others clearly shows.

Calvin does no justice to the variety of Anabaptist views, including those which recognized the legitimacy of Christian participation in civil government, but simply attacks the most extreme expression of Anabaptist thinking. If truth be told, the early Anabaptists were much more serious advocates of religious tolerance than was Calvin. He gives no recognition to Anabaptist respect for government but engages in bitter polemic because of their withdrawal.

Dr. Loewen's paper very adequately demonstrates the variety of views within the Anabaptist movement, from the Dordrecht Confession of 1632 to the contemporary Confessions of the Mennonite General Conference and the Mennonite Brethren Conference, with their respective resolutions of the Church-state dilemma.

It should be kept in mind that, behind all of the conflicting views between Calvin and the Anabaptists, there was a conflicting ecclesiology, that of John Calvin being inclusive, a "both-and" ecclesiology which at least made room for believers and not-yet believers, and that of the Anabaptists which was an "either-or" ecclesiology, insisting that the true Church is made up of believers only, and excludes all who are not true believers.

In attempting to relate the implications of the two papers, the first of which is a treatment of a very limited Reformed position and the second of which is a highly representative demonstration of the rich variety of Anabaptist thought, it is clear to me that the polemical spirit of the sixteenth century has, in large measure, given way to the more appropriate agreement to allow for diversity without the denunciation or castigation of divergent theological positions.

Dialogue between these two historic theological traditions is of the greatest importance for the enhancement of Christian understanding and the effectiveness of the church within the state.

The Reformed position has much to commend it in terms of its positive affirmation of the sovereignty of God over all of life, personal, social, moral, and political. It is a salutary reminder to the believers' Church position that separation from civil power and the eschewing of civic responsibility does nothing to increase the penetration of human society by the kingdom of heaven, which "is like yeast that a woman took and mixed into a large amount of flour until it worked all through the dough" (Matthew 13:33, N.I.V.)

The Mennonite presentation is a very powerful contemporary reminder of the ways in which Mennonites are resolving their own struggle between those who have advocated non-involvement in government and secular society and those who have advocated selective participation by the increasingly active involvement in municipal, provincial, and federal levels of government.

Possible Convergence
Let me suggest three areas where, from the presentations before us, I see potential for theological convergence. These possibilities exist, in my view, because of the basically Reformed theology they share and because of the dynamic changes taking place within the Mennonite movement as part of its spiritual and social development.

1. Their Understanding of the State
Loewen indicates two major attitudes within Anabaptist thought: "the one which generally followed Schleitheim stressed withdrawal and non-involvement in matters of secular society and the state; the other, while most sympathetic to the Swiss position, stressed what might be called selective participation and involvement in matters of government."

He points out that, under pressure from governments and society, the Anabaptist leaders backed away from radical reform into withdrawal from the hostility of the world and became sectarian. Clearly, however, despite the conservatism of Schleitheim, the Anabaptists, such as Hübmaier, recognized the divine establishment of the state.

Of course, the Reformed position recognized, from the beginning, that God is at work in both Church and state, and Calvin taught that both were obligated to live under the rule of God. So Christians were seen to belong to both societies, the divine and the earthly.

While the idea of two opposed kingdoms is generally rejected, the twofold government, spiritual and civil, is acknowledged. While the Reformers saw the state as a transitory and provisional establishment, they saw it, nonetheless, as divinely established.

Calvin's willingness for the state to have a part in reforming the Church is problematical, but has a partial counterpart in Mennonite thinking which accepted the ordering of God in the state and the Christian's obligation to be submissive to it. It seems clear to me that there is ground here for constructive discussion.

2. Their Concepts of the Church's Role
While Reformed and Mennonite Christians differ on the nature of the Church, Mennonite hesitancy about involvement with the state has altered significantly in recent years, indicating a communion intent on applying its faith to the real world. Although as prominent a Mennonite

scholar as John Howard Yoder questions how long a Christian might survive in politics, he does not resist participation. In Canada, John Redekop, a Mennonite political scientist, has become one of the clearest and most convincing Christian voices on matters of Christian involvement in the life of the state.

Professor Nicol very clearly states the Reformed position as first, to pray for those with political power, second, to call political authorities to obedience under God, and third, to be a prophetic voice calling the state to give special attention to the needs of the poor and the powerless.

Although the Reformed churches have tended, historically, to accept a closer relationship to the states in which they exist than Mennonites, who experienced rejection and opposition in the early years of their witness, I see a distinct possibility of real advance in the contemporary context in the development of a shared position built around the idea of the Church's prophetic role in the nation and the world.

3. Their View of Civic Responsibility

Both have a high view of Christian responsibility to and within the state. Mennonites, however, have been known as pacifist, while the Reformed churches are frequently somewhat nationalistic in their loyalty, and nationalism does not sit very well with pacifism in times of international tension.

However, committed as they are to a pacifist position, Mennonites, who recognize the need for patience and restraint in times of national difficulty, also acknowledge the legitimacy of passive, and even active, but not violent, resistance where the divine honour seems to be at stake.

I take the risk of suggesting that there is a real challenge to Reformed Christians to find ways of being identified as distinctively Christian in the context of their state and political settings rather than being recognized, as they sometimes are, by their state identity more than by their distinctiveness as the people of God.

Likewise, I see a real challenge to Mennonites to find ways of maintaining a pietism appropriate to the discipline of a believers' Church, without abandonment or neglect of the Christian roles of being salt and light in the world for which Christ died.

Possible Convergence

Perhaps, at this juncture, both parties to this consultation may be able to commit themselves to the following propositions, or, at least, to their serious consideration. I take the risk of advancing them as having a legitimate place on their joint agenda for working out a dynamic and distinctive contribution to the understanding of Church and state.

1. The Church is part of God's divine plan for bringing the redemption which is in Christ to the world.

2. The Church is, in all spiritual matters, subject only to God, through Christ, the head of the Church.

3. The Church is intended by God to be a responsible part of human society, and, therefore, a positive contributor to the welfare of the state in which it is placed at any given time.

4. The Church is not to seek to dominate human society, but to be a prophetic voice within it, bringing to bear on the life of the state the divine word and authority under which every human institution is established.

5. The Church is not to be identified with the state in such a way that it is subservient to the state, but must, at all times, accept that God may, in his wisdom, use such influences as the state to challenge the church to be reformed. If, as most Reformed Christians believe, the church is *"semper reformanda,"* such a conclusion should not be either surprising or unpalatable.

6. The state exists under the hand of God and is obligated to honour him. While the emergence of the consciously secular state challenges such a view, the Church, while not entitled to control the state, is bound to insist on the state's existence as being conditional upon the divine appointment, and therefore, under divine authority.

7. While the state may legitimately make the same demands upon Christian citizens as it does upon all its other citizens, it has no inherent right to challenge the Church's primary loyalty to God, nor any proper role in demanding the compromise of that loyalty to meet the arbitrary demands of a society which itself exists only with the divine permission.

8. The state exists, under God, for the right ordering of society, and for the maintenance of that order against all lawlessness which disrupts or denies the welfare of the community at large.

9.   The state's right to order human society always carries the overriding obligation to recognize and uphold individual human rights, including political and religious liberty.

II. Baptism

I acknowledge with appreciation the contributions both of Dr. West from a Reformed and covenantal perspective and of Dr. Miller from a Reformed and Mennonite perspective. The common ground is that both speak from a Reformed perspective. Although deep divergences exist, especially in matters of ecclesiology and, in particular, the nature of the Church, it is clear to me that both presentations may equally claim to be written from a Reformed perspective. The implication of that may be that some are more Reformed than others, but that is another issue.

Although my own theological training was predominantly in the context of Reformed theology, albeit with a strongly Barthian emphasis, I confess to having some real theological concerns about the presentation by Dr. West. I greatly appreciate the personal reflections with which the paper begins and ends which indicate clearly the writer's stance and which provide a personal rationale for that stance.

He is right to recognize a high degree of Calvinism among Baptists as well as among Presbyterians. I believe he fails to recognize the seriousness with which such Baptists take the divine initiative in salvation, and makes an assumption common among Reformed theologians that the believers' Church subjectivizes the Gospel and the church too much, to the point of making human response more significant than the Divine grace. Such a conclusion is hard to justify from a careful examination of the writings of advocates of the believers' Church. It simply cannot be sustained from a reading of Dr. Miller's presentation.

It is of considerable interest to me that the paper opens with a question from the Heidelberg Catechism, which states that "faith alone makes us share in Christ and all his benefits," and of which faith that Confession states, "The Holy Spirit creates it in our hearts by the preaching of the Holy Gospel and confirms it by the use of the Holy Sacraments." This is the more interesting in the light of later affirmations about infant baptism which is legitimized "in the context of the salvific life of the church" a position which is somewhat at a distance from the Heidelberg statement.

Understandably, I do not share his ambivalence as to the clarity with which the New Testament implies that baptism is a rite appropriate to conscious believers and that its form of administration was by immersion. If the Reformed churches of a pedobaptist variety are really to do justice to the understanding represented in a significant part of Mennonite life, they must do something with the very plain descriptions of baptism in the New Testament, in description of which the word "baptizein" is repeatedly used, before ecclesiastical influences had eroded its stark and unmistakable meaning, and also to clear descriptions such as that in Acts 8, where the baptism of the Ethiopian eunuch is described thus: "Then both Philip and the eunuch went down *into* the water and Philip baptized [immersed] him." Also, various references to the baptism of believers need to be considered in the light of the believers' baptism position, whether *individually*, in the context of *believing households* or large groups of *believers*, as in the record of the early Church. The witness of such evidence seems clearly to point to the practice of baptism by immersion, although I would be the last to argue that the *form* of baptism is as vital as its *content*. The apostolic and theological evidence of such passages, and notably of the baptismal passage in Romans 6 with its dramatic description of burial and resurrection in baptism, provides evidence which is much more specific, I believe, than Professor West acknowledges when he contends, "There is no evidence as to how the ceremony was performed except that water was used." I make this plea, not to engage in theological confrontation, but to plead that, in such a forum as this, every possible and positive consideration should be given to the known position of the other consulting party, and that justice be done to well-known biblical evidence and its interpretation.

Dr. West's emphasis on the prevenience of the Divine grace is, of course, shared strongly by Dr. Miller, although the *essential* juxtaposition of Divine grace and human faith is more firmly demanded in the Mennonite position. This reflects, I believe, what may be the most basic divergence between the two positions. The matter is essentially ecclesiological. In the Reformed understanding of the Church here presented, "the absolute priority of divine action and divine grace *over* human response" (emphasis mine) is affirmed. This may be read as implying the relative inferiority of faith in the salvation process. The Mennonite position would undoubtedly endorse the absolute priority of divine action and grace *in* human response, but would stop short of any kind of dichotomy between them. This can be illustrated from Dr. Miller's paper when he says, "Baptism...refers to the divine initiative of grace which initiates and established this covenant," but expands the matter thus: "water baptism as a sign of the believer's commitment to this covenantal transaction thus presupposes the action of divine grace in initiating the covenant, forgiving the sinner, and *in enabling the believer to respond him- or herself to the purpose for which God has given the covenant.*"

Dr. Miller puts the divergence very clearly when he writes,

> Even though both the Mennonite and Protestant traditions can...agree on the priority and the gift-quality of divine grace in the relationship between grace and the response of faith, the *nature* of God's grace and its *effects* in the lives of Christian believers have usually been understood differently by these traditions.

To carry this "bottom line" issue a little further, let me advance the view that for pedobaptist and believers' baptist advocates to make meaningful headway in understanding calls for a continuous attempt to reach some shared *modus putandi* in relation to the Church. The pedobaptist position, with its strong insistence on the divine initiative and convenant, sees the infant of the Christian community as legitimately in the sphere of divine grace by birth and makes way for a much wider range of church membership than the believers' baptist position allows. It is argued, with Calvin, that the Church is a both-and institution. Sometimes this had led to the establishment of state churches where it is hard to distinguish between church membership and citizenship. (Even in my native Scotland, where the National Church repudiates the description of "State Church," there are many people who know they are "Church of Scotland," without appearing to be at all sure they are "Presbyterian.")

The believers' church position recognized only a "regenerate" membership, and Dr. Miller puts his understanding of the contrasting views quite pointedly when he writes of "a qualitatively different ecclesiology, namely from the church as faith community to the church as an ethnic community (or at best a confusing mixture of the two)."

The Mennonite position quite legitimately challenges a Reformed theology to come to terms with the possibility of faith and unfaith within the body of Christ, based on a both-and view of the church where, as some have put it, "the wheat and tares grow together until harvest." The Mennonites may legitimately ask, "Are we to conclude that, on the basis of physical birth within a Christian family, the child enjoys some potential favour with God which the children of non-Christian parents do not enjoy? Is this part of "election?" And how can the Church be a mixture of the convinced and the not-yet convinced, remembering that the

Church is the people of God, and what does that make of Divine election? Are the children of Christian parents safe in God's care, whether or not they are baptized? If they are not, does that mean, after all, that baptism actually changes their status with God? If it does, how do we avoid the dangers of an *ex opere operato* sacramentalism, and how do we, with Calvin, see it as the *cognitio salutis* and not the *causa salutis*?

If it does not change their status with God, what is the difference between them and the children of pagans before God? Does God have his favourites, and are they "elected" on the basis of their physical lineage? If so, where do atonement and reconciliation lie? Moreover, what is the status of those unbelievers who, having been baptized in infancy as the offspring of Christian parents, are therefore claimants to a share in the people of God? Who constitute the Church?"

For the Reformed churches, the answer seems to suggest a mixed collection of people of faith and unfaith, sometimes hard to distinguish from the community at large by any definitive distinctiveness, while, for the Mennonites, the Church consists of those persons who have received the grace of God in Christ, and have made commitment of their lives to His Lordship in the fellowship and service of the Church, by the support and discipline of which they covenant to live as Christ's people.

Now the Reformed position may, with equal legitimacy, ask the Mennonites, "What do you make of the status of children, if the Church comprises only believers. Are the children of believers in no better case than the children of unbelievers? Are they part of the Church, or aren't they? If they are not eligible for the initiatory rite of Christian baptism, where do they belong? Is the grace of God ineffective in their case? Are they outside the sphere of saving grace until they make a conscious, individual, and intelligent response to the claims of Christ in years of discretion? If so, has not their 'faith' become a 'work,' by which they are saved? If they are not outside the sphere of Divine grace from birth, ought their inclusion not to be recognized in baptism? Or are they safe in God's care through the merits of Christ's death until such time as they can choose for or against the Gospel for themselves? If that is the case, are they then 'saved' in a theological sense in infancy, only to lose that salvation if they choose not to follow Christ in later years? And what does that do to the effectiveness of the Divine grace, or the convicting power of the Holy Spirit who gives faith to all believers?"

If I may say so, both authors seem to be somewhat uncomfortable with some of the deviations from the expected norms, theologically. Dr. West mentions Karl Barth at length, only to make it clear, discreetly of course, that he regards Barth as something of a deviant, for all his scholarship and influence, and there is a sense of dismissal of Barth as a result. He says, to my great pleasure as one who owes much to Barth's influence, "Barth has picked up the Baptist side of the Reformed tradition and given it fresh twentieth-century expression. He has done so without delivering the ceremony of baptism into subjectivism."

What Barth holds in his "twentieth-century expression" is really the same as what Dr. Miller holds in his tenacious insistence that the biblical and apostolic witness supports the believers' baptism position. Barth has simply gone back to the New Testament when he insists that in the New Testament people *came* to baptism: they were not *brought* to it!

Incidentally, I am fascinated that the Reformed presentation should major on the significance of the word "sacrament" in terms of the "mystery" of the Gospel, leading to an emphasis of the imponderable and unfathomable grace of God, while the Mennonite presentation lays emphasis on "sacrament" as "oath or pledge" and therefore as denoting commitment to discipleship, based on a faith response to God's grace within the fellowship and discipline of the Church.

It should be noted that the Mennonites stand much more comfortably with Barth than do his own people within the "Reformed" family. They, too, believe very strongly in a covenantal relationship, but for them, it is a covenant of grace, experienced through faith (*sola fide*). Indeed, a major difference between the two groups appears to be that, while the Reformed people believe in a covenant of grace, based entirely on the Divine initiative, the Mennonites seem, while arguing just as strongly for a covenant of grace, to carry it to the point where they believe that a covenant involves a two-sided agreement, and that it is really quite meaningless to rest our covenant theology on grace alone (*sola gratia*) if we have not embraced that grace through faith (*sola fide*), since only the response of faith can bring any awareness that the grace is real!

All of this reinforces my concern that you should seek progress by wrestling together with the question of the Church. If it is a *community church*, of which the individual is a part, and a relatively passive and subservient part, then you may base your sacramental theology on the traditions of the institutional church. If it is a believers' church, then you will base your sacramental theology on the experience, individual and corporate, of the grace of God through faith in Jesus Christ. That will determine both who may be baptized and who may be entitled to share in the Lord's Supper.

I believe Karl Barth could help you both, if you can come to share an understanding of the Church which recognizes the primacy of grace, the necessity of faith, and the incorporation into the people of God as his *ekklesia*, his called-out people, his people with a mission, his chosen band, his "task-force" in, to, and for the world.

I have to say that, if Reformed theologians are really serious about interacting with Mennonites, they would really make much greater progress by paying greater attention to Barth at this point than, with great respect, to the *Baptism, Eucharist, and Ministry* document, which does less than justice to considering in depth the believers' baptism position. Barth does what he does, however uncomfortable his fellows in the Reformed churches may be with him, while remaining absolutely true to his Calvinist roots. He remains much more true to them, in my view, than those Reformed theologians who seem more intent on achieving common certificates of baptism and common recognition of ministries with the "mainline" and "established" churches of their regions and countries than the achievement of real theological understanding with those who share much more closely the Reformed faith which gave birth to both in the Reformation period.

While the two papers before us are largely confrontational, they have so much common ground that, given the will to listen to the other, and the resolve to wrestle with the central, rather than the peripheral issues, they can lead to substantial progress.

III. On Peace

In the presentations by Max Stackhouse and Howard Loewen on the subject of peace, there is an underlying awareness of the crucial importance of securing peace among the divergent parts of the Church if we are to achieve a meaningful approach to peace issues in society and the world. Although neither paper spells out this idea specifically, it is evidenced both in the honest wrestling with the issues and in the eirenic tone of the presentations, illustrative of the desire of both contributors to contribute not only to Christian understanding but to the *shalom* of the church.

I applaud that, and feel that in the face of a number of somewhat intransigent issues facing Reformed and Mennonite Christians in these discussions, the peace of the Church is a very important issue.

I belong to a part of the universal body of Christ which has demonstrated considerable hesitancy in ecumenical relationships, frequently fearing ecumenism. It is sometimes felt that ecumenism has tended, historically, to be a means of pressurizing the Independents, the Congregationalists, and the non-creedal segments of the church to bow to the attempted accommodations of one another by the so-called "mainline" churches. This is itself an offensive and pejorative term in its implications for other Christian bodies, especially when used as a club to beat the "sectarian" fragments into line.

While I understand the grass roots hesitancies which sometimes exist, I give it as my conviction that any contribution we can make to peace and peacemaking in the world is largely dependent on how seriously we recognize, and how intentionally we seek, the peace of the Church.

I affirm the appropriateness of these discussions between Christian groups who are concerned about the issue of peace, since Christians have no right to expect their efforts to bring peace and reconciliation to a broken world if they are themselves unreconciled. As we explore the issue of peace as it affects our presence in, and mission to, the world, we must first resolve to demonstrate the reality of that peace in our own relationships as Christians.

I acknowledge freely that I am almost haunted by several biblical emphases at this point.

First, the dominical prayer "that they all may be one, that the world might believe" is an immense challenge to conflicting, competing Christians, with a clear mandate to bring Christ's reconciling Gospel to a broken world, calling them to demonstrate that oneness in their own mutual acceptance and relatedness.

Second, the insistence of the letter to the Ephesians that God, in Christ, has broken down all the walls, all the barriers, and has made even Jews and Greeks one in Christ is surely a rebuke to the lingering tendency for conflicting Christians virtually to disown one another on intellectual, philosophical, theological, liturgical, or ecclesiastical grounds. If there is any objective reality in the saving events of God's self-revelation in Jesus Christ, his life, death, and resurrection, then the walls *are* broken and the barriers *are* down! We must live in relation to one another in the light of the peace Christ has made real if we are ever to convince anyone of a Gospel of peace.

Third, the foundational affirmations of 2 Corinthians 5 concerning the reconciliation accomplished in Christ, and entrusted to his ambassadors to share, demand a people themselves reconciled if they are ever to contribute effectively to reconciliation in the world.

The honest wrestling with some of the divisive issues in these two presentations is vitally important. I have chosen to reflect briefly on these two papers as they relate to the peace issue. I do, however, offer some side comments on the Stackhouse paper as it relates to baptism and Church and state since he spends considerable time on these issues and makes some significant contributions.

The whole tone of his paper is eirenic and conciliatory without the abandonment of his own distinctive and denominational perceptions and is, for me, especially effective in its discussion of the responsibilities of Church and state in the peacekeeping task in the world. I greatly appreciate the emphasis on family and Church, but need to sound some caution about the way baptism is related to these. It needs to be noted that in his discussion of baptism, his persistent use of the term "adult baptism" to describe the Mennonite position clouds and confuses the real issue in some measure. While it may be argued that "adult baptism" and "believer's baptism" are interchangeable terms, this is manifestly not so for many Mennonites and others who practise believers' baptism.

The real divide between these two communions on the sacrament of baptism is not primarily related to chronology or age, but to position. Mennonites advocate a Church composed of believers. They may or may not be adults. That is never the point, as I understand their position. They hold, however, to an ecclesiology of regeneration and conceive of baptism as being the "birthright," if so it may be described, of those who are part of the family of God by virtue of a covenant of grace through faith. The covenant is incomplete without the two-sidedness of the covenant relationship. As Abraham entered into a covenant with God which was entirely based on the divine initiative, but was only entered by faith (which, incidentally, made him "the friend of God"), so Mennonites and other advocates of the believers' church, believe that the new covenant in the Gospel is also entirely of God's grace, but is not entered except by faith. While the love, acceptance, and forgiveness which express the Divine grace come all from the one side, the side of God, the response of faith to that proffered grace is an essential part of the ontological relationship established through the saving activity of Christ. To call it "adult baptism" is a theological, and not a semantic issue. It is the response to grace that is important for the believers' church tradition, and not the physical maturity of the person baptized.

Dr. Stackhouse's argument for infant baptism seems to be driven by a concept of the Church, and of the family as expressions of a faith community. The question of what is meant by a faith community is the real issue that seems to me to remain unresolved between Reformed and Mennonite thought. Is it a community characterized by certain theological and doctrinal content as its heritage and even its ground of existence, a community in which the content of the faith is enshrined in the Creeds of the Church, the Westminster Confession of Faith, or some such authoritative and agreed source of orthodoxy? Or is it a community made up of persons who have responded to the grace of God in Jesus Christ in a response of faith which is much more a matter of trust in Jesus Christ as Saviour and Lord, in a personal sense and with collective effects, than it is an endorsement of a faith position or a creedal statement? It seems to me that the first of these is largely the way current Reformed and Covenantal theology *tends* to think, while the second is much more the way the believers' church, in its various forms, *tends* to think.

If progress is to be made, the implications of such trends on both sides of the dialogue need to be taken seriously and worked out openly and honestly. Otherwise, the Mennonites will find themselves confronted with a concept of inter-church or ecumenical relationships which seems to be more intent on finding common and acceptable certificates of baptism, or common and acceptable criteria for ordination to what the Reformed churches call "the ministry of the word and sacraments," or common and acceptable ways of achieving inter-communion. All these emphases have featured prominently in the story of the ecumenical movement, when, for the believers' church the nature of faith, and the necessity of a committed or "regenerate" membership is the bottom line in matters of inter-church understanding and co-operation.

I am impressed by Dr. Stackhouse's handling of the peace question and its relevance to the Church and state question. His statement that "there should be an institutional separation of church and state" is very helpful, though I suspect Calvin would have some questions for clarification. He reinforces that position by indicating that membership in one of these does not carry the automatic benefit or obligation of membership in the other. His argument that both state and Church are to work for peace and justice, but that "the Church pursues peace in terms of love and justice by the powers of the word and the spirit," while "the state pursues peace in terms of law and order...enforced, when necessary, by the power of the sword" suggests a kind of separation which might well commend itself to Mennonites. In the remarkable development of their understanding in recent years, Mennonites argue, as never before, for involvement in society and its structures, but nonetheless want to clarify the nature of Christian belonging and distinctiveness before determining how Christians relate to the state, or before deciding on major issues, such as peace. Howard Loewen says that the real question to be asked by the Christian is not, Who am I?, a fashionable North American question, but, Whose am I? Only this question will help us to understand our distinctiveness in a pluralistic world; that is most important if we are to contribute authentically to the peace of the world.

Loewen makes it clear that his tradition rests its confidence, and its case, on the authority of Holy Scripture; any meaningful discussion between Reformed and Mennonite Christians will have to clarify the measure of agreement on this crucial issue. Are we to build our views and our *modus vivendi* on Reformed theology, on covenant theology, on separatist theology, on conversion theology, or are we to come with openness to seek our authority in the authority of Scripture, as free as we can be of a spirit of protectiveness of our cherished heritages and traditions? It seems clear to me that, whether Reformed or Mennonite, the source of our authority has to be established, and agreed, if we are to make progress in a spirit of trust.

Now this is easy to say but inordinately difficult to implement, since there are not lacking, in both traditions, those who readily agree on the authority of Scripture, but who apply that belief by the application to the issues under discussion certain carefully selected "proof-texts," even parts of "proof-texts," to establish their points, instead of on the cohesive teaching of Scripture taken as a whole.

To illustrate, I have vivid memories of the Report on Baptism of the Church of Scotland which appeared in the 1950s, and which actually argued for infant baptism on the biblical ground that Peter, on the Day of Pentecost, instructed his listeners to "Repent, and be baptized...and you will receive the gift of the Holy Spirit, for the promise is unto you *and to your children.*" That, it was argued, validated infant baptism. The authors omitted to point out, however, that that very verse, in its completeness, actually says, "the promise is unto you and your children, *and to all who are afar off, as many as the Lord your God shall call.*" Clearly, on the basis of THAT "proof-text," baptism may be argued to be for everybody in the world, or for those the Lord calls, whoever they may be! I am suggesting, however, that we need seriously to address the source of our authority!

Returning to the matter of peace, Howard Loewen argues that the Mennonite position has always been "that peace is at the heart of the Gospel and that the nature and mission of the Church leads to the way of non-violence." He later argues that the Mennonite emphasis, including its emphasis on peace, with its rejection of revolutionary violence, is transformationist in its intention. He says, "For Mennonite social ethics the biblical concept of *shalom* is the primary point of reference for giving definition to a transformationist theology of peace." Allied to that, and vital for an understanding of Mennonite social ethics, is the quoted affirmation of J. Lawrence Burkholder, that "the main impetus of social thought and action in the Mennonite tradition has been the endeavor to carve out a total way of life in accordance with the biblical doctrine of nonresistance." This is clearly a point of strain in the views of the two traditions, since the Reformed tradition has had less difficulty in identifying with the state in its pursuit of justice, even when it has been enforced by violent coercion.

The Mennonite understanding of a transformational theology of peace is expressed by Loewen in a commitment to "practise the following virtues: social transformation in the context of non-conformity; transnational identification in the context of cultural particularity; and responsible non-violent action in the context of violence," a challenging and humbling agenda for social change. Its description as involving *concern for the physical and material well-being of persons and society,* his view of the church as *agent of conversion and transformation,* and his application of the biblical images of salt, light, and witness in terms of *a full-orbed cultural embodiment of the Gospel in its physical, material, and organic form* provide a basis for creative thinking between two traditions committed to the transformation of the world in the name of Christ.

I have deliberately selected from these two papers facets which seem to me to be particularly promising as bases for constructive discussion between Reformed and Mennonite Christians. I am encouraged to believe that the contributions of both presenters provide excellent stimuli for constructive progress in understanding. I pass no judgment on the specific conclusions of the two traditions, but I see, in the commitment of both traditions to a transformationist view of the Christian mission of peace in the world, a basis for an ongoing search for ethical and pacific mission.

I believe the Mennonite position on pacifism needs to be presented, and understood, not at all as a separatist withdrawal from society but as a positive description of mission under a mandate from one who said, "Blessed are the peacemakers". Pacifism as a concept has been degraded by being interpreted simply as a refusal to resort to violent force or to take up arms. In Christian, and, I believe, in Mennonite terms, it is a mission involving Christians in the conflicts and alienations of the world with a view to bringing the reconciliation of Christ to bear on the divisions and brokeness of humanity.

With great sympathy for such a position, I enter a plea for a conscious development of the concept of pacifism on a christological basis, as expressed in the life, death and Resurrection of Him who "made peace through the blood of his cross," and who, in doing so, has "broken down the walls" in such a way that "his purpose was to create in himself one new man out of the two, thus making peace, and in this one body to reconcile both of them (i.e., Jews and Greeks) to God through the cross, by which he put to death their hostility" (Ephesians 2: 16). On the basis of such a theology and understanding, there is room for new and shared consensus between these two traditions, I believe.

Chapter XI

A CHURCH HISTORIAN'S RESPONSE

Tom Sinclair-Faulkner

For four centuries, Reformed and Mennonite theologians have been striving to refine and bring coherence to the faith of their people, so far as that faith can be formulated reasonably in words. The image that springs to my mind is the shaping of two circles: strong, integrated, symmetrical, and self-contained. The six essays on the state, baptism, and peace presented in this volume are clear and eloquent statements of the Reformed and Mennonite traditions, presented with *caritas* to those who would understand the two circles that have come together at this symposium.

As an historian responding to these theological statements, I take it that I have two tasks. One is to probe the elegant abstractions for evidence that they truthfully reflect the messy complexity of historical reality. I am glad to say that these six essays are already historically sophisticated and are therefore in little need of assistance from someone like myself, though from time to time in the space that follows I will suggest ways in which our historical perspective ought to shift a little. The second task, however, is to find ways in which the histories of these two circles may be helpfully construed as part of a larger circle: the history of all Christians, or Church history in its broadest sense. Where can Mennonite experience and Reformed experience enlarge each other? And when they do, will the two circles share even more than they already do?

I.

In light of what Nicol and Loewen have told us about the Reformed and Mennonite understandings of the state, let me propose that they hold in common what I might call the *boot theory of the state*. Without wishing to minimize either the importance of the Schleitheim Confession or its uncompromising rejection of the Christian's participation in the state and all its works, Harry Loewen reports that in 1527 Balthasar Hübmaier published a booklet entitled "On the Sword" in which he asked rhetorically, "What good is a shoe if one dare not wear it?" Loewen concludes that "Hübmaier believes that in discharging his duty as a magistrate a Christian can and must act in love and for the good of his fellowmen." Coincidentally, Iain Nicol informs us that John Calvin, in a sermon on Daniel 6:22, argued that when magistrates rise up against God, "They must be put down, they must be held of no account, no more than boots." I regard the "boot" as a marvellous metaphor for the state. Neither pretty nor delicate, it is enormously useful; we can try to get on without it but we get farther with it. So long as it serves God's justice we should make use of it, but neither awe nor sentimentality should deter us from changing it when it ceases to serve.

One cannot help but speculate how *The Leviathan* might have looked if Thomas Hobbes had been more interested in boots than in earthly gods.

In the light of our histories, surely the great debate among Reformed and Mennonite Christians should be over how to participate in the state, not whether to do so. If that is the case, then we need to ask what life in the modern *civitas* is like. For purposes of our discussion, let me suggest that it is both democratic and alienating.

I am persuaded that Reformed Christianity has played a distinctive role in fostering the development of the democratic state. Although I agree in general with the picture that Iain Nicol has painted of Calvin's contribution to political theory, I think that he has underestimated Calvin's importance in fostering political democracy, even political revolution. Prior to Calvin few had argued that lower magistrates should overthrow the higher magistrate who violates God's justice. *Magna Carta*, for example, binds the monarch to behave justly vis-à-vis the nobility and the people but does not provide for the overthrow of the monarch. This notion that revolution could come from below flowered in the chaos of the English Civil War of the seventeenth century when Presbyterians and Independents—alike, the children of Geneva—determined to overthrow King Charles I and ultimately to execute him for treason.

The Puritans went beyond the King's execution for treason to lay the basis of political democracy. For example, the General Council of Cromwell's new Model Army met in Putney on the outskirts of London on 28-29 October and 1 November 1647. The purpose of the gathering was to determine what direction the Puritan revolution would take and the debate was taken down in shorthand, a record readily available to us today in *Puritanism and Liberty* (1950), edited by A.S.P. Woodhouse.

The rank and file were represented at the Putney debates by the so-called Agitators, elected under the provisions of the *Solemn Engagement of the Army*, a covenant that provided for a formal debate before the Army should be ordered to undertake a new strategy. The Agitators presented *The Case of the Army Truly Stated*, supported by Levellers such as Thomas Rainborough. Woodhouse describes the meetings as a church gathering in which the Puritans tried to reach agreement on how a holy community might be realized in England at this moment when the Civil War seemed so uncertain of resolution.[1]

At a key point in the debate, Cromwell's brother-in-law and second-in-command argued that only those men with substantial property should determine the course of the state in England. One of the Levellers, Colonel Thomas Rainborough, rebutted him:

> For really I think that the poorest he that is in England hath a life to live, as the greatest he; and therefore truly, sir, I think it's clear, that every man that is to live under a government ought first by his own consent to put himself under that government; and I do think that the poorest man in England is not at all bound in a strict sense to that government that he hath not had a voice to put himself under; and I am confident that, when I have heard the reasons against it, something will be said to answer those reasons, inasmuch that I should doubt whether he was an Englishman or no, that should doubt of these things.[2]

I note in passing that two years later a *Petition of Women* was presented to the House of Commons offering these arguments:

> Since we are assured of our creation in the image of God, and of an interest in Christ equal unto men, as also of a proportionable share in the freedoms of this commonwealth, we cannot but wonder and grieve that we should appear so despicable in your eyes as to be thought unworthy to petition or represent our grievances to this honourable House. Have we not an equal interest with the men of this nation in those liberties and securities contained in the *Petition of Right*, and other the good laws of the land?

The twentieth-century editor of this document expressed the opinion that it "is improbable that this petition was actually composed by the women. Its principles are nonetheless interesting."[3] I am not competent to judge whether Woodhouse was right to draw this conclusion but, even if he was, we can probably assume that such thoughts of political equality had occurred to some other seventeenth-century Puritan women.

The point that I want to make is that this is the moment when Reformed Christians began to consider seriously that everyone should be a magistrate. I would go further than Max Stackhouse does in his statement that today "everyone is a magistrate—at least episodically." The kind of political responsibility demanded by Rainborough must be exercised between elections through careful attention and comment, not just at the ballot box.

If the state today aspires to be democratic, we must remember that it is also alienating. I recall that when I was a socialist candidate in our provincial election in 1981 I was cautioned to watch out for the citizen whose position is, "I never vote. It only encourages them." In this respect our political order is faced with the same problem that our churches confront: the privatizing tendencies of modern life. Here I follow the argument of Thomas Luckmann who says that modern persons characteristically consider themselves to be "real" only in the private realm—where, incidentally, religious life is lodged.[4] Elsewhere they are at best playing a role from which they feel personally distant.

Historically, Reformed Christians have placed a good deal of emphasis upon the importance of responsible Church government. The teaching elder who may be tempted to think that ordination confers divine right is required to share power with the ruling elders of the congregation who are members of the laity. Everything is done decently and in right order by the courts of the Church. Things never work that smoothly in real life, of course, but Presbyterian theory is persistent in its effort to remind Presbyterians of what Presbyterian practice ought to be. Since democracy is so patently strained and subverted by the privatizing tendencies of modern life, the Reformed churches may have a calling to serve as schools in which genuine democracy is taught. Given their traditional penchant for reshaping society as a godly commonwealth, Presbyterians should have no hesitation in suggesting that their own practice of active and responsible Church citizenship should model behaviour for citizens of the state.

And how much more, then, might Mennonite churches offer civil society? In my lack of experience of congregational life among Mennonites I do not know, but my imagination tells me that Mennonites expect each Mennonite to share responsibly and actively in the common life of their gathered congregation. If the black Americans who were first enslaved and later disenfranchised in American history could learn the lessons of practical politics within their churches—the only political institution permitted to them until comparatively recently—what can Mennonites teach us who have governed themselves for four hundred years? Even those who hew to the Schleitheim Confession rather than to Balthasar Hübmaier have something important to contribute to our understanding of the state.

II.

One of the reasons that I love the study of history is that it liberates us from the enervating argument, "But we have always done it this way!" Alas, I think that the essays by Miller and West—indeed, I would add Stackhouse—demonstrate that whatever diversity we uncover in the theory and practice of baptism in the Mennonite and Reformed traditions, it is unlikely that either one will be led to a radical restructuring of its most common view of baptism. Presbyterians are extremely unlikely to adopt Karl Barth's view that believers' baptism is essential, however hedged about with Barth's affirmations concerning the objective efficacy of the rite. With all due respect to West I ask, if Barth could not move the Reformed on that point, who can? And it would appear from Miller's report that the most likely alteration in Mennonite practice is already under way in those North American churches where new communicants are not always required to be baptized, giving an implicit recognition that their baptism as infants was valid. Let us note that this is a long way from adopting the practice of pedobaptism; only those who view the change as the first step on a slippery slope are likely to view it with great alarm; personally I have found that few slopes are as slippery as some would have us believe. Mennonite history and tradition provide too many toeholds to leave us with much concern on this point, I think. Believers' baptism may become routinized but it is unlikely to be abandoned.

Marlin E. Miller's account of baptism as the doorway into disciplined congregational life is very helpful. His essay makes it clear that baptism is not a kind of sheep dip that acts objectively to prevent further sickness. Nor is baptism a covenant between an isolated Christian and God. What Mennonites may have to teach the Reformed is not the necessity of believers' baptism—here we must surely thank Charles West for reminding us of Karl Barth's rousingly Protestant affirmation that Jesus Christ is the only sacrament and that therefore all sacraments are merely means to an end—but instead Mennonites might teach the Reformed how to foster "supportive congregational accountability and discipline," whether believers are initiated into it as adults or as children.

The Reformed tradition clearly needs the lesson. In Nova Scotia 150 years ago, Presbyterians used to leave their farms four times a year and come together outdoors in crowds of several thousand. After a day of singing and a further day of debate among the ruling elders on some scriptural question, they would celebrate the Lord's Supper. Or, to be precise, between thirty and two hundred persons who had been judged to be in a satisfactory state of uprightness were furnished with silver communion tokens that permitted them to pass the bar of the communion rail to share in the sacrament. While those few score celebrated, the remaining thousands watched quietly from beyond the pale, no doubt comforted as only Presbyterians can be comforted by the thought that high standards of Christian behaviour were being affirmed.[5] I would not want my home congregation in the United Church of Canada to replace the paper communion cards distributed as invitations by our elders with those old silver tokens that customarily barred 95% of the congregation from full participation in the Lord's Supper. Surely there is some happy medium to find between the Reformed practice of the early nineteenth century and my own experience of accountability in a Reformed church today. (During the past fifteen years of my active membership in a congregation of the United Church of Canada I have been visited only twice by my Elder; and on one of those occasions the visit was provoked by my objection to the Elder's conduct, not by his objection to mine.)

I do not want to romanticize the effectiveness of Mennonite congregational accountability and discipline. Indeed, if I may take Rudy Wiebe's fictional but semi-autobiographical account of Mennonite congregational life[6] to be in some measure accurate, Mennonites have as many difficulties on this side of Jordan as the rest of us. However, they appear to be working at the issue of congregational accountability and discipline in a way that the Reformed no longer do. In my view, the Reformed should seek to know more about how the Mennonites do it. If adopting believers' baptism is essential to the task, then I for one would be tempted to shrug my shoulders in the manner of that unreformed Christian magistrate, Henri IV, and say, "Well, Paris is worth a mass."

What might the Reformed teach the Mennonites in return? Marlin E. Miller makes it plain that Mennonites have a richly diverse tradition concerning many aspects of baptism, but the best of Mennonite teaching understands the specific order of baptism to be "*normative* because it is *the New Testament order.*" I think that Mennonites who make such an affirmation about New Testament norms should ask Reformed Christians how they have come to the view of Scripture that they have.

To that end I should like to ask Charles West how he as a Reformed Christian comes to the point of saying that we ought to regard, for example, Mark 16:16 as a second-century addition and therefore not helpful in defining baptism. I happen to agree with Charles West; and I have no difficulty recognizing him as a thoughtful and committed Reformed Christian. However, it is not easy to square his biblical stance with that of John Calvin who wrote in *The Institute of the Christian Religion*,

> When that which is set forth is acknowledged to be the Word of God, there is no one so deplorably insolent — unless devoid also both of common sense and of humanity itself — as to dare impugn the credibility of Him who speaks....
>
> But a most pernicious error widely prevails that Scripture has only so much weight as is conceded to it by the consent of the church. As if the eternal and inviolable truth of God depended upon the decision of men![7]

Nor is it easy to square it with the position of another distinguished Princeton professor and Reformed theologian, Bejamin Breckinridge Warfield (1851-1921), who wrote in *The Inspiration and Authority of the Bible* that Christians know that they need

> a Word of God in which God speaks directly to each of our souls. Such a Word of God, Christ and his apostles offer us, when they give us the Scriptures, not as man's report to us of what God says, but as the very Word of God itself, spoken by God himself through human lips and pens. Of such a precious possession, given to her by such hands, the church will not lightly permit herself to be deprived. Thus the church's sense of her need of an absolutely infallible Bible has co-operated with her reverence for the teaching of the Bible to keep her true, in all ages, to the Bible doctrine of plenary inspiration.[8]

What route has the Reformed tradition taken that it can include Calvin, Warfield, and West as legitimate guideposts along the way? We must not be satisfied with the legendary reply of the cabby from Brooklyn, "But you *can't* get there from here." Reformed Christians have fought more important battles over the understanding and authority of Scripture than any other Christian communion in the past 100 years has. We need to know more of the history of their struggles so that we may all learn how to be properly submitted to the guidance of Scripture when we wrestle with particular problems such as baptism or — as I would prefer to do — congregational accountability and discipline.

III.

Max Stackhouse was assigned the topic of peace in the Reformed tradition but in fact he has produced a paper that deals with the state and baptism as well. Has he been sloppy? No, instead he has indirectly made the point that the issues of Church-state relations, baptism, and peace cannot be left in isolation from one another but must be dealt with together.   What this conference has separated for purposes of convenience must not remain separate for lack of understanding.

In my two earlier responses I have touched upon some points that Stackhouse has made. There are two others that I would like to raise here: the Reformed understanding of worldly vocations and the high vocation of the family.

Calvin's contribution to our understanding of the spiritual character and importance of vocations in the world has the status of a truism today. Stackhouse points out that the Reformed churches have from time to time held different views on how godly this or that vocation may be, but then he adds the interesting statement that "a decided moral preference is given to church members who refuse to work for any company engaged in the design, manufacture, or sale of military weaponry." Coming as I do from the Canadian city that depends more heavily upon military institutions for its living than any other — estimates suggest that 40 percent of the people in the Halifax area depend upon the military for their income — I should like to hear more about this. My suspicion is that the "decided moral preference" described by Stackhouse is to be found among those in central ecclesiastical institutions who are actively and professionally involved in peace work, not among those who sit in the pews. In fact, I would suggest that the Reformed tradition has become increasingly delinquent over the centuries about its duty to reflect carefully upon the spiritual character of earthly callings. The capitalists whom Max Weber described as being trapped in John Bunyan's "iron cage" were not former Calvinists who had left the churches; most of them were Reformed Christians whose churches had forgotten how to support their spiritual development properly.

Compare, for example, the Mennonites and the Reformed on this matter. Mennonite business folk are gathered together in Mennonite Economic Development Associates (MEDA) where they foster programs of international economic development. There is a clear institutional role for Mennonites who would understand and practise the spiritual dimension of their worldly activity. It may be that they fall short of their duty to take stock of their business practices at home but at least they are engaged at some level of theological theory and practice. In contrast, the Reformed denominations in Canada have devoted considerable energy to challenging the practices of private corporations trading with South Africa, manufacturing Cruise missile components, etc., but have not fostered a body of business folk who formally consider what they might do as Christians together. Instead, the churches provoked the establishment of the Confederation of Church and Business [*sic*], an organization devoted to fending off the public criticism of business people by ecclesiastical leaders. If Mennonites seek what Howard Loewen calls a "transformational" role in society today, perhaps their efforts may stimulate Reformed Christians to do the same in a way that enlists the aid of more lay people from the business world, the military, etc.

On the matter of the family's high vocation, Stackhouse is right to remind us of the pressures on families today, including the high divorce rate and the expectation that parents grow as individuals and achieve success outside the home. My impression is that the visceral response of the churches to these pressures is to condemn them and to commend — practically as a sacrament — the two-parent family with a mother who stays at home. Apart from public pronouncements of one sort or another, the loudest statement made by the churches in this regard is in the unstated but clear expectation that the minister of each congregation shall (a) model family behaviour as stated above, and (b) work the number of hours that a celibate monk would be hard put to wring from a day that only has twenty-four to distribute himself among sleep, work, family, care of self and praise of the Lord. The acronym "PK" is widely recognized in our society as a symbol for the preacher's kid whose father's holy calling left little room for childrearing. "PK" is rarely a badge of pride; all too often it is merely a certificate of survival.

I am grateful to Howard John Loewen for his careful and persuasive effort to explain the historical transition of the Mennonite community from those who are quiet in the land following the First World War to those who feel themselves called to transform the larger society under the banner of *shalom*. As an historian it particularly delights me to hear that this laudable transition was stimulated largely by a reappropriation of sixteenth-century Mennonite history. Let me suggest an additional strategy for Mennonite historians that may at first appear to be perverse but will prove, I hope, to be wise. Since non-Mennonite historians have often used their accounts of the terrible events at Münster under John of Leiden to discredit and marginalize Mennonites as an unrealistic and ineffective sect, Mennonite historians have shied away from that unhappy figure. Now, however, it is time for some Mennonite historian to study John of Leiden.

In traditional psychotherapy, the one who suffers learns to acknowledge, understand, and finally move beyond the tragedies that most human beings simply try to forget. "Moving beyond" does not mean denying their real connection with the patient's life but giving them their due — no more and no less — and knowing how to act rightly when circumstances arise in the present that stimulate echoes of the past. John of Leiden was an Anabaptist. What experience of Jesus led him to chart the course that he did? What terrible circumstances drove him to violence, authoritarian rule, sexual excess, and morbid self-sacrifice?

It may be that groups as well as individuals must confront a dark night of the soul, just as individual mystics do in their response to God. Teresa of Avila studied and analyzed the life of prayer with systematic care and found that the dark night of the soul comes without warning upon the spiritual adept, not upon the spiritual novice. It is an experience of thoroughgoing isolation from God, with all the attendant temptations to despair, and only the carefully cultivated habits of the past and the knowledge that this too shall pass will enable the devout to pass beyond the dark night, strengthened by its violence and grief as iron is tempered by fire and water. No proper historical reappropriation of the past can select only the good — the Pilgram Marpecks, Balthasar Hübmaiers, etc. Whether as individuals or groups we are what we are, and the search for a usable past must include everything.

The same may be said of the Reformed, of course. Those who love Calvin must remember Michael Servetus; those who love John Knox must remember the young woman to whom he preached the Word before she was led to her execution by fire. The Reformed do remember these things. It is why their representatives are here today, speaking with the representatives of those whose ancestors were drowned by Reformed Christians for daring to baptize those who had been sprinkled once before.

When the Reformed look around this table they see the faces of Mennonites who were martyred, leaving the imprint of their names and stories on the flesh that carries on today's dialogue. When you Mennonites look at each other, can you see John of Leiden as well as Menno Simons? Can you see the heart of darkness as well as the heart of faith?

Notes

1. A.S.P. Woodhouse, ed., *Puritanism and Liberty: Being the Army Debates (1647-9) from the Clarke Manuscripts with Supplementary Documents* (Chicago: University of Chicago Press, 1950), pp. 36-37.

2. Ibid., p. 53.

3. Ibid., p. 367.

4.   Thomas Luckmann, *The Invisible Religion: The Problem of Religion in Modern Society* (New York: Macmillan, 1967).

5.   D. Campbell and R.A. MacLean, *Beyond the Atlantic Roar: A Study of the Nova Scotia Scots* (Toronto: McClelland and Stewart, 1974), p. 202-203; Laurie Stanley, *The Well-watered Garden: The Presbyterian Church in Cape Breton, 1798-1860* (Sydney, N.S.: University College of Cape Breton Press, 1983), p. 139-49.

6.   Rudy Wiebe, *Peace Shall Destroy Many* (Toronto: McClelland and Stewart, 1972).

7.   John Calvin, *The Institutes of the Christian Religion*, J.T. McNeill, ed., book I, chapter VII (Philadelphia: Westminster Press, 1960), pp. 74-75.

8.   Benjamin Breckinridge Warfield, *The Inspiration and Authority of the Bible*, Samuel G. Craig, ed. (Philadelphia: Presbyterian and Reformed Publishing Co., 1948), p. 125.

PART THREE:
THE FINDINGS OF THE PARTICIPANTS

Chapter XII

CONCLUSION

The following are the findings of the consultation on "Baptism, Peace, and the State in the Reformed and Mennonite Traditions" held at the University of Calgary, 11-14 October 1989.

This concluding statement attempts both to reflect the life of their communions as they are, and to articulate a vision of what they ought to be. It became clear that both Reformed and Mennonites own a common Reformation heritage. It was realized that while there is a Mennonite spectrum of views and a Reformed spectrum of views, there is also a considerable area of common ground. The old sense that the two parties are rigid and bitter enemies is gone. Reformed and Mennonites now accept one another as brothers and sisters in Christ.

Baptism
Concerning baptism, it was agreed that neither the Mennonite nor the Reformed traditions can properly be understood apart from a doctrine of prevenient divine grace. It was agreed that further discussion should be devoted to this question, especially as it impinges upon a correlative understanding of baptism and the nature and place of human response; and in relation to the question of divine initiative and human response *vis à vis* Christian initiation as a process in which there is mutual involvement and interaction between the communities of Church and family.

It was noted that both traditions insist upon the connection between baptism and Church membership. However, within the Reformed family of churches, not only are there different views as to precisely who is a member of the Church, but there does not as yet appear to be any clear consensus with respect to the place and function of the practice of confirmation in relation to baptism. On the basis of the practice of believers' baptism Mennonites are able to answer questions about Church membership less ambiguously. It is suggested that Reformed churches give further attention to resolving confusions and disagreements within their own ranks, and that Mennonites reconsider their position *vis à vis* other churches, especially with respect to baptizing believers who have received infant baptism according to the theology and practice of other communions. Both communions need seriously to address the question of whether and with what ecclesial consequences the Gospel breaks down barriers which the respective doctrines and practices of baptism have erected.

The Reformed house clearly emerged as one in which there are many ecclesiological mansions, and each ecclesiology (established or free, gathered or connectional) reflects differently nuanced understandings of the nature and function of baptism. Whereas in all Reformed churches baptism is seen as the sacrament of incorporation into the Church, and hence as the basis of the nurture of the child (or older believer) in the community of faith, in Reformed churches which are national in character, baptism *per se* may be viewed as constituting membership, and may in practice be a terminus. In Reformed churches which have adopted the ecclesiology of the gathered church, the role assigned to baptism is sometimes viewed as minimal. For their part, those Mennonite circles which are strongly ethnically conscious sometimes reduce believers' baptism to a mere formality. In order that serious dialogue may continue, the question of how a tradition which includes a variety of ecclesiologies may engage in discussion with one which is much more homogeneous is of primary importance.

It emerged from the papers and discussions that from the beginning of the Anabaptist movement, Church discipline has been closely linked with baptism. Congregational discipline has also figured prominently in traditional Reformed ecclesiology and practice. However, both the misuse of disciplinary measures within the churches of both communions and the "spirit of the age" have either undermined the practice of congregational discipline, or contributed to its discontinuation. Both Mennonite and Reformed churches need a renewed theological understanding of baptism as entailing supportive parental and congregational accountability and discipline; and such an understanding needs to be practised consistently. Mennonites should view and practise discipline as a means of restoring an erring brother or sister in compassion and love. The Reformed should regain and reinstitute a supportive and corrective practice of discipline as a part of normal congregational life. Both communions urgently need to examine the relation between baptism, the Lord's Supper, and discipline.

The dialogue participants have been challenged to re-examine the biblical foundations for Christian baptism, and to clarify the hermeneutical context within which Scripture is heard. Both Mennonites and Reformed acknowledge the Bible as the primary rule of faith and life in seeking further clarification, mutual correction, and a greater measure

of unity in their views and practices of baptism. However, full agreement has not yet been reached on the following points:
- whether and in what sense baptism in the NT may be understood as analogous to circumcision in the Old (Col. 2: 9-15);
- whether the NT teaches believers' baptism as the normative order;
- whether the NT understandings and accounts of baptismal practice allow for infant baptism;
- the sense in which baptism as "mystery" or "sacrament" may be grounded in the NT concept of "mystery" or the NT concept of "pledge" (I Pet. 3: 21);
- the degrees to which differing views of covenant and of the relation between divine grace and faith comport with Scripture.

The scriptural foundations for the above issues need further examination.

Peace and the State
The realities of a nuclear age have prompted many in the Reformed family to address the peace question with greater urgency, and to take account of the fact that violence can be institutional, economic, and systemic as well as military. This recognition has prompted a fresh investigation of the strategies of active non-violence, and has greatly facilitated dialogue with the Mennonites.

If the issue of peace is adequately to be addressed, the Gospel must be related not only to questions of war, revolution, and military affairs, but also to an expanded theological understanding of the institutions of civilization—for example, families, economic and technological systems, cultural patterns, and political regimes. These were intended by God to be preservative and enhancing of human life, but are too often characterized by conflict, hostility, division, and violence. Believers, congregations, and the peoples of the world are thereby victimized. The vocation of all Christians to be peace-makers in all arenas of life requires careful consideration.

The Reformed have traditionally held that there are situations in which it becomes necessary for the Christian to take up the sword. The Mennonites have not traditionally endorsed this view. The establishment of a just order which entails the use of violent force is still, in the eyes of many of the Reformed, an obligation in a sinful world. However, some in the Reformed family adopt a stance which is in complete harmony with that of the Mennonites. Reformed scholars need to respond to the

Mennonite challenge concerning the consistency of their stance(s) on peace, and the degree to which they are faithful to Scripture.

It became clear that there are differences in the way in which Scripture is read, both within the Reformed and Mennonite traditions and between them. Nevertheless in general it can be said that both traditions take their stand on the Christ event, including the life and example of Jesus, his atoning death on the Cross, his Resurrection and lordship over the powers. Within this understanding Mennonites, and some parts of the Reformed family, have emphasized the obligation of non-violent action in accordance with the teaching in the Sermon on the Mount. Other Reformed Christians would claim that free responsibility in Christ may involve violent action at times, undertaken in repentance, and confident in the forgiving mercy of God.

Despite the elements of convergence noted above, it was admitted that some continuing mutual suspicion remains, involving a partially articulated attribution of moral inadequacy. The Mennonites suspect that the Reformed-Puritan traditions sell out biblical principles too soon to the strictures of necessity. The Reformed heritage suspects that the Mennonite tradition says that it wants to be socially responsible and engaged, but is not in fact ready to take full responsibility for justice in society.

The Mennonites' theological understanding of revolution requires clarification. Though not wishing to surrender their peace principle, they must ask: How are unjust rulers, who understand nothing but force, to be dethroned? It became clear that Mennonites are not abandoning traditional Anabaptist pacifism, but they are struggling with the question how to apply the peace principle concretely in today's situation. The Reformed noted that the Mennonite Central Committee is with the oppressed in its programs, but that Mennonites are at a loss in some situations where the regime is unjust.

Both traditions are changing, the Reformed realizing that they must pay more attention to the integrity of the Church as a witnessing and nurturing community than they have sometimes done, the Mennonites recognizing that they have to participate and act responsibly in society and culture. The traditions are converging on the conception of Christ as transforming culture, as opposed to his being over, against, or above, it.

Reformed and Mennonites are coming together in understanding of what it is to be *in* but not *of* the world. There is acknowledgement on both sides of the dual membership of the Christian believer in the secular community and in the society of the redeemed. It is agreed that the state is needed in a fallen world, as a positive but provisional institution, to maintain some relative order, justice, and peace, and that some degree of coercion is legitimate in the attainment of this end.

Pacifism is the crucial element of the witness of Mennonites to be listened to by the Reformed. It is to be noted that there are sections and groups for peace-making already at work in the Reformed context. Mennonites could greatly advance the discussion of this crucial issue if they would undertake scholarly work to show how the concern for peace is rooted in, and derives from, the whole work of Christ—his life and ministry, and his atoning death and final victory. The implications of God's redemptive Act in Christ for the mission of Christians as agents of peace and reconciliation need clearly to be worked out. Further work might be done on the analogy between the place of peace in the Mennonite tradition and that of the sovereign grace of God in the Reformed.

While there is convergence on the *role* of the church, differences remain as to its *nature*, and on the terms most appropriately used to express it. Hence the need for further analysis of this matter both within the two traditions and between them. It would seem that the Reformed tend to have a more social understanding of the catholicity of the Church, while the Mennonites tend rather to emphasize the discipleship of believers in the context of commitment to community. In the effort to relate to culture, the Reformed have sometimes identified themselves too closely with it, while the Mennonites, in their effort to challenge culture, have sometimes distanced themselves too far from it.

Recommendations

The following recommendations, addressed to the Executive Committees of the World Alliance of Reformed Churches and the Mennonite World Conference, were unanimously approved by the Reformed and Mennonite participants in the consultation on "Baptism, Peace, and the State in the Reformed and Mennonite Traditions," held at the University of Calgary, 11-14 October 1989.

1.   That in gratitude for the unity into which God, by grace, has called us, and with a view to urgent and credible mission, Reformed and Mennonites engage wherever possible in united witness and common study at all levels, from the local to the international.

2. That the Executive Committee of the World Alliance of Reformed Churches promote a discussion among Reformed churches on the nature of the Church, having regard to the varied ecclesi-ologies — established and free, gathered and connectional — that are to be found in that communion, the objective being to reach a biblically grounded ecclesiology which will take due account of the realities of the several societies within which the churches are currently called to serve. That the question of church establishments be raised with the Anglican Consultative Council and the Lutheran World Federation.

3. That the Executive bodies of the World Alliance of Reformed Churches and the Mennonite World Conference promote a joint discussion between their member churches on the nature of the Church and baptism in relation to Christian incorporation and nurture, the Lord's Supper, and church discipline.

4. That the Executive Committee of the World Alliance of Reformed Churches urge member churches of the Alliance clearly to articulate their understanding of baptism, and to revive and practise that understanding of the Church as God's covenant people, within which the integrity of infant baptism is actualized.

5. That the Executive Committee of the Mennonite World Conference urge its member churches seriously to examine their attitude towards Christians baptized as infants who wish to exercise their church membership in a Mennonite church, in relation to the questions of the nature and mode of baptism, and in the light of the Gospel which has made us one.

6. That the Executive Committee of the Mennonite World Conference initiate a discussion among Mennonites on the possibility of a theological understanding of revolution, and the application of the peace principle in face of economic, institutional, military, and cultural violence.

7. That the Executive Committee of the World Alliance of Reformed Churches initiate a discussion among Reformed churches on the possibilities in, and applications of, just war theory, and on Christian participation in the responsible use of coercive power.

8. That the results of the consultations urged under 2 and 7 above be shared with the Mennonite World Conference as a basis for further joint discussion.

9. That the results of the consultations urged under 5 and 6 above be shared with the World Alliance of Reformed Churches as a basis for further joint discussion.

PARTICIPANTS IN THE CONSULTATION

For the Mennonite World Conference

Harry Loewen (Mennonite Brethren Church), Professor and Chair in Mennonite Studies, The University of Winnipeg

Howard John Loewen (Mennonite Brethren Church), Associate Professor of Theology, Mennonite Brethren Biblical Seminary

Marlin E. Miller (General Conference Mennonite Church and Mennonite Church), President and Professor of Theology, Associated Mennonite Biblical Seminaries

For the World Alliance of Reformed Churches

Iain G. Nicol (Presbyterian Church in Canada), Professor of Systematic Theology, Knox College, Toronto

Max L. Stackhouse (United Church of Christ), Herbert Gezork Professor of Christian Social Ethics, Andover Newton Theological School

Charles C. West (Presbyterian Church USA), Stephen Colwell Professor of Christian Ethics, Princeton Theological Seminary

Respondents

Harry H. Hiller (Baptist), Professor of Sociology, The University of Calgary

Andrew D. MacRae (Baptist), Principal and Dean of Theology, Acadia Divinity College, Acadia University

Hugo Meynell (Roman Catholic), Professor of Religious Studies, The University of Calgary

Tom Sinclair-Faulkner (United Church of Canada), Associate Professor of Comparative Religion, Dalhousie University

Together with

Ronald W. Neufeldt (Mennonite), Professor and Head of the Department of Religious Studies, The University of Calgary

Ross T. Bender (Mennonite Church), President of the Mennonite World Conference; Professor of Christian Education, Associated Mennonite Biblical Seminaries (Co-secretary)

Alan P. F. Sell (United Reformed Church in the UK), Professor and holder of the Chair of Christian Thought, The University of Calgary (Co-secretary); formerly Theological Secretary of the World Alliance of Reformed Churches

INDEX

Also published by Wilfrid Laurier University Press
for The Calgary Institute for the Humanities

BAPTISM, PEACE AND THE STATE IN THE REFORMED
AND MENNONITE TRADITIONS
Edited by Ross T. Bender and Alan P. F. Sell

Essays by: Alan P. F. Sell, Charles C. West, Marlin E. Miller, Max L. Stackhouse,
Howard John Loewen, Iain G. Nicol, Harry Loewen, Hugo Meynell, Harry H. Hiller,
Andrew D. MacRae, Tom Sinclair-Faulkner

1991 / pp. xii + 248 / ISBN 0-88920-204-4

THE EDUCATIONAL LEGACY OF ROMANTICISM
Edited by John Willinsky

Essays by: Aubrey Rosenberg, Ann E. Berthoff, Clarence J. Karier, Diana Korzenik,
Edgar Z. Friedenberg, Johan Lyall Aitken, Richard L. Butt, John Willinsky, Anne
McWhir, Max van Manen, Jane Roland Martin, Madeleine R. Grumet, Deborah A.
Dooley, Kieran Egan

1990 / pp. xiv + 310 / ISBN 0-88920-996-0

SILENCE, THE WORD AND THE SACRED
Edited by E. D. Blodgett and H. G. Coward

Essays by: David Atkinson, Robin Blaser, E. D. Blodgett, Ronald Bond, Joseph Epes
Brown, Harold Coward, Monique Dumais, David Goa, Stanley Hopper, Doug Jones,
Smaro Kamboureli, Rudy Wiebe

1989 / pp. xii + 226 / ISBN 0-88920-981-2

THE EFFECTS OF FEMINIST APPROACHES
ON RESEARCH METHODOLOGIES
Edited by Winnie Tomm

Essays by: Margaret Lowe Benston, Naomi Black, Kathleen Driscoll and Joan McFar-
land, Micheline Dumont, Anne Flynn, Marsha Hanen, Jeanne Lapointe, Hilary M. Lips,
Pamela McCallum, Thelma McCormack, Rosemary Nielsen and E. D. Blodgett, Lynn
Smith

1989 / pp. x + 259 / ISBN 0-88920-986-3

RUPERT'S LAND
A Cultural Tapestry
Edited by Richard C. Davis

Essays by: Richard I. Ruggles, Olive P. Dickason, John L. Allen, Clive Holland, Sylvia
Van Kirk, James G. E. Smith, Robert Stacey, Irene Spry, Fred Crabb, Edward Cavell,
R. Douglas Francis, Robert H. Cockburn

1988 / pp. xii + 323 / ISBN 0-88920-976-6

THINKING THE UNTHINKABLE
Civilization and Rapid Climate Change
Lydia Dotto

Based on the Conference Civilization and Rapid Climate
Change, University of Calgary, August 22-24, 1987

1988 / pp. viii + 73 / ISBN 0-88920-968-5

GENDER BIAS IN SCHOLARSHIP
The Pervasive Prejudice
Edited by Winnifred Tomm and Gordon Hamilton

Essays by: Marlene Mackie, Carolyn C. Larsen, Estelle Dansereau, Gisele Thibault, Alice
Mansell, Eliane Leslau Silverman, Yvonne Lefebvre, Petra von Morstein, Naomi Black

1988 / pp. xx + 206 / ISBN 0-88920-963-4

FRANZ KAFKA (1883-1983)
His Craft and Thought
Edited by Roman Struc and J. C. Yardley

Essays by: Charles Bernheimer, James Rolleston, Patrick O'Neill, Egon Schwarz, Ernst
Loeb, Mark Harman, Ruth Gross, W. G. Kudszus

1986 / pp. viii + 160 / ISBN 0-88920-187-0

ANCIENT COINS OF THE GRAECO-ROMAN WORLD
The Nickle Numismatic Papers
Edited by Waldemar Heckel and Richard Sullivan

Essays by: C. M. Kraay, M. B. Wallace, Nancy Moore, Stanley M. Burstein, Frank Holt, Otto Mørkholm, Bluma Trell, Richard Sullivan, Duncan Fishwick, B. Levy, Richard Weigel, Frances Van Keuren, P. Visonà, Alexander G. McKay, Robert L. Hohlfelder

1984 / pp. xii + 310 / ISBN 0-88920-130-7

DRIVING HOME
A Dialogue Between Writers and Readers
Edited by Barbara Belyea and Estelle Dansereau

Essays by: E. D. Blodgett, Christopher Wiseman, D. G. Jones, Myrna Kostash, Richard Giguère, Aritha van Herk, Peter Stevens, Jacques Brault

1984 / pp. xiv + 98 / ISBN 0-88920-148-X

IDEOLOGY, PHILOSOPHY AND POLITICS
Edited by Anthony Parel

Essays by: Frederick C. Copleston, Charles Taylor, John Plamenatz, Hugo Meynell, Barry Cooper, Willard A. Mullins, Kai Nielsen, Joseph Owens, Kenneth Minogue, Lynda Lange, Lyman Tower Sargent, Andre Liebich

1983 / pp. x + 246 / ISBN 0-88920-129-3

DOCTORS, PATIENTS, AND SOCIETY
Power and Authority in Medical Care
Edited by Martin S. Staum and Donald E. Larsen

Essays by: David J. Roy, John C. Moskop, Ellen Picard, Robert E. Hatfield, Harvey Mitchell, Toby Gelfand, Hazel Weidman, Anthony K. S. Lam, Carol Herbert, Josephine Flaherty, Benjamin Freedman, Lionel E. McLeod, Janice P. Dickin McGinnis, Anne Crichton, Malcolm C. Brown, Thomas McKeown, Cathy Charles

1981 / pp. xiv + 290 / ISBN 0-88920-111-0

CRIME AND CRIMINAL JUSTICE IN
EUROPE AND CANADA
Edited by Louis A. Knafla

Essays by: J. H. Baker, Alfred Soman, Douglas Hay, T. C. Curtis and F. M. Hale, J. M. Beattie, Terry Chapman, André Lachance, Simon N. Verdun-Jones, T. Thorner and N. Watson, W. G. Morrow, Herman Diederiks, W. A. Calder, Pieter Spierenburg, Byron Henderson

1985, Revised Edition / pp. xxx + 344 / ISBN 0-88920-181-1

SCIENCE, PSEUDO-SCIENCE AND SOCIETY
Edited by Marsha P. Hanen, Margaret J. Osler, and Robert G. Weyant

Essays by: Paul Thagard, Adolf Grünbaum, Antony Flew, Robert G. Weyant, Marsha P. Hanen, Richard S. Westfall, Trevor H. Levere, A. B. McKillop, James R. Jacob, Roger Cooter, Margaret J. Osler, Marx W. Wartofsky

1980 / pp. x + 303 / ISBN 0-88920-100-5

THE NEW LAND
Studies in a Literary Theme
Edited by Richard Chadbourne and Hallvard Dahlie

Essays by: Richard Chadbourne, Hallvard Dahlie, Naïm Kattan, Roger Motut, Peter Stevens, Ronald Sutherland, Richard Switzer, Clara Thomas, Jack Warwick, Rudy Wiebe

1978 / pp. viii + 160 / ISBN 0-88920-065-3

RELIGION AND ETHNICITY
Edited by Harold Coward and Leslie Kawamura

Essays by: Harold Barclay, Harold Coward, Frank Epp, David Goa, Yvonne Yazbeck Haddad, Gordon Hirabayashi, Roger Hutchinson, Leslie Kawamura, Grant Maxwell, Cyril Williams

1978 / pp. x + 181 / ISBN 0-88920-064-5